FOR GOD AND COUNTRY

Co bardziej dokuczy, to ruchlej nauczy.
(What hurts most, teaches soonest.)

HELEN S. ZAND
Polish Proverbs

FOR GOD AND COUNTRY

The Rise of Polish and Lithuanian
Ethnic Consciousness in America
1860–1910

Victor Greene

The State Historical Society of Wisconsin
Madison   1975

Library of Congress Cataloging in Publication Data
Greene, Victor R
For God and country: the rise of Polish and Lithuanian
ethnic consciousness in America, 1860–1910.
Bibliography: p. 180
1. Polish Americans—History.
2. Lithuanian Americans—History.   I. Title.
E184.P7G73   973'.04'9185   75–19017
ISBN 0–87020–155–7

For Jessica and Geoffrey

PREFACE

LIKE SO MANY other historical monographs, this work now bears only a faint resemblance to its original design. As conceived over a decade ago, the study was to be a sequel to *The Slavic Community on Strike: Immigrant Labor in Pennsylvania Anthracite,* my first book on the East European American workingmen. It was to be a further examination of the impact they had on industrial disputes and the organization of labor. Having moved to the Midwest I seemed to have the opportunity to make another test of my hypothesis on the organizability of immigrants, this time in the Chicago area. The prospects for research and analysis were especially attractive since the Illinois metropolis was a more concentrated geographical setting than the sprawling, diffused Pennsylvania anthracite region and the source materials, too, would be less scattered. Further, the location had particular significance for Chicago was in fact the heartland of Slavic America.

As I reviewed the East European groups' living and working conditions, the similar experiences of the Polish and Lithuanian communities became apparent. Clearly the most persistent and vexing concern to these peoples was the circumstances causing their mounting group awareness. As I proceeded with my study of community formation, this process of enlightenment and emerging group consciousness seemed a far more exciting, chal-

vii

lenging, and potentially rewarding path to pursue. My new objective, then, led me away from labor history and toward social and religious history, especially the place of the parish and Roman Catholicism in the immigrants' lives.

I began my study of ethnic consciousness just prior to the rise of the new ethnicity, a current national movement begun in the late 1960's, which, among other aims, has sought a redefinition of the country's non-Anglo-American groups. The persistence of ethnic loyalty among white immigrant groups caught most academicians by surprise. The majority of the sociologists, social scientists, and archivists had assumed that cultural diversity—although certainly not racial differences—had disappeared soon after the end of the open immigration policy early in the century.

When I began my research in the mid-1960's, I found once again, as I had in my earlier study in Pennsylvania, that locating source materials meant considerable preparatory field work. My previous experience had convinced me that most if not all of the research materials were extant, but that I would have to spend considerable time and energy in locating and getting access to the numerous private collections. At that time nearly all of these repositories were poorly organized and difficult to consult and use. Not being a member of either of the groups I was studying, I depended on the bountiful good will and generosity of many individual Polish and Lithuanian Americans. The experience was universally satisfying and the richness of my sources is in large part the result of their efforts for me. Therefore, to thank adequately all of my ethnic guides would require an inordinately long list of names. I will attempt to cite the most outstanding assistance, but I do so reluctantly because I fear I will omit some I ought to name.

Above all I am grateful to the staffs of the Polish and Lithuanian repositories in Chicago: Joseph Zurawski and the Reverend Donald Bilinski, OFM, president and curator, respectively, of the Polish Museum of America; Mrs. Josefa Rzewska of the Polish National Alliance Library; Joseph Białasiewicz of the old *Dziennik Chicagoski;* the Reverend Edward Janas of Weber High School; Alexander Ambrose and Martin Gudelis, editor, of *Naujienos;* Vincent Liulevicius of the World Lithuanian Archives; the Reverend Juozas Prunskis and Leonard Simutis, formerly of *Draugas;* the late J. J. Bachunas; Stanley Balzekas of the Balzekas Museum of Lithuanian Culture; Sister M. Timothy of the St. Casimir Sisters at Maria High School; and the late Archbishop S. A. Geniotis of the Lithuanian National Catholic Church. Ms. Ramona Juozevičius conscientiously assisted me by translating the more difficult Lithuanian sources. The Chicago Historical Society, especially Archie Motley; the University of Chicago Library; and the Chicago Public Library gave me every consideration possible. It was my extraordinary good fortune in Chicago to meet Jan Wepsięc, the distinguished Polish-American bibliographer, and the Rev. M. J. Madaj.

As I expanded the scope of my work from Chicago to the nation, I found it necessary to seek help from institutions and persons in many other cities. I received valuable service from Francis Czyzewski of South Bend; Arthur Waldo, then of Pittsburgh, now of Phoenix; the Reverend Joseph Swastek of the Sts. Cyril and Methodius Seminary Library in Orchard Lake, Michigan; Professor Szymon Deptuła of Milwaukee; Polish National Catholic clerics, the Reverends Francis Rowinski of Chicago, W. A. Slowakiewicz of Detroit, and Theodore Zawistowski of Chicopee, Massachusetts; Dr. Stephen Gredel of the Buffalo and Erie County Historical Society; Sister Ellen Kuznicki of Villa Maria College, Buffalo; Professor Walter Drzewieniecki of the State University of New York, Buffalo State College; Joseph Kij of Lackawanna, New York; Professor Antanas Kučas of the University of Scranton; Šimas Šuziedelis of *Darbininkas,* Brooklyn; Mrs. Bertha Pivaronas of *Tėvynė;* and Msgr. Francis Juras and the ALKA Archives at Putnam and Thompson, Connecticut.

I also gratefully acknowledge the support of various funding agencies: the American Association for State and Local History; the State Historical Society of Wisconsin and its Midwest History Research Program; Kansas State University; the National Endowment for the Humanities; and the International Research and Exchanges Board (IREX) of New York.

While I was in Eastern Europe I was aided substantially by

the Biblioteka Narodowy; the Jagellonian University Library; Professors Aleksander Gieysztor, Professor Stefan Kieniewicz, Dr. Irena Spustek, and Magister Bogdan Grzelonski of the Historical Institute, Warsaw University; Dr. Krzystof Groniowski of the Historical Section of the Polish Academy; Professor Jozef Chałasinski; and, particularly, Dr. Andrzej Brożek of the Opole Higher Pedagogical School and Dr. Hieronim Jakubiak of the Jagellonian University.

My American colleagues have also been especially generous with their criticisms and advice. They have saved me from many conceptual and contextual weaknesses. I am particularly indebted to Professor Philip Gleason of the University of Notre Dame, the most eminent Catholic-American historian. He and Professor Theodore Saloutos scrutinized the manuscript carefully and improved its quality immeasurably. I am very grateful, too, to my associates in the History Department of the University of Wisconsin—Milwaukee for their time and insights. The discussions on nationalism I had with Professors Walter Weare, Philip Shashko, and Bruce Fetter were invaluable. Professor Reginald Horsman gave me the benefit of his evaluation when the manuscript was in an early form. Though the work is far from his field, Professor James Brundage was kind enough to save me from some grievous errors in Catholic terminology and titles. Ms. Kathy Poplawski typed the difficult manuscript with exceptional patience and care.

My two children, to whom the book is dedicated, now know precisely what required so much of their father's attention over the last few years. The work was nearly another member of the family. My wife, Laura, with her own literary skill, unravelled much of my obscure thought and phrasing and acted once again as my best critic and reviewer.

VICTOR GREENE

The University of Wisconsin—Milwaukee
March, 1975

CONTENTS

A selection of illustrations follows page 116.

TABLES

INTRODUCTION

NOTED OBSERVERS of American society, writers such as Michel de Crèvecoeur, Alexis de Tocqueville, James Bryce, André Siegfried, and Samuel Lubell, have marveled at the seeming national cohesion of the American people. This unity is unusual because although American society functions as an integrated whole, it consists of numerous ethnic subgroups. There are, of course, cases where the many have not been as one. White-nonwhite relations have often broken down, producing racial unrest. Less apparent, and therefore more puzzling to the observers, has been the role of the many white ethnic elements in the New World and their adjustment to the new society. Certainly it is surprising that there has not been more friction and disorder. The arrival and intergroup contact between masses of English, Irish, German, Slavic, Italian, and other immigrants have not created the ethnic friction that might be expected from the many national enmities harbored in Europe.

Just how compatible the various ethnic groups were in America, among themselves as well as toward the native Anglo-American majority, is still a matter of dispute. Recent spokesmen for what has become known as "the new ethnicity," a movement to preserve and encourage the many ethnic subcultures, have offered one explanation for the relatively peaceful coexistence of the majority with minority groups.[1] They suggest

---

[1] Michael Novak, *The Rise of the Unmeltable Ethnics* (New York, 1971), expresses the new ethnic viewpoint best.

1

that the process of Americanization has had a devastating assimilationist impact upon most of the "ethnics," thus keeping
them silent and nonviolent. White Anglo-American Protestants
long ago adopted a feeling of superiority toward all other groups
and forced incoming members of minorities of whatever race to
adopt majority values and culture. Through a variety of pressures, broadly known as the melting pot, the dominant English-
speaking elements impressed upon the newcomers the necessity
of abandoning their cultural heritages and adopting the dominant Anglo-American one. According to these new ethnic
spokesmen, the melting-pot image confused minority group
members about their traditional identities and forced them,
under psychological and social pressure, to discard their Old
World folkways and "Americanize." The process caused millions of small, personal tragedies within immigrant families
which went on unnoticed by the larger society. The newcomers
put up little effective resistance. The few who did not reject their
group past eventually produced the ethnic pluralism that en-
dures in America today.

This new ethnic explanation of the non-Anglo-American experience, then, is a story of much human stress and anguish. It
suggests that the paradox which has attracted students to the
American enigma—diversity within unity—was in fact produced by a painful process of psychological trauma and discomfort affecting much of the population. Each successive
immigrant minority had to endure the ordeal of marginality;
each had to make the choice of identifying either with its traditional or adopted culture.

Whatever the validity of this pathology of adjustment, whatever the degree to which the immigrant was forced to forsake
his ancestry, certainly it is true that every newcomer had to deal
with the dilemma of group membership. Having moved from
one continent to another, every immigrant settler had to determine to which group he belonged: the people he left or the
people he met. It is a part of that intimate experience—specifically of learning about his ethnic group and realizing his membership in it—that is the subject of this book.

It is hazardous for the historian to generalize about and to describe the transformation of a psychological state of mind for individuals in a group. Over the years, each immigrant, from whatever foreign region, stepped ashore in America with a slightly different awareness of his ethnic heritage than any other newcomer. To determine how each person tried to accommodate his traditional culture with his new one, it is necessary to ascertain the newcomer's group consciousness upon arrival—what was his ethnic-national awareness when he came to America (to what extent did each consider himself part of a Polish or Italian "nation"), and how did that consciousness rise or fall over time?

An individual's ethnic awareness can be illuminated by dividing the more general feeling of nationalism into three subsidiary categories.[2] An elaboration of these subdivisions is necessary in order to clarify the entire nationalization process of which "ethnicization"—ethnic consciousness-making—the subject here, was a part.

The first level in the evolution of nationalism is ethnic naïveté. The overwhelming bulk of East European, German, and Italian immigrants were at this stage. They both possessed and practiced certain cultural characteristics of their group—for example, a common national language—but they had little or no feeling of membership in an ethnic nation. Whether in Europe or America, they may have sensed that they were different from other nationalities, but when asked for their own group identification, they probably would have responded by naming their regional or local origins—their village or more likely their province. Very few would have replied "Polish," "Lithuanian," "German," or "Italian."

A more advanced stage of ethnic feeling, which was much less evident among the immigrants mentioned above, could be termed cultural or polycentric nationalism. This feeling was evident among enlightened people who not only carried on traditional customs, as did the more naïve masses, but also those who considered themselves as ethnic. Their nation was one

---

[2] I use in part the breakdown offered by Anthony D. Smith, *Theories of Nationalism* (London, 1971), especially 158–164.

among many others. However, such an ethno-national awareness was not an aggressive, messianic attitude; it differed substantially from political nationalism, which sought to go farther and construct a sovereign nation-state.

This third feeling was the final level of nationalism, the most advanced national group sentiment. People with this feeling were a part of the migrating masses in the nineteenth century, but they were an elite segment, tiny in number, primarily refugee intellectuals. They were aware not simply of their membership in a separate nation; they also found considerable pride and satisfaction in feeling and broadcasting that identity. This handful of ethnic patriots worked enthusiastically to perpetuate their nation's name.

Unfortunately, historians of American immigration have paid little attention to this matter of national consciousness among the newcomers. The literature is not extensive, and although some authors mention ethnic group awareness at several levels, such references are no more than allusions. Most studies are still either introductory surveys of the various white subcultures or at best examinations of a group's social or political response in America. They assume that incoming group members had a generally well-developed sense of ethnic consciousness upon arrival and that the foreign communities remained essentially static over time.

Only one work, an exceptional, recent study of Irish-Americans by Thomas B. Brown, deals specifically with ethnic consciousness at the most advanced state of that feeling, immigrant nationalism. However, anyone seeking an understanding of the *process* of group ethnicization will be disappointed, for the author is more concerned with the strategies of the already committed group leaders, not the feelings of the immigrant rank and file.[3]

Of the several entering groups of foreigners who apparently did change their understanding of their native land—that is,

___

[3] See Thomas B. Brown, *Irish-American Nationalism, 1870–1890* (Philadelphia, 1966), and particularly his "Origins and Character of Irish American Nationalism," in *Review of Politics*, 18: 327–358 (July, 1956).

raised their level of ethnic consciousness—the Poles and the Lithuanians were outstanding. Over the era of the immigrant generation, they appear as models of this awareness process.[4] When they first entered the United States, just after the middle of the nineteenth century, they had no strong ethnic feelings or interest in politics; they made a decided shift in sentiment within a few decades. By the start of World War I the two communities were enthusiastically supporting ethnic nationalism—an independent homeland.[5] The process of ethnicization had taken place in America. This book will examine how this heightened ethnic consciousness took place, and offer an hypothesis about the compatibility of ethnic awareness and American identity, not only for these two peoples but for all Americans who endured a similar process.

The sources of this rising ethnic consciousness lay in local, neighborhood developments which affected all immigrants, even the most inarticulate. It was widespread activities in nearly every turn-of-the-century Polish and Lithuanian settlement in America that brought about this enlightenment of the masses, who then began to realize their membership and participation in an ethnic nation. Of course, as the three levels of consciousness and plain common sense would suggest, there was a small minority of Poles and Lithuanians who already possessed a sophisticated understanding of nationalism when they came to the United States. These few ethnocentric nationalists also played a significant part in stimulating the enlightenment process. They became active in even the earliest phases of Polish and Lithuanian America, in the 1860's and 1870's. Throughout they dedicated themselves to the task of arousing their more apathetic countrymen. However, the educational campaign by ethnic patriots was

---

[4] I am excluding Jews from my work; generally, they existed apart from the Polish- and Lithuanian-American communities.

[5] See Stanley R. Pliska, "Polish Independence and the Polish Americans" (D.Ed. dissertation, Teacher's College, Columbia University, 1955), ii and *passim;* Henry J. T. Dutkiewicz, "Main Aspects of the Polish Peasant Immigration to North America from Austrian Poland between the Years 1863 and 1910" (M.A. thesis, University of Ottawa, 1958), 97, for the Poles; Constantine Jurgela, "Lithuania and the United States" (Ph.D. dissertation, Fordham University, 1954), *passim,* for the Lithuanians.

not the only, and was certainly not the most effective, source for
stimulating the rank and file to ethnic consciousness.

Since ethnic awareness is an early form of nationalism, the
theoretical formulations of the general topic of nationalism are
important to this study of two East European groups in America. Scholars of nationalism have offered models of the entire
enlightenment process, from an awareness of nation onward to
the most spirited, aggressive political nationalism. They generally agree about the origins of national consciousness: nationalism, and therefore its less-developed form, ethnic awareness,
is born out of hostility toward another group.[6] A people must
feel some sense of oppression and bitterness before it can develop an idea of nationhood. From this some historians have
concluded that ethnic awareness—membership in a Lithuanian
or Polish totality—if it took place in America, developed out of
friction with the Anglo-American majority.

The idea that group hostility produced group consciousness
arose just before World War I when so many oppressed nationalities were struggling to win self-determination, particularly
in Central and Eastern Europe. As early an observer as Lord
Acton designated the source of mass support for nationalist
movements when he said, "A national impulse . . . is only awakened when there is an alien element, the vestige of foreign do-
minion to dispel."[7] And another scholar observed about the
initial stage of nationalism that "a common hate is one of the
most effective factors in making or uniting a nation."[8] According to this view, people first sense membership in a nation when
they respond to external domination. In other words, consciously felt Irishness began with animosity toward the English; Polish
feeling was essentially anti-Russian or anti-German; Slovak
sentiment was anti-Hungarian, and so forth.

A few students of ethnic group behavior have applied this

---

[6] The best-known essay on the subject emphasizes the psychological nature
of the idea. See Hans Kohn, *The Idea of Nationalism* (New York, 1967), 12,
16, 18.

[7] John E. E. Dalberg-Acton, *The History of Freedom and Other Essays*
(reprint edition, Freeport, New York, 1967), 272, 278.

[8] W. B. Pillsbury, *The Psychology of Nationality and Internationalism*
(New York, 1919), 81. See also Max S. Handman, "The Sentiment of Nationalism," in the *Political Science Quarterly,* 26: 105–106 (March, 1921).

hypothesis to the development of group awareness among America's white minorities. Noting a similar emergence of ethnic consciousness among many groups in the United States up to the 1920's, they argued that its source lay in Anglo-American hostility. A number of early American sociologists insisted that the New World experience was similar to the Old; the dominant power in both places, the imperial rulers in Europe and the Anglo-Americans in the United States, oppressed their minorities, thereby causing ethnic group consciousness. American intolerance, quite evident in the form of anti-Catholicism, anti-Semitism, and a variety of discriminatory laws, simply devised new forms of Old World oppression of subject nationalities.

The well-known early student of urban society, Robert E. Park, was a leading proponent of the thesis that an immigrant's awareness of his ethnic group originated in his maladjustment to his adopted country. According to Park, the newcomer suffered emotionally from conflicting group loyalties, the one in which he was raised and the one to which he came. Such a marginal man had to make the difficult decision of which society to join, since the majority and his minority were not only different but also antagonistic.[9] Down to recent times most observers have followed Park, maintaining that rejection by the American majority sparked minority-group awareness.[10]

[9] See particularly his introduction to the standard work on the subject, E. V. Stonequist, *The Marginal Man: A Study in Personality and Culture Conflict* (reprint of 1937 edition, New York, 1961).

[10] William Carlson Smith, *Americans in the Making: The Natural History of the Assimilation of Immigrants* (New York, 1939), 57–58, 60; H. Richard Niebuhr, *The Social Sources of Denominationalism* (reprint edition, Hamden, Connecticut, 1954), 222–223; Donald Taft and Richard Robbins, *International Migrations* (New York, 1955), 112–113; Louis Wirth, "The Problem of Minority Groups," in Ralph Linton, ed., *The Science of Man in the World Crisis* (New York, 1945), 347–348; Arnold and Caroline Rose, *America Divided: Minority Group Relations in the United States* (New York, 1948), 3, 35, 179, 182. Glazer feels that identity is gained when the group member recognizes that he has to choose between his own and the native American culture as a "marginal man." See Nathan Glazer, "Ethnic Groups in America: From National Culture to Ideology," in Morroe Berger *et al.*, *Freedom and Control in Modern Society* (New York, 1954), 164. See also Marvin Harris, "Caste, Class, and Minority," in *Social Forces,* 37: 248 (March, 1959). One of Glazer's recent comments on the subject still eschews any mention of internal group divisions. "The Peoples of America," in Milton Barron, ed., *Minorities in a Changing World* (New York, 1967), 144.

But not all have accepted this conventional thesis that group friction was the source of group consciousness. One sociologist, writing in the wake of the Nazi holocaust in Europe, suggested that the oppression of white minorities in America was hardly equivalent to the situation of minorities in the Old World. The Americanization of minorities here was benign; the brutal conformity enforced on the other side of the Atlantic was "alien to the American tradition."[11] A former proponent of immigrant disorientation, Oscar Handlin, has similarly modified his views. He, too, rejects the polarity between natives and white aliens, asserting that earlier observers have dwelled excessively upon majority hostility, social conflict, and those areas where American pluralism broke down. Viewing the immigrant experience at the level of the rank and file, he concludes that relations among this nation's white groups displayed an unusual flexibility and openness. The dominant majority, then, did not provoke ethnic group consciousness directly; rather, the origins of such awareness lay somewhere in the aliens' natural yearning for comfort and security, particularly at critical times such as birth, marriage, sickness, and death. It was not necessary for the white newcomers to make an unequivocal choice between two hostile communities, their traditional and their adopted. Rather, group consciousness arose in a host of social contexts, in social organizations which individuals could associate with whenever and to whatever extent they wished.[12]

Another revisionist, the sociologist Milton Gordon, also downgrades the supposed instantaneous friction between natives and aliens upon arrival. Contact in the early years, he points out, was very likely mutually apathetic for the ordinary newcomers. Psychologically at least, the aliens were able to live for

[11] Oscar I. Janowsky, *Nationalities and National Minorities* (New York, 1945), 5.

[12] Oscar Handlin, "Historical Perspectives on the American Ethnic Group," in *Daedalus,* 90: 220–232 (Spring, 1961). However, a recently revised edition of his work on the Boston Irish still refers to Protestant coolness as the source of that minority's self-consciousness; see *Boston's Immigrants* (revised and enlarged edition, New York, 1969), Chapter VI, especially 176. On the other hand, Handlin does condemn the "new ethnic" protest as unjustified. See *The Uprooted* (enlarged edition, Boston, 1973), 322, 330n.

a while in their own ethnic world, showing little interest in the dominant culture. Natives, too, on the whole cared little positively or negatively about immigrants. The result was a cultural standoff.[13]

It is difficult to apply any current theory of group consciousness to the experiences of an immigrant community such as the Poles' or Lithuanians', for the formulations themselves are in transition and necessary evidence on the groups is lacking. The most recent suggestions have minimized, but not discarded entirely, the theory that outgroup friction was the cause of ethnic awareness. Yet if such hostility was insignificant or unimportant, the sources of ethnic consciousness are still unknown. In the midst of the present uncertainty about the immigrant experience, a recent sociologist has observed that all the judgments seem hardly more than educated guesses, for they are really devoid of much hard evidence; scholars simply know too little about American ethnic communities to speak with any assurance about their origins.[14]

A closer look at the early history of Polish and Lithuanian immigrants may help to explain the process of ethnic enlightenment in America. The traditional view that majority rejection was the major cause appears to have considerable validity when applied to Poles and Lithuanians. Anglo-Americans did fear and condemn East Europeans, endowing them with an inferior and uncomplimentary public image that persists to the present day. At the turn of this century, American intellectuals and publicists exposed what they believed was Polish and Lithuanian inferiority and its deleterious effects upon the United States. Middle-class spokesmen castigated these immigrants for their lowly peasant origins, their intemperance, and their rigid adherence to Catholicism. Even social reformers, originally empathetic toward these urban poor, quickly grew suspicious of their charges, fearing the newcomers' baneful influence, their high illiteracy, their chronic poverty, their innocence of democratic traditions. The so-called "Hunkie" then evoked consider-

[13] Milton Gordon, "Assimilation in America: Theory and Reality," in *Daedalus*, 90: 281 (Spring, 1961).
[14] Glazer, "Ethnic Groups," 173.

able native hostility; in turn the foreigners' reaction to this pressure could very well have led to a raised group consciousness.

Unquestionably native American hostility and criticism leveled at them stimulated an ethnic group *defensiveness* among East European immigrants. But it is the principal thesis of this book that the major source of heightened group awareness came from the groups' inner experience in America, from their internal development. Briefly stated, in order to trace the growth and diffusion of ethnic group consciousness, it is useful if not imperative to concentrate on the social history of the Polish and Lithuanian immigrant communities in America. A deep-rooted conflict *within* these groups brought about national awareness; inter-ethnic friction was minimal and much less significant.

The process by which the ordinary immigrants came to realize their ethnic membership is somewhat involved. To understand it one must keep in mind that both incoming groups—Polish and Lithuanian—consisted of essentially three social segments: two small elites in continual dispute and the great rank and file. The disagreement was over the role of their community in America, specifically what qualities constituted membership and how the group should function as a Roman Catholic minority. The interminable, heated debate between the elites occasionally drew the masses into the controversy. It was because the issue touched upon a vital element in peasant-immigrant psychology, control of the parish, that the ordinary group members (parishioners, fraternalists, and readers of the ethnic press) became deeply involved. It was this experience that forced the immigrants to confront the notion of their ethnic identity. It was this inner ordeal that revealed to all immigrants the parameters of their group.

To comprehend fully this internal controversy and particularly its pervasive ramifications and impact upon everyone, one must look closely at the evolving disagreement. The dispute began immediately, virtually at the inception of the settlement of these two groups in America—the mid-1860's for the Poles and the 1870's for the Lithuanians. When they discovered in the new land that their primary social institution, the parish, was under alien control, group leaders had to make some adjustment. Immediately two factions arose in conflict over the objectives of their neighborhood and community. One camp, the "clericalists" or "religionists," defined the colony as a part of and synonymous with Roman Catholicism. All group members must be of that faith, and that meant complete loyalty to the American Church hierarchy regardless of the ethnic background of that authority. Opposing them were the ethnic patriots or "nationalists," who argued that faith was separate from nationality. While they admitted that Catholicism was the religion of most group members, it was not necessarily that of all. Further, the Church ought to recognize ethnic pluralism among its communicants, for American Catholicism should be primarily congregational not hierarchical. In short, the dispute centered on the place of American Catholicism among Polish and Lithuanian immigrants. Religionists insisted that since all group members were Catholic they must obey Church rules; nationalists responded that the Church had to adapt to the ethnic needs of its communicants, whether they were Poles, Lithuanians, Germans, Italians, or other nationalities.

This controversy over religion and ethnicity, which was really over Polish and Lithuanian identity, was far more than an abstract debate between a divided group elite. The matter became of vital concern to all members of these communities, for it involved the control of that cherished primary institution immigrants had carried to America, their neighborhood parish. In Europe ordinary parishioners did not have to consider the ethnic constitution of their local house of worship; their own spiritual leaders administered and owned the church. In the New World, however, the immigrant had to erect his desired ethnic community *de novo*, yet place it in an alien, American Catholic setting. This adjustment was uncomfortable. The problem originated in the Church rules which gave parish ownership to the diocesan Bishop, who was usually not a member of the incoming immigrant group. This ecclesiastical requirement divided the groups into two camps. The ethnic clerics who stressed Catholic loyalty agreed to diocesan title; nationalists condemned such ownership as outside interference. The disagreement produced an impasse that affected every parishioner. Eventually the tense atmosphere exploded into violence and disorder as parishioners took sides. It was in the crisis of having to choose which faction to support that ordinary Polish and Lithuanian immigrants became educated to their ethnic identity, and thereby raised their ethnic consciousness.

The disturbances followed a fairly common pattern. A few lay leaders usually allied with a parish assistant and bitterly attacked their group pastor for insufficient ethnic feeling and as a traitor to his nationality because he upheld the bishop's authority (which of course was his own) and gave his unalterable support to the American hierarchy. The layman-pastor friction escalated to the point that physical assaults took place between pro-nationalist and pro-pastor advocates fighting for possession of the parish property. They were especially bitter exchanges where brother fought brother.

The setting of all these verbal and physical battles may have been local, but the factionalism and disorder in ethnic neighborhoods expanded widely during the last third of the nineteenth century. The unrest first arose in just a few colonies, in the 1860's and 1870's, but continued later in ethnic newspapers and magazines on a national level. The intensity of the conflict reached a critical point in the mid-1890's. By that time the matter affected all Polish America; the similar Lithuanian upheaval came around 1900. The disorder then engulfed nearly every colony throughout the country. Nationalists and their allies even went so far as to join in their own separate "independent" Roman Catholic parishes. These unauthorized takeovers of or defections from older neighborhood churches were viewed by Catholic authorities as schism and apostasy, and they proceeded to widen the divisions further by excommunicating some of the independent leaders. A divided ethnic leadership then became a divided ethnic community, as the Polish and Lithuanian masses had to choose to whom their central neighborhood institution should belong—their pastor allied with their bishop, or the nationalist-independents. Fearing massive defections from Roman Catholic parishes, group religionists fought the schism on two fronts: they intensified their direct verbal exchange with the independents, and beseeched the Church hierarchy to grant more ethnic recognition.

Out of this group distress American Catholic leaders brought

Polish ethnic divisions to some resolution in 1908 by appointing the first Polish bishop. In so doing the Church also sanctioned ethnic group consciousness and stimulated its spread by official ecclesiastical recognition. Polishness now had its recognized place in the American Church hierarchy. The divisive ordeal of the immigrant Poles in America was over. The experience of the related minority, Lithuanian-Americans, was similar but with a less happy outcome. They, too, went through a consciousness-making process—a religionist-nationalist conflict within their community over church control which also educated their members to group awareness. However, the Church did not resolve Lithuanian-American divisions as satisfactorily, and failed to appoint an ethnic bishop. Still, the tension between ethnicity and religion subsided in time, and the prospect during World War I of an independent Lithuania tended to unify religionists and nationalists in America.

The inner group violence, riot, and disorder which drew the masses to the issue of who owned the parish raised their ethnic awareness. In order to demonstrate this agonizing experience among ordinary immigrants, this work focuses at the neighborhood level. In sum, there were approximately one thousand Polish and Lithuanian settlements in the country by the early 1900's, but the colonies in Chicago stand out as the most prominent, formative, and representative. In fact it was really in this midwestern metropolis that these subcultures were born. By 1900 the Chicago settlements had the most inhabitants and the two largest group parishes in America. In these two so-called mother churches from which most others in the city emerged, Polish St. Stanislaus and Lithuanian St. George, lived the groups' most powerful Catholic clerics, Fathers Vincent Barzynski and Matas Kraučiūnas. Chicago, too, was the home of the two leading Polish fraternal organizations, the Polish National Alliance and the Polish Roman Catholic Union, and of the important Lithuanian Roman Catholic Alliance. Chicago was the major battlefield for these two nationalities to thrash out their ordeal of "God and Country," and the experience there was a pattern to be followed in similar intra-group clashes around the nation.

ONE

The Soil and the Spirit

ANY STUDY of American immigration must recognize that how emigrants lived in the Old World conditioned their values and behavior in the New. In the Old World, Norwegians and Swedes had been dissatisfied with their established church, Greeks and Italians had had intense family attachments, East European Jews had lived in ghettos, and the Irish and others had suffered rural poverty. The most significant feature of the Polish and Lithuanian masses in Europe was the peasant quality of their lives.[1]

Anthropologists have already suggested the cultural dynamics of peasant life, and these appear to be the fundamental principles of the Polish and Lithuanian masses. Two important values—a strong attachment to property and a fervent devotion to religion—were the touchstones of peasant life.[2] The broader but less immediate issues of nationality conflict and politics were of little interest to them.[3]

---

[1] One must agree with Florian Znaniecki and William I. Thomas's classic, *The Polish Peasant in Europe and America* (1918), that peasant life in Eastern Europe holds an important key to behavior in America.

[2] A convenient recent summary of anthropological theory is John Powell, "On Defining Peasants and Peasant Society," in *Peasant Studies Newsletter*, 1: 94ff (July, 1972).

[3] I am also combining the opinions of Eric Wolfe, *The Peasants* (Englewood Cliffs, New Jersey, 1966), 106–108; Robert Redfield, *Peasant Society and Culture* (Chicago, 1956), 112, 140; Irwin T. Sanders, "Characteristics of

It is of course difficult to discern and identify values of a largely inarticulate mass such as peasants. However, it is clear that nineteenth-century Poles and Lithuanians gave a high place to the possession of property. Their past itself showed that they cherished and loved land and passionately sought to acquire it. For centuries, both as serfs under a feudal system and later as free peasants, they not only lived on the good earth but derived much of their identity from it. Agriculture characterized their entire world and had an enduring impact on their life.

Admittedly not all peasant folk enjoyed cultivating the land; some nationalities who were basically agrarian suffered painfully before coming to America, and upon their arrival readily forsook their rustic existence. The awful misery of the Irish cotter and the Italian *contadini* may have caused an aversion to farming. However, even for them rural folk traditions remained. And the Poles especially, despite an increasingly niggardly patrimony and agricultural distress as East Europeans, clung doggedly to the landholding ideal whether in Europe or in America, in the city or on the farm.[4]

Certainly, the peasant heritage of the Poles and Lithuanians, just as for other groups, grew out of a land-based culture; their folklore, customs, and habits were inextricably bound up with nature. Such a fixation with the soil did not lead to improved agricultural productivity; these men of the earth were more interested in farming as a way of life than as a business enterprise. They sought in agriculture the philosophical rationale for their existence, not greater crop production through progressive methods. Land had a weighty psychological as well as economic

---

Peasant Societies," in Edumund de S. Brunner *et al.*, *Farmers of the World: The Development of Agricultural Extension* (New York, 1945), 37–40; and M. E. Opler, "The Place of Religion in a North Indian Village," in *Southwestern Journal of Anthropology*, 15: 226 (1959).

4 Evidence for this assertion will be offered below, but the general statements are in Stefan Wloszczewski, *History of Polish American Culture* (Trenton, New Jersey, 1946), 112; Andrzej Brożek, "Początki Emigracji z Górnego Śląska do Ameryki w Swetle Współczesne Prasy Polskiej na Śląsku," in *Kwartalnik Historyczny* 75: 5 (Warsaw); and Peter Paul Jonitis, "The Acculturation of the Lithuanians of Chester, Pa." (Ph.D. dissertation, University of Pennsylvania, 1951), 8, 29, 83.

significance. The masses deliberately sought and created in country life an elaborate system of folk myth, legend, and superstition to illuminate the mystery of being. Such a complex network of customs suited their needs and insecurities admirably.[5]

A particularly attractive quality of the land for the masses was the soil's productive function, a feature that certainly intensified the peasants' reverence for the good earth. Ploughmen glorified the concept of fertility, biologically in humans as well as agriculturally in nature, so the property of the soil to bring forth a crop continually must have stimulated their admiration. The reproductive process in plants and animals was always a fascinating mystery. While East Europeans praised a bountiful harvest in crops and in children, they simply could not produce enough of the former to feed the latter, so the result was ever-increasing misery.

In addition to the compelling magic of soil chemistry, the Slavs' high regard for landholding came from their esteem for what productive land required—hard work. Although they may not have enjoyed the necessary effort, field workers valued manual labor. To them a good day's labor on the land was very satisfying.[6] They would retain that penchant for heavy manual work in America, too, although there it was performed in the mine and factory rather than on the farm.

The land, then, occupied a central and honored place in peasant culture. Both Polish and Lithuanian masses were men of the soil with a deep psychological identification with it. "To win a . . . piece of fertile soil was the cherished dream of . . . a peasant." "He knows the land and loves it." "What is it men quarrel for, work for, and make every attempt to get? Why,

[5] Sanders, "Characteristics of Peasant Societies," 38; Sula Benet, *Song, Dance, and Customs of Peasant Poland* (New York, 1952), 20, 24–25; William Rose, *Poland, Old and New* (London, 1948), 164–165; William I. Thomas and Florian Znaniecki, *The Polish Peasant in Europe and America* (5 vols., Chicago, 1918–1920), 1: 173.

[6] I am applying the generalizations of Redfield, *Peasant Society*, 63–64, and Thomas and Znaniecki, *Polish Peasant* (reprint edition, 2 vols., New York, 1958), 1: 173ff.

[7] The quotations are from Jonitis, "Acculturation," 83; Sister Lucille Mar-

what, but property alone!"[7] Such land hunger was important also to the peasant who left for America, for the immigrants did not divest themselves of their agrarian past. They merely transformed their passion for land in Europe to a yearning for acquiring American real estate.

The familial and local political organization of these European peasants further demonstrated the importance of landed wealth in their life. The supreme authority in family matters was the father, whose major administrative role was to supervise the property. The land, however, was in no sense his personal possession, for ownership was not individual. The family head never thought of himself as the proprietor but rather as a temporary manager. The soil was ancestral land, not private property, and the father's task was to assure that the land would sustain the family members. In time, of course, when he grew old and infirm, he was obliged to give up his role and to divide the estate among his children. Sometimes the eldest son would be the sole recipient and he, in turn, would subdivide the patrimony among his younger brothers or buy them off in other ways. The parents would end their days in the home of the new land manager.[8]

Even in decline, during the late nineteenth century, the Polish and Lithuanian peasant village played an important role in enforcing traditional practices and thus sustaining the esteem for land. The local community upheld a very fixed social order. Community opinion, formed by local figures, such as the priest, petty officials, and even gossipy women, sanctioned the paternal authority within the family. Through the 1880's, Polish and Lithuanian villages were less and less self-sufficient and more dependent on external commerce, but the *okolica* (wider region)

---

gin, C.R., "The Polish Immigrant in the American Community" (M.A. thesis, DePaul University, 1948), 31; and the famous novel of Ladislas Reymont, *The Peasants: Autumn,* trans. by Michael H. Dziewicki (4 vols., New York, 1925), 1: 206.

[8] The traditional practice is in Rev. Casimir Peter Sirvaitis, "Religious Folkways in Lithuania and their Conservation among the Lithuanian Immigrants in the United States" (Ph.D. dissertation, Catholic University, 1948), 29–30, and Rev. Joseph Bogusas, "The Lithuanian Family in the United States" (Ph.D. dissertation, Fordham University, 1942), 13–19.

which replaced the *osada* (local colony) as "home" was still essentially an agrarian community.[9]

The most important proof of the sanctity of property-holding in peasant culture was its function in determining status. As such an indicator, it must have affected immigrant psychology profoundly. Polish agrarian society based its regard for the family largely on the size of its land holding. The estate owner, the Pan (Lord), ranked at the top of the peasant social order, while the landless, *komorniki,* occupied the bottom. This high regard for a landed aristocracy, whatever its nationality, may have inhibited peasants from becoming supporters of ethnic revolutionaries. In any event, to the peasant land meant position. When in need of funds in the nineteenth century, selling land was the last alternative; for cash the peasant preferred to borrow on or sell livestock and produce. Clearly, the "Poles saw in the possession of land a sign of social superiority."[10]

The Polish and Lithuanian peasants in the mid-1800's were in a difficult position. By that time the landed masses saw that economic conditions threatened their cherished, traditional way of life. As hard times spread throughout Eastern Europe's agrarian districts, they feared losing their land. To lose land was to lose status, and some landowners decided to take the unprecedented action of traveling elsewhere to maintain their position. They rationalized their uprooting by considering it a temporary means to retain their patrimony. Their earliest moves were relatively easy and scarcely disruptive; they found employment in nearby districts. Later they would traverse continents. But almost always their ultimate goal was winning, maintaining, or enlarging their homesteads.

A combination of a rising birth rate and an excessive parcelization of land was the major cause of the move beyond the

[9] The best description of the typical village setting is by a Polish mayor, Jan Slomka, *From Serfdom to Self-Government,* trans. by William John Rose (London, 1941), especially chapter II. The village's social function is in Florian Znaniecki, "The Poles," in Henry P. Fairchild, ed., *Immigrant Backgrounds* (New York, 1927), 204–205; and R. A. Schermerhorn, *These Our People* (Boston, 1949), 272.

[10] Henryk Frankel, *Poland: The Struggle for Power, 1772–1939* (London, 1941), 62; Benet, *Song and Dance,* 20–21.

okolica. These two factors continually made village life economically intolerable and forced inhabitants to travel to acquire income.[11] Population was expanding in all of continental Europe in the nineteenth century, and the Polish increase was one of the highest.[12] Parcelization was the twin problem. The average size of the peasant family holding was incredibly small, whether they lived in Austrian, Russian, or German Poland. In the Galician area, for example, almost 90 per cent of all holdings were below subsistence in the late 1800's.[13] In the Polish and Lithuanian sectors of the Tsardom, peasant conditions were only slightly improved.[14] The imbalance in landholding was least in the German sector, but even there it was clearly inadequate for many.[15]

The outlook for the Slavic peasants working the land was not bright during the nineteenth century. They had to find other means of support, and that meant moving elsewhere to earn an income. For centuries the district had been their world, so the prospect of moving, even if only temporarily, could not have been appealing. Now they must admit the inadequacy of their home and look for work, leaving the familiar church, cottage, family, and friends behind.

Not all of the migrating masses were indigent or landless, seeking to avert outright starvation. Those on the move were largely members of propertied families of the village who went

[11] Good statistical reviews of the process are in Paul Fox, *The Poles in America* (New York, 1922), 38–43, and Polish National Committee of America, *Polish Encyclopedia* (3 vols., Geneva, 1924).

[12] About 43.5 per 1000 in 1896–1900 for Poland. *Concise Statistical Yearbook of Poland, 1937* (Warsaw, 1937), 40, 45.

[13] Fox, *Poles*, 39.

[14] The population density in 1909 was 250 per square mile, with the peasant masses owning only one-half the entire territory. From Arthur E. Gurney, "The Population of the Polish Commonwealth," in Polish Information Committee, *Poland's Case for Independence* (New York, 1916), 138, and Krzysztof Groniowski, *Kwestia Agarna w Krolestwa Polskim, 1871–1914* (Warsaw, 1966), 106, 121. In what would be Lithuania, only 450 families held over one-fifth of the land. Goeffrey Drage, *Russian Affairs* (London, 1904), 323; Anicetas Simutis, *The Reconstruction of Lithuania After 1918* (New York, 1942), 25.

[15] M. Erasme Piltz, *Petite Encyclopedie Polonaise* (Paris, 1916), 124; Bogusław Drewniak, *Robotnicy Sezonowi Na Pomorzu Zachodnim, 1890–1918* (Poznań, 1959), 44–46.

abroad to avoid descending the social scale. There may have been many who were completely landless, but considerable evidence indicates that the overseas migrants particularly left for psychological rather than simply material reasons.[16]

The early migrants moved to areas which offered them employment, usually the more industrialized sectors of their own region—the manufacturing district around Łódź and Silesia, the mills of western Germany, the factories in St. Petersburg, or even the larger, more efficient estates of Prussia. The American-bound emigrant was more venturesome, and went farther, but whether in Chicago, the Ruhr, or on a Prussian estate, the Polish and Lithuanian worker had the same goal—to earn enough to return to his village, buy land, and live as an independent farmer.[17] It was not uncommon for some peasants actually to carry a handful of East European soil with them to a foreign land so that if they did not return home, they could still be buried with part of their native village. The masses on the move were willing to sacrifice much in order to acquire property: "The peasant eager for land, attached passionately to the earth, makes for himself every possible sacrifice [for it]," even the crushing labor of American mines and factories.[18] But wherever he went, assuredly he was still a peasant at heart.

Additional proof of the importance of property in the goals of the masses is the subsidiary role that politics played for most emigrants. The American arrivals for the most part had no

[16] Joseph Roucek, *American Lithuanians* (New York, 1940), 5. Roucek's "Lithuanian Immigrants in America," in *American Journal of Sociology*, 41: 447ff (January, 1936), and Fabian Kamesis, *Cooperation among the Lithuanians in the United States* (Washington, D.C., 1924), both refer to material deprivation as the cause of movement. The psychological motivation is in E. J. Harrison, *Lithuania, 1928* (London, 1928), 88; William P. Shriver, *Immigrant Forces* (New York, 1913), 12; Rev. Jozef Chodkiewicz, *Polacy w Ameryce Północnej* (Warsaw, 1914), 13; and references in Victor Greene, *The Slavic Community on Strike* (Notre Dame, Indiana, 1968), chapter II.

[17] Bogusas, "The Lithuanian Family," 22; Zdisław Ludkiewicz, *Kwestia Rolna w Galicia* (Lwow, 1910), 123; Roman Dyboski, "The Peasant in Modern Poland," in *The Slavonic Review*, 2: 107 (June, 1923). The German Polish migration abroad was the most permanent. See Stefan Barszczewski, *Polacy w Ameryce* (Warszawa, 1906), 20.

[18] Stanislaus Posner, "Les Forces de la Pologne," in *Revue Internationale de Sociologie*, 24: 238, (April, 1916). See also Thomas and Znaniecki, *Polish Peasant* (1958), 1: 386–387n.

interest in the romantic national movement of the young liberals; they had little sense of and certainly did not support any Polish or Lithuanian "nation."

Austria, Russia, and Germany, the three empires which partitioned Poland in the 1790's, understood and acted shrewdly in dealing with the agrarian masses on the nationality question. Recognizing the danger of an enlightened and aroused peasantry, the governments sought to maintain the distance between nationalist enthusiasts and the bulk of their people. To avert the possibility of mass discontent and to hold their loyalty, the three empires engaged in a surprisingly liberal land policy, abolishing feudalism in the early 1800's and initiating land reform. As a result Vienna, St. Petersburg, and to a lesser degree Berlin all were able to avert widespread peasant dissatisfaction toward established authority. Imperial land reform was hardly a radical move; in fact it was more apparent than real. The three governments made only slight modifications in landholding, just enough to silence discontent. To midcentury the major guidelines of peasant policy were to emancipate the serfs and to transfer property only slowly to the villager. The first Prussian province to release the masses from their feudal dues did so in 1807; Austria followed in 1848, Russia in 1861. Active revolutionary movements in the two latter cases spurred imperial liberalization.[19]

Not all Polish peasants remained apathetic to politics; some in Prussia developed a national consciousness before 1890 as a result of Bismarck's Germanization campaign in the churches and schools, and his colonization of Germans to replace Poles in the region. This ethnic awakening was not widespread even in that sector, and was evident only in Silesia and around Poznan.[20] The masses of Europe remained unenlightened until far into the next century.

[19] Adam Zoltowski, *Border of Europe* (London, 1950), 121–122, 142; Edwin A. Pratt, *The Organization of Agriculture* (London, 1904), 215; and especially W. F. Reddaway *et al., The Cambridge History of Poland* (Cambridge, 1941), 382–383, 419.

[20] Aleksander Gieysztor *et al., History of Poland*, trans. by Krystyna Cekalska *et al.* (Warszawa, 1968), 471–472, 494, 542–543, 582. The campaign is in Richard Tims, *Germanizing Prussian Poland* (New York, 1941), 108–109.

In addition to official efforts to inhibit nationalism among the masses, ethnic patriots found other difficulties in winning the peasants to their cause. One drawback was that the leadership of the liberal movement did not come from the rank and file. Polish and Lithuanian patriots in particular were generally aristocrats and intellectuals rather than rural proletarians. Normally and historically the cleavage between these two classes was distinct and even hostile. The upper classes in Poland during the eighteenth and early nineteenth centuries had very little contact with the majority of their countrymen. No middle class existed, so an enormous social gulf separated economic groups at the upper and lower levels.[21] The efforts of enthusiastic liberals to arouse the people to those broader political and cultural issues were clearly unfruitful until very late in the nineteenth century. An ardent promoter, Jan Stapiński, of peasant stock himself, tried to mobilize the *chłopi* (peasant folk) through political organization, but he labored in a lonely cause until the middle 1890's when his Peasant Party took firm shape.

Peasant behavior and attitudes in the several liberal uprisings of the nineteenth century provide additional evidence for the general lack of interest in the national question. For example, in a poorly organized effort in 1863, the famous January Insurrection, Polish and Lithuanian patriots joined in trying to overthrow Russian rule. Although some peasant representatives in Austria showed sympathy, the masses inside Russia where the revolt took place hardly stirred. In fact the lower classes aided the repression by the authorities. As late as 1895 a Danish visitor to the Lithuanian region described the inhabitants as having "no national idea as such."[22] The Lithuanians in Prussia never developed any strong ethnic consciousness.[23]

Ethnic identity developed very slowly among peasants at the turn of the century. A local Polish politician noted that his own

---

[21] Francis H. E. Palmer, *Austro-Hungarian Life in Town and Country* (New York, 1903), 77–78; Dutkiewicz, "Polish Peasant Immigration," 42, 71.

[22] Their folk culture was not self-conscious. Jack Stukas, *Awakening Lithuania: A Study of the Rise of Modern Lithuanian Nationalism* (Madison, New Jersey, 1966), 38.

[23] Alfred Senn, *The Emergence of Lithuanian Nationalism* (New York, 1959), 75.

personal conversion to the cause was exceptional and developed rather late in the nineteenth century through literature. Originally he and his class "cared nothing for the nation. I . . . did not know that I was a Pole . . . till I began to read books and papers, and I fancy that [the few] other villagers [who] came to be aware of their national attachment [did so] much in the same manner."[24] A Galician observer suggested that emigrants were just too concerned with earning bread to care about national matters.[25] A student of Polish folklore has dated the start of the massive national awakening after the onset of the Great War of 1914:[26]

> Peasants do not share the passionate national patriotism of the nobility and the intelligentsia. Nor do they share the concept of the Poles' role as sacrificial crusaders among nations. For centuries the peasants were without civil rights and accordingly without national awareness or any urge toward political participation. . . . Only after World War I did [they] step into the arena of public life.

The peasant apathy toward national animosities, along with their quest for land, illuminates their motivation for leaving Europe and coming to America. They came not for political justice or because of some abstract urge for ethnic freedom. Their passion was to obtain income for land, and thus status.[27]

[24] Slomka, *From Freedom to Self-Government*, 171. See also Mieczysław Szawleski, *Wychodźtwo Polskie w Stanach Zjednoczonych* (Lwów, 1924), 171, and Ludkiewicz, *Kwestja*, 129.

[25] P. Panek, *Emigracya Polska w Stanach Zjednoczonych Ameryki Północnej* (Lwów, 1898), 28. See also the comments of a contemporary visiting American expert, Emily Greene Balch, *Our Slavic Fellow-Citizens* (New York, 1910), 20; of a Polish-American nationalist leader, Stanisław Osada, *Na Rok Grunwaldski* (Chicago, 1910), 13; and the 1867 lament of the newly formed Polish National Committee in New York in Jerzy Borejsza, *Emigracja Polska Po Powstaniu Styczniowym* (Warsaw, 1966), 87.

[26] Benet, *Song and Dance*, 35. Additional support is in Louis Gerson, *Woodrow Wilson and the Rebirth of Poland, 1914–1920* (New Haven, 1953), 8–9, and Thomas and Znaniecki, *Polish Peasant* (1958), 2: 1580–1582.

[27] Obviously one generalization cannot apply to every case. Some migrants were not peasants but adventurers and fugitives from military conscription and the several insurrections. But the masses were overwhelmingly of peasant stock, traveling for the most material and therefore psychological reasons. The exceptional migrants are described in V. K. Rackauskas, "Lithuanians in America," in Harrison, *Lithuania*, 85; Lopata, "Polonia," 60; and V. Bartuśka, *Les Lituaniens d'Amèrique* (Lausanne, 1918), 5–6.

The nearly exclusive quest of migrants to the New World to satisfy immediate needs may appear strange to the observer who knows that East European Americans fervently supported homeland independence by 1914. By that date the awakening of the masses which had just begun in Europe was well developed in America. That such ethnic sensitivity developed over such a short space of time in the New World is astonishing for a group which had been so a-nationalistic on its arrival. Why was a social class which had once been so apathetic to patriotic appeals in Europe so receptive to them in America?

The wide response of the ordinary immigrant rested upon another important element that Polish and Lithuanian newcomers brought with them in their cultural baggage: a profound religious fervor. Religious convictions among the newcomers were just as integral to peasant temperament as were material wants; and just as they had brought with them their desire for land, they carried, too, their deep spiritual convictions. While these two factors, land and faith, were entirely compatible in Europe, normally producing little discomfort, their juxtaposition in America caused widespread conflict, leading Poles and Lithuanians to a heightened ethnic consciousness.

In the peasant districts, the church served its members' spiritual requirements without disturbing their agrarian values. In fact the fervent Polish and Lithuanian piety nicely complemented the peasant attachment to land. Religious observance enabled the superstitious peasant to deal with the mysterious and the unexplainable, and provided a force to be called upon in man's battle with evil, suffering, and pain. Thus religion offered a measure of security for the uncertain future. With a daily life that was filled with the unknown and doubt, the peasants, with the help of their church, could gain greater power over what would be. At least religious observance provided a sanction for the benchmarks of the life cycle—birth, marriage, and death.

Besides its function of assuring the communicant about the future, the faith also provided an earnestly sought instrument for metaphysical expression, diversion, and entertainment. Attendance at the local parish was a part of the peasants' day of rest where they could commune with the holy spirit in a state of wonderment and awe. Even though the village house of worship was small, the peasants never ceased to be affected by the elaborateness of the interior. The service, as well as the ritual, transported the lowly from their own drab environment into the sphere of the strange and supernatural. In addition to offering some diversion from a hard agricultural life, the church also served a specifically extra-religious function as a family social center.[28]

The faith of the Poles and Lithuanians, Roman Catholicism, or rather its complex system of venerated saints, added further variety to the peasants' spiritual existence and provided specific remedies for particular ills. God, the Father, stood at the apex of the communicants' spiritual hierarchy. He had the power to solve all the world's problems with His omnipotence and His ability to perform miracles. Jesus, His Son, acted as the mediator between man and God. But to have those divine remedies applied to the sufferings of peasant life, the ploughman had to petition one of an array of saints for assistance. These celestial figures handled particular problems with a lower order of miracles.

The exalted place of the Holy Mother most accurately demonstrates the profound awe peasants had of religious matters. The Virgin Mary was particularly revered by both Poles and Lithuanians. In fact so intense was the worship of Her that a cult of the Virgin, and even Mariolatry, developed in those East European districts in the nineteenth century.[29] Poles and Lithuanians attached great significance to regular pilgrimages to religious shrines. The most hallowed Polish place was the Mother of God Church on Jasna Góra in Częstochowa. Visitors would travel hundreds of miles to ask the picture of the Black Madonna within the church to cure some special ailment or to give their family a son. The atmosphere of tinkling bells, burning incense, and the gilded representation of the Virgin framed in precious stones always provided an appropriate setting for

---

[28] Schermerhorn, *These Our People*, 149; Jonitis, "Acculturation," 116.

[29] The place of the saints and the Virgin is described in Joel Hayden, *Religious Work Among the Poles in America* (New York, 1916), 14, and Thomas and Znaniecki, *Polish Peasant* (1958), 1: 249–252.

spiritual experience.[30] Our Lady of Siluva was to the Lithuanian masses what the Black Madonna was to the Poles.[31]

The most informed guide for determining which saint to petition in this intricate religio-magical system was the local curate. Peasant devotion to the faith showed itself in their high regard for their clergy. As God's mortal representatives on earth, the clergy demanded, and received, the utmost respect in the Old World. The cleric more than any other person in the community was the common man's guide in the mysterious world and as a result exerted more authority over his parishioners than probably the cleric himself realized.[32] The great hope of all Polish peasant families was that one of the males might take the vows, for "more than anything else a man of the cloth raises the social standing of the family. . . . Every peasant, when giving instructions to his son, dreams that the latter will become a priest."[33]

The critical area of church activity that might have caused social dissatisfaction was financial support. Even during hard times in the nineteenth-century Polish districts, however, the peasants rarely objected to contributing to the local parish. Unlike later events in the New World, little friction arose between the pastor and his flock. The ploughmen readily offered their Christian dues when the pastor and his organist made their periodic rounds. Such aid was more likely in kind than in money, since barter was the normal exchange in the districts. During good harvests and on holidays the peasants treated their curate and his assistants with exceptional generosity. Part of the reason for general harmony between the laymen and their cleric was

[30] See C. B. Bailey, *The Slavs of the War Zone* (London, 1917), 34–39; Louise Van Norman, *Poland, The Knight Among Nations* (New York, 1907), chapter X; and Kenneth D. Miller, *Peasant Pioneers* (New York, 1925), 41ff.

[31] Henry M. Malak, *Apostle of Mercy of Chicago* (London, 1961), 42; Slomka, *From Serfdom*, 142; Sirvaitis, "Religious Folkways in Lithuania and Their Conservation in the United States," 263–264, 286. Compare the immigrant's Black Madonna in Daniel Marsh, "The Problem of Polish Immigration . . ." (M.A. thesis, Northwestern University, 1902), 13.

[32] Compare the etiquette of greeting the pastor at the beginning of Władysław Reymont's epic novel of Polish peasant life, *Chłopi;* there the people threw themselves at the feet of the priest.

[33] Thomas and Znaniecki, *Polish Peasant* (1920), 12: 141–143; 1: 273; and Sirvaitis, "Religious Folkways," 308, 424.

village custom, which enforced family support. Inhabitants considered a cottage in disgrace or in sin if the priest avoided the dwelling on his regular visitations.[34] Finally, the Roman Catholic institutions were theirs; parishioners did not need to separate their group and their faith.

The oppressive, anti-Catholic policies of two partitioning powers, Prussia (later Germany) and Russia, did not weaken the religious devotion of the masses. Bismarck's Protestant and Prussianizing drive in the *Kulturkampf* and the Russification policy from 1863 to 1904 still left the agrarian masses strongly Roman Catholic. As the standard study on Polish peasant life has pointed out: "Religious attitudes prove . . . the most lasting of all traditional components of the peasant's social psychology."[35]

For ordinary Polish and Lithuanian peasants, then, two basic urges constituted their psychology as they left for America: the drive for land and the necessity of religion in their existence. They dearly cherished the soil, its mystery of productivity as well as its status implications. And they revered their faith, a spiritual tradition which provided them with continuity wherever they went. These two values were an integral part of their heritage and, even more, dominated their peasant consciousness. Regrettably, but perhaps inevitably, it was to be these very basic Old World characteristics that would collide and disrupt their community in the New.

---

[34] Slomka, *From Serfdom*, 29, 141–142.

[35] Thomas and Znaniecki, *Polish Peasant* (1918), 4: 136. See also Władyslaw Grabski, *Historia Towarzystwo Rolniczego 1858–1861* (Warszawa, 1904), 1: 152, quoted in S. M. Bronisława Dmowski, "Rozwój i stuletnia działalność Zgromadzenie Siostr Felicjanek w Polsce," in *Sacrum Poloniae Millenium* (1962), 8–9, 45n.

TWO

America's Impact on Rural Aliens

POLISH AND LITHUANIAN IMMIGRANTS brought with them to America a profound religious devotion and a passion for land. The long journey to a new location was not a rejection of tradition but rather a new means of attaining their old, rural end—earning income to buy land. In that sense they were still conservative, for though they settled largely in unfamiliar American industrial centers, they retained the vital spiritual and material needs they had in the Old World. By about 1900 they had made substantial progress toward such religious and secular goals. Polish and Lithuanian America by then consisted of hundreds of ethnic parishes, which were evidence of vast Polish and Lithuanian real wealth.[1]

But the New World society in which the East Europeans now lived was not entirely satisfactory. The immigrants would have

[1] The use of the term "parish" here and later is likely to be misunderstood. I use the word with its sociological connotation to mean a neighborhood, rather than simply a unit of church government. The frequent reference ought not to suggest, as non-Catholics might assume, that religious authorities, particularly the priest, directed the locality. Polish immigrants, for example, often labeled something by the name of the neighborhood parish, as "Stanisławowo" ("Stanislavian," literally translated). The designation did not mean that the individual in question submitted to the dictation of the priest or even that he was a regular churchgoer; it merely meant he lived in the section served by that house of worship. See Stefan Barszczewski, *Polacy w Ameryce* (Warsaw, 1902?), 29; Włodzimierz Wnuk, *Szarotki Rosna w Chicago* (Warszawa, 1964), 22.

preferred to reconstruct in the United States an exact replica of their Old World community, but such replanting was impossible. Their primary settlement in America was in a radically different environment, for most a complex urban center rather than a peasant village. The new arrivals could and did fashion their American neighborhood upon the traditional bases they had known, with an accessible church and property of their own in the form of real estate. As best they could, Poles and Lithuanians did re-establish their communities in the unfamiliar environment of Anglo-America. To some arrivals the majority culture was hostile, but it was not an insurmountable barrier to the re-creation of their traditional way of life.

An earlier theory of immigrant adjustment stresses the devastating effect of American culture. It views the arrival in America as a cultural shock to all new immigrants. The impact upon East Europeans was especially disturbing, producing much emotional, psychological disorientation. Far from friends and relatives, a greater distance from home than most Europeans, having had to endure a long and disruptive ocean voyage, ignorant of the basic features of American life, thrown into a teeming and unfamiliar slum in a strange metropolis, and forced to labor in the gruelling conditions of a mine or factory, the East European suffered considerable mental distress. It was therefore entirely understandable that these immigrants would become delinquents, even criminals, and engage in generally antisocial behavior, as American nativists and other unfriendly sources alleged.

In spite of its emphasis upon the uprooting, this interpretation suggests that the newcomers did benefit a little from their experience. Through all the hardships of adjustment, the migrants realized that there were others very much like themselves culturally, with the same traditions, language, and customs, who generally were undergoing the same alienation. It was the realization of this common cultural conflict that taught the East Europeans that they were members of a nationality. The common denominator, then, of ethnic consciousness—Polishness for the immigrant Pole, Lithuanianness for the incoming Lithuanian—was an outgrowth of psychological torment. They realized their own distinctive culture by confronting an alien one.[2] Such an interpretation exaggerates the disruptive impact of the new environment and misleadingly subordinates certain aspects of cultural continuity. The newcomers' entrance into American life was hardly destructive to their temperament, and though there was some maladjustment, the distress was not a major foil for ethnic consciousness. The realization of national identity among Polish and Lithuanian immigrants resulted essentially from a dramatic polarization over objectives that disturbed these nationality communities at the end of the nineteenth century. The stress which produced national consciousness came from within, not without, the immigrant communities.

The earliest critical moments for testing identity-making occurred during the very formation of immigrant Polish and Lithuanian settlements.[3] These nationality subgroups emerged gradually, almost imperceptibly, out of a familiar cultural environment. Even though "Americanization" demanded the rapid assimilation of newcomers, the ordinary immigrant pioneers actually experienced far more continuity than shock. The impact of the New World was to reinforce the arrivals' traditional quest for economic accumulation and their Old World ideals of religiosity and property holding.

The American social fabric was already pluralistic by the time these East Europeans came to the New World. By 1864, for example, at the birth of the major Polish parish in Chicago, the nation included not only the older communities from northern and western Europe—the English, Scotch, Welsh, Scandinavians, and Irish—but also others from the central and even the eastern areas of the continent—Germans, Jews, and Czechs. Even earlier there were no completely isolated Polish settlements. Thus the Polish vanguard in Chicago and many other centers did not have to strike roots in a completely alien, Anglo-American environment, nor even in the more familiar Irish

---

[2] Thomas and Znaniecki, *Polish Peasant* (1918–1920), 3: 1476–1477; Joseph Wytrwal, "Two American Polish Nationality Organizations," 68; and Helena Z. Lopata, "The Function of Voluntary Organizations in an Ethnic Community: 'Polonia' " (Ph.D. dissertation, University of Chicago, 1954), 13.

[3] See Chapter VIII below for a detailed review of Lithuanian development.

Catholic community, for a much more closely related Central European element was already in the New World to help cushion cultural shock. There were peoples from both their own and adjacent regions with whom they were familiar. Understandably, it was within or very close to these Prussian-American centers that Polish America began. The succession of ethnic communities in the United States developed out of nationality subsocieties which the emerging group was geographically closest to, and were thus most familiar with, in Europe. Nationality fragmentation was hardly a product of cultural disorganization.

Even more significant evidence of cultural continuity is the adaptable quality of the pioneers themselves. The early Poles and Lithuanians were from German-speaking borderlands—the Prussian, Silesian, and Pomeranian districts. The pioneers probably already knew the language and perhaps some of the customs of the nationality within which they settled. Some of the vanguard had a bicultural identity, partly Polish and partly German.

The earliest Polish settlers in America (disregarding individual arrivals before the 1850's) were the best equipped for cultural adjustment. Down to 1890 the overwhelming majority originated in the eastern German borderlands. Normally they had considerable personal resources, brought their families, became permanent residents, and had a higher literacy level and more skills than their countrymen from Austria and Russia who came later.[4] Similar generalizations can be made about the earliest Lithuanians who emigrated from near the Prussian border in the Suvalki district.[5] It is beyond the scope of this work

4 Note particularly the Silesians, Kashubes, and Mazovians. Joanna Ladomirska, "Z Dziejów Śląskiej Emigracji do Ameryki Północnej," in *Studia Śląskie*, New Series, 274 (1966); Felix Seroczynski, "Poles in the United States," in Charles G. Herberman, ed., *The Catholic Encyclopedia* (1911), 12: 205–206; Barszczewski, *Polacy*, 12–13; Jan Perkowski, "The Kashubes— Origins and Emigration to America," in *Polish American Studies*, 23: 4–7, (January–June, 1966); and Stefan Wloszczewski, "The Polish Sociological Group in America," in *The American Slavic and East European Review*, 4: 142–143 (August, 1945).

5 A. Kaupus, "Les Colonies Lituaniennes aux États-Unis," in *Annales des Nationalities*, Année 2e: 231 (Mai-Juin, 1913).

to trace in detail the origins of every Polish and Lithuanian colony in America. However, a summary view of the major settlements leads one to conclude that these new immigrant communities developed from within related nationality settlements, and that it is likely that German and Czech America had far more to do with the construction of Polish and Lithuanian America than did Anglo-America.

The very first Polish parish—at Panna Maria, Texas, in 1854 —and many of the other early ones demonstrated the kind of cultural transition that every later group settlement experienced. A Polish priest, Father Leopold Moczygęba, a cleric in a German Franciscan order (the ethnic contacts of these first Polish regulars is characteristic), led his countrymen into an area that he had known well as a member of the religious community. Similarly, the other pioneer colonies—in Wisconsin, Michigan, and Nebraska—began in agriculture under German-American influence.[6]

In the larger city settlements to which Poles came later the so-called first or "mother" Polish parishes emerged from neighborhoods which had a clearly German or Bohemian character. Omaha Poles, for example, must have known other languages because they attended services at the German St. Mary Magdalene's and later at St. Wenceslaus.' The important Polish St. Stanislaus parish in New York had noticeable Moravian as well as German origins. Detroit Poles refer to a West Prussian as the founder of that colony, which was located within the German St. Joseph parish. The Milwaukee Polish founder assisted both his countrymen and Germans in getting settled. Father Wolfgang Jamietz help start Cleveland's first Polish parish in 1875, and in Scranton, Wilkes-Barre, Pittsburgh, Buffalo, St. Paul, St. Louis, and South Bend the Poles first attended Czech or

---

[6] Albert Hart Sanford, "The Polish People of Portage County," in *Proceedings of the State Historical Society of Wisconsin, 1907* (Madison, 1908), 274. Parisville, Michigan, begun in 1852, probably included some German families. From a report quoted in Reverend Wacław Kruszka, *Historya Polska w Ameryce* (13 vols., Milwaukee, 1905–1908), 11: 144–151; and Henry W. Casper, *History of the Catholic Church in Nebraska: Catholic Chapters in Nebraska Immigration* (Milwaukee, 1966), 145–147.

German services.[7] Lithuanian newcomers, who first arrived about 1868, usually settled as a part of various Polish nuclei until the 1880's, and they too met familiar German hosts.[8] Besides entering an ethnically familiar rather than a strange Anglo-American community, the Polish and Lithuanian peasants relied upon the immigrant letter. In fact very likely East Europeans knew of the economic conditions in the New World even before they received American correspondence personally. They may have heard of overseas opportunities through their frequent movement to and settlement in German lands. The potential migrants accumulated a considerable fund of information over time, for letters and news from countrymen began arriving in Polish areas surprisingly early in the century—during the 1850's from American agricultural regions and the 1860's from cities. The knowledge East European migrants had about traveling and settling in the United States has been greatly underestimated.[9] It is true that members of these nationalities who arrived after 1890 were less literate, less sophisticated, and more subject to the shock of an alien world; but at least their

---

[7] An illustrative, though perhaps apochryphal, story tells of an early Polish family lost in Detroit, looking for their settlement. They finally found directions to the neighborhood by asking a passerby in German. Kruszka, *Historya,* 11: 167, as well as 6–7; 12: 43–45, 124; 13: 7, 24; 2: 121–123; Thaddeus Borun, *We, the Milwaukee Poles* (Milwaukee, 1946), 1–3; *1885–1935, Souvenir of the Golden Jubilee of Most Sacred Heart of Mary Parish in Scranton, Pa.* (Scranton, 1935), 6; Sister Mary Remigia Napolska, *The Polish Immigrant in Detroit to 1914* (Chicago, 1946), 26–30; Casper, *Catholic Church in Nebraska,* 184; Frank Renkiewicz, "The Polish Settlement of St. Joseph County, Indiana, 1855-1935" (Ph.D. dissertation, University of Notre Dame, 1967), 34, 45; *1875–1950, Diamond Jubilee, St. Stanislaus Church, B.i.M. Nanticoke, Pa.* (n.p., 1950), 34; J. Mierzynski *et al., Polacy w New York* (New York, 1908?), 46; *Parafia Św. Stanisław B.i.M. w New York, 1874–1949* (New York, 1949), 53–54.

[8] Joseph S. Roucek, "American Lithuanians," in *Baltic and Slavic Countries,* 4: 348 (September, 1938); *Pittstone Lietuvių Istoria, 1885–1935* (Pittston, Pennsylvania, 1935), 12; Greene, *Slavic Community,* chapter III.

[9] Stefan Wloszczewski, *History of Polish American Culture* (Trenton, New Jersey, 1946), 19; *Emigration Conditions in Europe* (61 Congress, 3 session, Senate Document no. 748, Washington, D.C., 1911), 56; Peter Roberts, *The New Immigration* (New York, 1913), 11; Brożek, "Początki Emigracii z Górnego Śląska do Ameryka . . ." in *Kwartalnik Historyczny* No. 1 (1968), 12, 15; Balch, *Slavic Fellow Citizens,* 53.

own ethnic community was well established in America by then. To be sure, the existence of familiar though differing ethnic institutions and the foreknowledge of conditions in America did not guarantee a totally comfortable transition for Poles and Lithuanians. The long journey over land and sea was normally fraught with unexpected difficulties, and individual tragedies occurred. Living among Germans and Czechs in the New World also produced some group discord and antagonism. But on the whole, Anglo-American culture had little impact on the ethnic consciousness of the Poles and Lithuanians, for the established English-speaking majority existed some distance away, separated by other nationalities. Another segment of the American population—one might call it "central European America"— served as a transitional subculture for East Europeans. The Poles and Lithuanians did not have to make the traumatic choice between "drowning in the Anglo-Saxon sea" and making their own self-conscious community.

But if the East Europeans did not experience severe cultural shock, was their quest for income and savings thwarted? And if they were exploited as dollar-a-day Slavs, did this encourage group consciousness? The answer appears to be no. While industrial employers frequently did abuse and mistreat employees at the turn of the century, the feeling of anti-American resentment among foreign-born workers existed mostly in the minds of the reformers.[10] East European immigrants on the whole had little reason for massive dissatisfaction. They achieved the income accumulation they sought, even if the means of acquisition was something other than they had anticipated. In any event economic exploitation was not the catalyst of nationality awakening.

Although the Poles and Lithuanians originally came to America to earn money to buy European land, most stayed in Amer-

---

[10] Elsewhere I have indicated the militancy of Slavs in labor unrest. Certainly they had grievances and acted vigorously to have them resolved, but their resentment toward their employer was on economic not nationality grounds. In fact, immigrant strike demonstrations preceded by the stars and stripes were a common sight in Pennsylvania. Greene, *Slavic Community*, chapter VII, especially 132ff.

ica, where they successfully purchased property. Their plans changed, but they maintained their traditional land hunger and love of the soil.[11] The "soil" now was not land in the usual sense of property for cultivation, but real estate, a home. In short, the Polish and Lithuanian immigrants transformed their original intention of owning an estate in Europe to living here as Americans, with homes of their own. It would be this enduring concern for property, and particularly property in their ethnic parish, that would produce internal friction, rioting, and ultimately ethnic consciousness.

The destination of early Poles in America demonstrated their land hunger. In the major wave of the 1870 to 1914 era (approximately 3 million persons), the majority headed for the urban centers of the East and Midwest; a large minority of several hundred thousand located initially in rural areas. The first settlements were in the Texas, Wisconsin, and Michigan countrysides. Even the later urban immigrants probably would have preferred open areas, but most remained in cities. While a few eventually reached rural America, many more kept that destination in mind.[12] For the Polish-Americans, becoming a rural proletariat in agricultural regions was not simply an attempt to find employment but also a means to re-establish their traditional way of life. They sought hired work on farms on their way to becoming proprietors.[13]

[11] See the observations in Immigration Commission, *Recent Immigrants in Agriculture* (61 Congress, 2 session, Senate Document no. 733, pt. 24, Washington, D.C., 1911), 2: 108; William Seabrook, *These Foreigners* (New York, 1938), 241, 261–264, 293–294; and the quoted newspaper in Kruszka, *Historya*, 3: 111–112.

[12] Balch, *Slavic Fellow-Citizens*, 333.

[13] Note the movement out to Long Island and the Connecticut River valley in particular. Joseph Wytrwal, *America's Polish Heritage* (Detroit, 1961), 85–86; Szawleski, *Wychodźtwo*, 21; Edward Kirk Titus, "The Pole in the Land of the Puritan," in *New England Magazine*, 29: 13 (October, 1903); Balch, *Slavic Fellow-Citizens*, 240, 324; William Shriver, *Immigrant Forces* (New York, 1913), 82–85; V. Bartuśka, *Les Lituaniens d'Amerique* (Lausanne, 1914), 8, 14; Grace Abbot, "The Chicago Employment Agency and the Immigrant Worker," in the *American Journal of Sociology*, 14: 292 (November, 1908); Wloszczewski, *Polish American Culture*, chapter VI; Victor Greene, "Polish American as Peasant American," paper given at State Historical Society of Wisconsin meeting, Stevens Point, June 16, 1973.

Even when they remained in America's new urban-industrial centers, the ex-peasants retained their agrarian culture and values. However, it took a keen eye to detect in the ethnic slums the Polish and Lithuanian love for rural life; the new factory workers displayed their pastoral attachment in an inconspicuous manner. The standard social study of the Pennsylvania minefields, for example, pointed out the vegetable garden and birdhouse which often complemented the "Hunkie" shack.[14] In still more congested urban surroundings, the Slavic practice of raising livestock such as goats, chickens, and even a cow was not uncommon.[15]

In addition to retaining agrarian practices in an urban setting, East European newcomers doggedly worked for that nest egg with which to purchase property, and their success was surprising. Unquestionably the impressive savings record of these "urban poor" would have silenced critics of the immigrants had they known it. These unskilled, foreign laborers accumulated sizable funds which they either sent abroad or invested as proprietors here. Regrettably, a precise accounting of Polish and Lithuanian immigrant wealth is nearly impossible to obtain. Official statistics are lacking since neither group had a sovereign homeland, and determination of nationality for East Europeans by last name is very inaccurate.[16] Therefore estimates must be based upon a careful assessment of knowledgeable contemporary observers and group members. Their conclusion is that the Slavic immigrant did accumulate considerable capital.

Early in the century an authoritative source stated that the total amount of the remittances sent back to Europe and funds

---

[14] Peter Roberts, *Anthracite Coal Communities* (New York, 1904), 107–108; Peter Roberts, *The New Immigration* (New York, 1912), 106; Balch, *Slavic Fellow-Citizens,* 372–373.

[15] Balch, *Slavic Fellow-Citizens,* 372–373; Bessie Olga Pehotsky, *The Slavic Immigrant Woman* (Cincinnati, 1925), 45; Laura B. Garrett, "Notes on the Poles in Baltimore," in *Charities,* 13: 237; Leila Houghteling, *The Income and Standard of Living of Unskilled Laborers in Chicago* (Chicago, 1927), 189; Joseph Chałasinski, "Parafja i Szkola Parafjalna Wśród Emigracja Polskiej w Ameryce," in *Przegląd Sociologiczny,* 3: 637 (1935).

[16] See the discussion on the matter in Balch, *Slavic Fellow-Citizens,* 458–459.

on deposit in the United States was "imposing" and "enormous."[17] In addition, a flood of money orders was sent from America to Austrian Poland in 1907 in answer to widespread economic suffering in Galicia. The deluge of funds was so great that the Austrian postal service feared a sizable misplacement of the monies. A commission of the Galician provincial diet looking into the matter estimated yearly transfers at about $4,000,000.[18] Even during the hard times of the previous decade, a Prague bank reported that just over $1,000,000 per year was sent to the Polish province at the turn of the century.[19] Other observers estimated that in about 1900 Polish workers, mostly unskilled laborers, were able to save almost half of their income —the average family then possessing about $1000 in wealth.[20]

A number of writers recognized that by using their savings to purchase farmland and homes, immigrants were achieving a modified realization of the old peasant dream. "Again and again," said an observer in 1895, "our emigrants have interests in purchasing land. Many such arrivals from overseas scrape together a few *grosz* and purchase a lot in the wilderness."[21]

Other writers also spoke of the Polish-American paradox: abnormal means for traditional ends. The ex-peasants lived and worked in the American cities so that they could one day resume their rural way of life. "It is the dream of each Pole to acquire one of these [city] lots to construct a cottage . . . and a little garden. . . ." A Polish newspaper editor wryly explained to an

---

[17] *Ibid.*, 303–309.

[18] Zygmunt Gargas, *W Sprawie Ruchu Pieniężnego Między Ameryka a Galicya* (Kraków, 1907), 1, 4, 10. There were then about 500,000 Austrian Poles in America and only a handful of Galicians of other nationalities, Jews and Ruthenians. If one considers the average income at less than $300 per breadwinner, the total sent to the Old Country showed real determination. Compare Jan Pietka, *Z Galicyjskiego Bagna Emigracyjnego* (Kraków, 1912), 22, who says the yearly return was 80 million crowns.

[19] *Emigration Conditions in Europe*, 387. One should not take the list of immigrant bank remittances in Immigration Commission, *Immigrant Banks* (61 Congress, 3 session, Senate Document no. 753, Washington, 1911), 19: 206, 209, 277, as indicative, for the sampling of 116 banks of eight nationalities was too small.

[20] Panek, *Emigracya Polska*, 20; Chałasinski, "Parafja," 636–637.

[21] Ludwik Krzywicki, *Za Atlantikiem* (Warszawa, 1895), 270.

inquiring non-Pole the incongruous yearnings of a factory worker: "Industrial employers will tell you that Poles are good workers . . . but they dream at night of growing potatoes and cabbages."[22] Lithuanians, too, were known to have such "dreams."[23]

The nestor of Polish-American historians, Father Wacław Kruszka, attempted to calculate the total real wealth of his group at the end of the century. After admitting the possible inaccuracy of his conclusions, he extrapolated from an 1887 Polish reference to give the property accumulation for 1901. The figures probably are inflated, but even though they were not precise, they do suggest that the Polish immigrants' landholding was impressive. The 1887 source places the number of group farmers at 2,500 who own on the average of eighty acres each, and insists that this sum of 200,000 acres is really too conservative. By 1901 Kruszka reckons there were about 700 group agricultural colonies, and about 70,000 farming proprietors, who held over 5 million acres with a value of over $200,000,000.[24]

Far more sophisticated research is necessary to establish the precise amount of farmland owned by the American Poles, but the great influence of peasant tradition—the urge to own soil— in the New World is apparent. Other statistical evidence illustrates that land hunger among the more urbanized Poles and Lithuanians was nationwide, and that the immigrants fulfilled their wishes by purchasing their own residences. Home buying by the Slavs in Pennsylvania impressed an authority concerned with the social composition of the anthracite fields. After little

[22] Kowalczyk, "L'Emigration Polonaise," 54, 52; and Seabrook, *Foreigners*, 262, 294.

[23] Peter Jonitis, "The Acculturation of the Lithuanians of Chester, Pa." (Ph.D. dissertation, University of Pennsylvania, 1951), 274–275; Bartuśka, *Lituaniens*.

[24] His extraordinary effort to make a census of the Poles in America persuades his reader that his estimates are reasonable. Kruszka, *Historya*, 3: 120–122. Note his reputation in Balch, *Slavic Fellow-Citizens*, 262–265, and general assessments in Rev. Alexander Syski, "Nestor of Polish Historians in America: Rev. Wacław Kruszka," in *Polish American Studies*, 1: 62–70 (1944).

more than a decade in the region "Sclav acquisition of real estate is . . . general all through the coal fields." In four supposedly typical towns, Poles and Lithuanians possessed title to $2,500,000 worth of property, and over 98 per cent of the owners were meeting their mortgage obligations.[25] Other authorities attested to the immigrants' goal of acquiring real estate in other communities.[26]

Incoming aliens acquired land at times by utilizing the ethnic building-and-loan society. The popularity of this institution of immigrant adjustment is still little known, but it appears to have been a common agency in significantly easing East Europeans into American surroundings. The building and loan association among Eastern Europeans was really another form of the mutual-aid principle that American immigrants used to meet economic needs. Shortly after its arrival every group established "self-help societies" to which members made contributions and from which they received minimum security in times of emergencies, such as sickness, accident, or death. From its birth almost every local and national fraternal union had mutual benefit features. There were ample precedents for mutual aid in both the European and American experience. The Poles had formed land committees to combat Bismarck's colonization program through group purchase, and German- and Czech-American fraternal organizations, earlier societies in which Poles participated, had used the mutual-benefit idea extensively.

The Polish- and Lithuanian-American building-and-loan associations originated as neighborhood organizations to accumulate capital to buy homes. They remained grassroots, not nation-

---

[25] Roberts, *Communities*, 41–43. Note, too, Sister M. Theodosetta Lewandowska, "The Polish Immigrant in Philadelphia to 1914," in *Records of the American Catholic Society of Philadelphia*, 65: 83 (June, 1954).

[26] Barszczewski, *Polacy*, 85, 87; Edmund de S. Brunner *et al., Immigrant Farmers and Their Children* (New York, 1929), 215–216; R. A. Schermerhorn, *These Our People* (Boston, 1949), 281–284; Panek, *Emigracya Polska*, 21; Paul Fox, *Poles in America* (New York, 1922), 77–78; Napolska, *Polish Immigrant in Detroit*, 44–45; Renkiewicz, "Polish Settlement of St. Joseph County," 37; Daniel Katz and Niles Carpenter, "The Cultural Adjustment of the Polish Group in the City of Buffalo," in *Social Forces*, 6: 79 (September, 1927); Bartuśka, *Les Lituaniens*, 12.

wide, bodies, democratically organized by ethnic members. Meeting regularly in churches or some other central location, the immigrants pooled their money by purchasing shares. After a time the shareholders could withdraw what they had paid, plus interest, and also secure a home loan. Essentially, the fund was a savings as well as a lending agency for home buying by local nationality members. This building and loan idea was not a Slavic immigrant creation; it had come to America from England about 1830.[27] Yet in the middle and late nineteenth century these new ethnic groups utilized it widely as a mechanism for buying homes.[28]

The long tradition and the large sums of money accumulated by the Polish-American societies indicated the home-buying mania of the group. One Polish historian, writing in 1920, termed the institution "very successful" in the years before the First World War, particularly among the Chicago population.[29] A 1925 report listed 550 societies with 400,000 members and $330,000,000 in assets. An incomplete breakdown of the location of these institutions showed sixty in Chicago, eight in Milwaukee, seven in Baltimore, six in Pittsburgh, four in Cleveland, and two in Buffalo.[30] The enthusiasm and impressive results of the Polish building-and-loan societies in at least two colonies, South Bend and Baltimore, have been noted by others. The South Bend Polonia established their two co-operative societies early, 1882 and 1893. The initial institution was of particular importance as it constituted the cornerstone of the nationality's

[27] See the official history: H. Morton Bodfish, ed., *History of Building and Loan in the United States* (Chicago, 1931), chapter I and *passim*.

[28] One must carefully distinguish between the building-and-loan and the better-known "immigrant bank." The latter was usually a privately managed and owned agency to retain deposits of group members temporarily for safe-keeping. Its purpose was to assist the immigrant in essentially financial matters other than home buying. Compare Immigration Commission, *Immigrant Banks*, 19: 203, 217. On the origin and the performance of the Polish immigrant building-and-loan association, see *Polska Przegład Emigracyny*, May 23, 1908, at the Kórnik Library, Poźnan, Poland.

[29] Jozef Okolowicz, *Wychodźtwo i Osadnictwo Polskie Przed Wojna Światowa* (Warsaw, 1920), 24.

[30] Computed from Rev. Francis Bolek and Rev. Ladislas Siekaniec, eds., *Polish American Encyclopedia, A–B* (Buffalo, 1954), 253–254.

economy and did more than any other factor "to satisfy the [drive] of the Poles to own their own homes." By 1903, with $1,500,000 in assets, it was the largest building-and-loan association outside of Indianapolis.[31]

The building-and-loan societies of Baltimore in 1925 were one of the Polish community's "outstanding features." The Poles there were "a thrifty people. Not many generations removed from the soil, their great ambition in life is to own land. They will go hungry and take their children out of school to work in order to secure money to purchase homes. . . . A very large percentage of the Poles in Baltimore own their own homes and have purchased them through their [thirteen] building and loan associations."[32]

This evidence suggests in absolute figures the determination and earnestness of Poles and Lithuanians to acquire property. Comparative information showing the Polish and Lithuanian ability to accumulate and purchase homes in relation to that of native Americans and other ethnic groups is equally impressive.

TABLE 1: Native and Immigrant Family
Home Ownership and Income, 1910

Nativity	Income	Number of Families	Rank	Homes Owned	Number of Families	Percentage of home owning families	Rank
Native white	$657	324	1	259	1187	21.8	5
Irish	557	464	2	222	734	30.2	2
Bohemian-Moravian Czech	552	384	3	328	515	63.7	1
Hebrew	463	615	4	48	764	6.3	10
Italian, North	449	47	5	182	655	27.8	3
Slovenian	433	98	6	46	182	25.3	4
Lithuanian	419	250	7	150	832	18.0	7
Slovak	402	288	8	239	1361	17.6	8
Italian, South	390	1190	9	239	1603	14.9	9
Polish	379	872	10	404	2233	18.1	6
Syrian	356	29	11	8	171	4.7	11

[31] Renkiewicz, "St. Joseph County," 127.

[32] Mary Laura Swanson, "A Study of the Polish Organizations in the Polish Community of Baltimore" (M.A. thesis, The Johns Hopkins University, 1925), 83.

The Federal Immigration Commission statistics for 1911 are useful, though there are some limitations: the sampling was fragmentary, the numbers both by group and as a whole were small, the representative quality by nationality of the subjects polled is now unknown. Nevertheless the table, comparing annual income to home ownership of family heads by nationality, offers some basis for testing home ownership interest.[33]

The Poles' record of low income and a high percentage of ownership indicated their strong desire for real estate. While next-to-last of the eleven nationalities in income, receiving $379 yearly, the Polish immigrants were sixth in the percentage owning homes, 18.1. Native Americans were highest in income but fifth in home ownership. Lithuanians were about average, ranking seventh in both categories. Their poorer performance may have been a reflection of their relatively late arrival in the United States—there was no Lithuanian-American community until about 1890—rather than disinterest in owning a home. A leading sociologist, reviewing the major study on the Polish peasant, concluded that "the Polish peasant tends to buy a house and lot more readily than an immigrant from some other society."[34]

This general survey, then, strongly indicates that landholding, whether in Europe or in America, in the country or in the city, was a mark of achievement for the Polish family. Passage to America reinforced rather than altered that passion.

If these immigrants extolled the landholding ideal for themselves, it is logical that they would regard the title to their religious institution, in America the local ethnic parish, with special sensitivity. Parishioners exerted considerable effort to support that other transplanted institution, their church. Polish

[33] Only eleven of the twenty-three groups had income listed. Calculated from Immigration Commission, *Abstracts of Reports of the Immigration Commission with Conclusions and Recommendations and Views of the Minority* (61 Congress, 1 session, Senate Document no. 747, Washington, 1911), 468, 767.

[34] Louis Wirth, in Herbert Blumer, "An Appraisal of Thomas and Znaniecki's The Polish Peasant in Europe and America," in *SSRC Bulletin*, no. 44, pp. 147–148 (1939).

laborers, although earning only a pittance, contributed a part of that hard-won income to their local parish. The donation signified a reaffirmation of the peasants' devotion to the spirit. The exact amount of the group's financial support of American Catholicism is difficult to estimate, because all immigrants did not live in group parishes. But some picture is possible. A 1905 observer judged the property value of Polish ethnic parishes and pastor maintenance at about $11,000,000. This figure, which excluded the cost of group hospitals, orphanages, seminaries, and the like, was equivalent to over two weeks' wages for every adult immigrant.[35] Thus, for themselves and their neighborhood church, the possession of property was of vital interest to former Polish and Lithuanian peasants, an interest that would be at the root of their difficulty with Catholic Church leaders.

[35] Kruszka, *Historya,* 2: 17.

—————————— THREE ——————————

Building the Immigrant Capital: Chicago, 1860–1900

THE EAST EUROPEAN rush to Chicago was a part of the great economic and social boom that revolutionized that city on Lake Michigan. In fact, if one can typify radical material change in America by reference to one urban center, for the late nineteenth century Chicago is the place. It characterized clearly the fundamental economic changes affecting all American development in that period. While never growing to become the nation's largest city, it was *the* metropolis of the new industrial order, gaining national leadership as America's major railway, grain, meatpacking, and steel-producing center. At the end of the last century Chicago surged forward more rapidly than the other American cities, especially those in the East, and as it did so it became an important magnet for workers, native and immigrant, who sought industrial employment. In the forty years before 1910 its population growth, coming heavily from abroad, was tenfold, reaching 2,000,000 and making it the country's second-largest city.[1] Any general study of late-nineteenth-century immigration must devote considerable attention to Chicago.

East Europeans were able to adjust satisfactorily to Chicago

———

[1] New York achieved its numerical superiority largely by annexing Brooklyn at the turn of the century. Bessie Louise Pierce, *A History of Chicago* (3 vols., New York, 1957), 3: 6.

without suffering severe disorientation. It is unlikely that their ethnic group consciousness developed because of a hostile American culture or economy, for both Poles and Lithuanians accomplished their cultural and material objectives. Simple population statistics indicate that the burgeoning metropolis on Lake Michigan was, more than any other industrial center, the mecca for Polish and Lithuanian newcomers. The tables below show not only the size of the East European influx into Chicago but also its beginning. The precise figures are difficult to obtain because surnames do not distinguish these two groups clearly from others or from each other. Therefore, the investigator must rely heavily upon nationality sources for estimates. This is not a serious drawback, however, for most group authorities were writing in their own language for their own countrymen, which may have minimized deliberate inaccuracies or inflated numbers.

Table 2 shows the major Polish population centers about 1905 and in 1920. Chicago far out-distanced the other colonies. Presumably all numbers include foreign-born and their children.[2]

TABLE 2: Major Polish Population Centers

City	1905	1920
Chicago	250,000	400,000
New York	150,000	200,000
Pittsburgh	70,000	125,000
Buffalo	70,000	100,000
Milwaukee	65,000	100,000
Detroit	50,000	100,000
Cleveland	30,000*	50,000*

*Toledo, Philadelphia, Baltimore, and Boston were below these figures.

Table 3 depicts the growth of the Polish and Lithuanian communities in Chicago—when they began, how quickly they developed. Although the figures below are again approximations, they do indicate an early beginning for the two ethnic settle-

[2] From my own calculations and those of Fox, *Poles*, 63; Balch, *Slavic Fellow-Citizens*, 264; and Kruszka, *Historya*, 1: 94ff.

ments, then moderate growth, and finally a rapid expansion at the turn of the century.[3]

TABLE 3: Polish and Lithuanian Population in Chicago
(Foreign born and their children)

Year	Poles	Lithuanians
1864	100 or less	—
1871	6,000	—
1880	30,000	—
1881	N.A.	20 or less
1883	N.A.	30
1886	45,000	N.A.
1890	90,000	2,000
1896	N.A.	8,000
1900	150,000	13,000
1908	N.A.	50,000
1914	300,000	75,000

A nucleus of the Slavic contingent existed in Chicago from the mid-1860's; Lithuanians first appeared in the mid-1880's. Chicago Polonia was already over thirty years old and the Lithuanian colony over ten when the large numbers of twentieth-century immigrants began inundating the midwestern metropolis. These statistics suggest, although they do not prove, early, sound nationality communities. The long period of

3 My figures are derived from the following: for Poles, *Report of the Select Committee on Immigration* . . . (51 Congress, 2 session, House of Representatives Report No. 3472, Washington, D.C., 1891), 2: 64; Ks. Władysław Kwiatkowski, *Historia Zgromadzenia Zmartwychwstania Panskiego* . . . , *1842–1942* (Albano, Italy, 1942), 340; Barszczewski, *Polacy*, 29; A. Bakanowski, *Moje Wspomnienia* (Lwów, 1913), 73; Panek, *Emigracya*, 12; Chodkiewicz, *Polacy*, 12; *Chicago Tribune*, March 14, 1886, in *Foreign Language Press Survey*, Chicago Public Library (hereinafter *FLPS*). *Dziennik Chicagoski*, November 21, 1945, Part 6, p. 12; and U.S. Department of Commerce, Bureau of the Census, *Thirteenth Census of the United States, 1910, Volume I: Population* (Washington, D.C., 1913), 1012; Karol Wachtl, ed., *1876–1917 Złoty Jubileuszy Najstarzy Polskiego Parafii Świetego Stanisława Kostki w Chicago, Illinois* (Chicago, 1917), 9, at the Polish Museum, Chicago; and for Lithuanians, "Valstija Illinois'o," in *Tevyne*, 4: 313 (Rugsejio, 1899); *Istoria Chicagos Lietuviu Ju Parapiju ir Kn. Kraučiunas Prova Su Laikraiciu "L"* (Chicago, 1900), 3, 8, 11, 579; *Lietuva*, December 11, 1908, *FLPS;* Paul Cressey, "The Succession of Cultural Groups in the City of Chicago" (Ph.D. dissertation, University of Chicago, 1930), 146.

gradual development, which was sufficient to establish and consolidate group institutions before the much larger immigrant waves appeared in the twentieth century, probably minimized disorganization.

To understand further the development of these groups in Chicago, and to determine the sources of self-consciousness, one must examine their economic adjustment. Further, one must survey the start of religious institutions in order to assess fully Polish and Lithuanian reactions to the nationalities they encountered. Despite vast cultural differences and few material resources, the Polish and Lithuanian peoples settled in Chicago without serious friction, and there they accumulated considerable capital.

The evidence in Chicago corroborates the two groups' providential nature, as indicated in the previous chapter. Throughout this period most members of the two immigrant groups worked at the lowest-paying industrial positions. An 1886 report listed few of the 45,000 Poles in the city employed above the menial level; only a "handful" were doctors; eight were druggists; and the rest priests or an occasional city employee.[4] The lower-class social structure for Lithuanians was similar; a detailed study of them in 1909 showed that only 322 were self-employed in a population of 50,000.[5] The overwhelming majority of both colonies were unskilled laborers, earning less than two dollars a day.

The availability of menial jobs determined the geographic clustering of the two groups in certain areas of the city. For example, three major Polish neighborhoods had appeared by 1900. The first and largest Polish colony in the 1860's was located near the many garment-making shops on Milwaukee Avenue on the near northwest side. By the next decade the emerging factory and slaughterhouse districts of the near west and southwest neighborhoods created a second area around Eighteenth and Allport streets and in Back of the Yards. The third and last area (about 1885) to draw East Europeans was

[4] *Chicago Tribune*, March 14, 1886, *FLPS*.

[5] *Lietuva*, August 20, 27, July 23, September 3, 17, October 10, 1909, *FLPS*.

south Chicago, with the rise of that area's rolling mills and steel plants, near Eighty-eighth Street and Commercial Avenue. The "mother" Roman Catholic parishes reflected the settlement pattern of Chicago Poles and Lithuanians. The first Polish church was St. Stanislaus, begun in 1866 on Noble Street near Milwaukee Avenue; the west siders formed St. Adalbert's in 1873; and the nucleus in the south was Immaculate Conception parish in 1883. The Lithuanians formed their first cluster among northside Poles at St. Stanislaus in the mid-1880's, although their largest neighborhood by 1890 was in Bridgeport on the west side. St. George's in Bridgeport was probably the largest Lithuanian church in America by 1900.

Whichever district the immigrants chose for employment, their pay was low, although the social character of the settlements differed slightly. Germans, Jews, Scandinavians, and Czechs ran the sweatshops in the northside garment district. This admirably suited the requirements of early arrivals, who had come largely in family units. Women and children sorted the rags that collectors brought them; men finished the cloth into clothes. The normal weekly income for a family of five was about twenty-five dollars. While reformers condemned the labor conditions and wages, the immigrants not only subsisted on the earnings but even saved. A group of seventy surveyed in 1892 stated that they put away on the average of forty dollars per year.[6] By stringent economies, such as using rags from work for clothing, they minimized their subsistence expenditures. The tobacco and candy industries in the vicinity further assisted family incomes by employing Polish girls at about the same wages as garment contractors paid.

The west side was more attractive to single foreigners looking for work. In the brickyards close to the railroads, at the Crane Plumbing Company, the McCormick Works, and the slaughterhouses pay was comparatively high for the unskilled, roughly fourteen dollars a week for men in about 1890. Girls could

[6] *Seventh Biennial Report of the Bureau of Labor Statistics of the State of Illinois, 1892* (Springfield, 1893), 108–109, 275–277, 363, 364, 368, 371, 380. Two-thirds of the working Lithuanians there in 1908 were listed as tailors. *Lietuva*, December 11, 1908, *FLPS.*

work in cleaner surroundings under more pleasant conditions.[7] Poles and Lithuanians entered that area in large numbers in the late 1880's, coming not only from outside the city but from other neighborhoods as well, especially to the north.[8] An average family saved about fifty dollars per year, a little more than in the garment district.

The third section of the city which drew Poles and Lithuanians, or, more accurately, all East Europeans en masse, was the Calumet district in the south with its steel and fabricating mills and car shops. Actually the region contained two Polish areas, the major center around Immaculate Conception Church in 1881 and another at St. Michael's in the vicinity of South Ninety-second Street and the lake.[9] In 1900 this region looked the most poverty-stricken of the three to many outsiders. It was the youngest community, and had had the shortest time to accumulate wealth. Many of the homes were built on stilts above the marshes, trash was everywhere, and the roadways were unimproved. But the workers were earning about two dollars a day in 1909, only slightly less than their countrymen to the north.[10]

Difficult living and working conditions did not discourage the Slav who was eager for income. A number of employers recorded their impressions of Polish and Lithuanian workers, whom they characterized as anxious for employment, loyal, persevering, and conscientious. In 1886 an executive of the

[7] *Lietuva*, August 20, 1909; *Tevyne*, 4: 311 (Rugsejis, 1899); *Istoria Chicagos* . . . , 580; *Seventh Biennial Report* . . . , 81–82; *Chicago Tribune*, March 14, 1886, *FLPS;* John R. Commons, "Labor Conditions in Meat Packing and the Recent Strike," in the *Quarterly Journal of Economics*, 19: 18–20, (November, 1904).

[8] Cressey, "Succession," 217; Pranas Garsva, *Negestanti Sviesa: Marijonu Vieka Amerikoje* (Chicago, 1964), 69; William Kucinski, "Polish People in the Town of Lake," in Town of Lake *Journal*, September 14, 1939, Chicago Historical Society.

[9] Rev. Alfred Abramowicz, *Diamond Jubilee, Immaculate Conception BVM Parish, 1882–1957* (Chicago, 1957), 21, 23.

[10] Chałasinski, "Parafja," 636–637; *Istoria Chicagos* . . . , 580; *Lietuva*, September 17, 1909, *FLPS;* Robert Hunter, *Tenement Conditions in Chicago* (Chicago, 1901), 181ff; Sophonisba Breckinridge and Edith Abbot, "Chicago Housing Conditions, V: South Chicago at the Gates of the Steel Mills," in the *American Journal of Sociology*, 17: 151, 154 (September, 1911).

large Chicago Rolling Mill Company explained simply, "[The Poles] are good workers or we would not employ them." John Cudahy, the meatpacker, agreed, with some minor reservations. While somewhat "hot-tempered," they were generally not "quarrelsome" but "excellent and faithful."[11] John Appleton, author of the standard work on the Calumet steel complex, judged the stolid East European ex-peasants as preferable to Negroes and Mexicans, who appeared to have less stamina for the arduous toil and less steady work habits.[12] However racist such comments may be, still they show the favorable reputation of Slavic laborers in heavy industry.

Both the immigrant settlement pattern in Chicago and the affirmative opinion of employers pointed to the laborers' objective: earning wages. Other evidence indicates not only their eagerness to accumulate savings but also their propensity to invest their earnings in land, thus retaining their Old World affection for real estate.

The manuscript census returns for 1870 list the real and personal property of all Americans. However, accurate nationality determination for East Europeans is nearly impossible since most persons from that part of Europe had no sovereign homeland. "Poland" is listed as an origin for some, though it probably refers to Congress Poland in the Russian sector, only a small part of the suppressed mother country. Non-Poles, such as Jews, some of whom are indistinguishable by name from Poles, compounded the difficulty by using that geographical designation for their birthplace as well.[13]

11 *Chicago Tribune,* March 14, 1886, *FLPS.*

12 John B. Appleton, *The Iron and Steel Industry of the Calumet District* (Urbana, Illinois, 1925), 93. See also Herman Feldman, *Racial Factors in American Industry* (New York, 1931), 160–161; and E. S. Clarke, "History of the Controversy Between Labor and Capital in the Slaughterhouse and Meatpacking Industries in Chicago" (M.A. thesis, University of Chicago, 1922), 28–29.

13 In addition many Prussian Poles, who made up the bulk of the Polish contingent in these years, had German names. For example, it was entirely possible for a man named Schmidt from Pomerania, to have been Polish. Anton Schermann, a leading Chicago Pole, stated that he was from Poland, but his wife, a Polish woman, stated her origin as Prussia. See the 15th Ward Manuscript Census for Chicago, Chicago Historical Society, from which I

Relatively accurate figures can be obtained for the north side, where the Polish cluster was very homogeneous. From a sampling of 128 Polish household heads in 1870 (10 per cent of the Poles then in Chicago), 107 were ordinary laborers. Thirty-eight of these unskilled owned a total of $8,725 in personal wealth and twenty-one had $14,100 in real property. Thus, if this is a representative sampling of the nationality in Chicago, 35 per cent of the group's lowest paid had accumulated surprising wealth, about $87,000 in personal property and $140,000 in land. These figures are particularly impressive because they exclude the group's few middle-class members and because it was only six years after the colony had begun. By 1870 the ordinary Polish immigrant had acquired an unusually large amount of real estate.[14] In 1886 an informed reporter estimated that just under half of the entire colony owned their own homes.[15]

Another measure of the Polish and Lithuanian drive for savings and property was the time taken to acquire title. Although a long period might show inability rather than determination, much early acquisition would at least demonstrate a

TABLE 4: Lot Transfers from Outgroup to Group Members

Years	Locality	Number of Transfers	Number of Ethnic Transfers		Per cent
*1864–1890	St. Stanislaus (north side)	406	269 (Polish)		68.7
1884–1913	St. George ⎱ St. Mary of ⎰ Perpetual Help (west side)	343	88 (Lithuanian) 25.7 ⎱ 119 (Polish) 34.7 ⎰		60.4
1881–1902	Immaculate Conception (south side)	267	191 (Polish)		71.5

*The initial dates are when the areas opened for residential development.

took my data. Note, too, that almost half of the 110 Polish founders of Immaculate Conception Parish, south Chicago's Polish "mother," had non-Polish names. Abramowicz, *Diamond Jubilee*, 25.

[14] Mieczyslaw Haiman, *Zjednoczenie Polskie Rzymsko-Katolickie w Ameryce 1873–1948* (Chicago, 1948), 28.

[15] *Chicago Tribune*, March 14, 1886, *FLPS*.

strong interest in land investment. The neighborhoods selected were three heavily Polish and Lithuanian districts: the St. Stanislaus Church vicinity on the north side, Polish-Lithuanian Bridgeport on the west side, and the area surrounding the Polish Immaculate Conception Church in the south.[16]

The table shows the rapid property acquisition of the two groups in the three districts. By 1890 the Poles had been the purchasers of just over two-thirds of the properties put up for sale in the St. Stanislaus area. In the smaller, more heterogeneous community of Bridgeport both Poles and Lithuanians are listed because it is difficult to separate them. It was normal for the latter to use Slavic names; for example, the leading Lithuanian there was Anton Olszewski, only later Olšauskas. In any event, even though the Lithuanian figure ought to be higher and the Polish one lower, together they had purchased three-fifths of the properties by 1913. And in south Chicago, the Poles had been proprietors of almost three-quarters of the available lots by 1902. Such homogeneous clustering by land title just two decades after their arrival suggests a strong interest in property acquisition, especially since the great percentage of landholders were simple laborers and the overwhelming percentage of purchases were one-lot acquisitions. Such lot buying was obviously not land speculation by developers; it was home buying by families. This tendency to buy property against all social and economic odds was more pronounced among Poles and Lithuanians than among Germans, Swedes, Irish, and Italians.[17]

A number of general observations by contemporaries familiar with the groups and the neighborhoods further confirms the East European passion for saving to buy real estate. A banker from the stockyards district, for example, told U.S. Labor Commissioner Carroll Wright in 1904 that "Slavonians and Gali-

---

[16] Cook County, Office of Recorder of Deeds: *North Side:* West ½ 4, Block 27, lots 1–3, Subsection Schultze; Canal Trustees Subsection Block 2; 5 ½ Block 11 Hurford; Canal Trustees Blocks 7, 8; Meyerhoff's Subsection North ½ Block 13. *West Side:* Egan's South Block 521 Addition to Chicago 32-39-14; Brown's Addition Northeast ¼ Section of Block 52113; Egan's Addition to Block 521, *South Side:* Calumet & Chicago Canal Subdivision 6-37-15, Blocks 8-12, 22–23.

[17] See Julius J. Ozog, "A Study of Polish Home Ownership in Chicago" (M.A. thesis, University of Chicago, 1942), 3, 15, 83–84, 138.

cians" (largely if not entirely Poles) had been buying homes recently "to a most remarkable and unprecedented extent," and that this was almost as true with Lithuanians.[18]

In the first decade of the century, social reformers surveyed the industrial districts of Chicago to designate those neighborhoods which were slums and needed improvement. They discovered some revealing yet bewildering paradoxes: first that there were numerous Polish and Lithuanian landlords, and second that these owners of unsanitary, overcrowded housing lived on the premises themselves. For example, the well-known social critic Robert Hunter condemned the generally unwholesome environment of the Polish north side, yet was forced to admit that the inhabitants appeared to be prospering. While nearly all were unskilled, the Poles were thrifty and industrious. "Property turnover was low and the houses are nearly all owned by the Polish people," he wrote, and in fact "the owners in most cases lived in their own houses."[19]

Two other investigations uncovered the same features in other East European neighborhoods. In 1910 Sophonisba Breckinridge and Edith Abbott discovered an even more unusual practice among immigrant landlords in the heavily Polish and Lithuanian Back-of-the-Yards quarter. They often rented out the better units to tenants but lived in the worst rooms themselves to minimize cost. Almost half the slum homes were owner-occupied.[20] A short time lated the unusually high percentage of Lithuanian home ownership in Bridgeport, "better . . . in that respect than any other foreign district of which a similar survey was made in that year [1914]," impressed another observer.[21]

Two other surveys were made which determined home own-

[18] The imprecise ethnic reference was likely about Poles. Quoted in Carroll D. Wright, "Influence of Trade Unions on Immigrants," in *Bulletin of the Bureau of Labor,* 56: 5, 8 (January, 1905).

[19] Hunter, *Tenement Conditions in Chicago,* 186–187.

[20] See their "Housing Conditions in Chicago: III, Back of the Yards," in the *American Journal of Sociology,* 16: 436–440, 461–463 (January, 1911).

[21] Joseph Perry, "Rents and Housing Conditions Among the Lithuanians in Chicago" (M.A. thesis, University of Chicago, 1925), 18, 37; Elizabeth Hughes, "Chicago Housing Conditions, IX: The Lithuanians in the Fourth Ward," in the *American Journal of Sociology,* 20: 293, 295–296 (November, 1914). See also the Roseland Lithuanian conditions in *Lietuva,* August 24, 1909, *FLPS.*

ership in Chicago by nationality. Both reported immigrant percentages clearly above the average for the city as a whole. The 1900 U.S. Census found that 18.3 per cent of 5,500 Polish households were proprietary; in 1910 Edith Abbott estimated that the Polish percentage was two points above the Chicago average.[22]

An additional and perhaps more accurate measure of the proprietary instinct than actual statistics of ownership was the significance attached to the building-and-loan society. While the home purchase percentage shows achievement, the importance of an instrument for purchasing real estate is probably a better indication of desire. The co-operative principle played a vital role in Chicago Lithuanian and Polish life, perhaps even more so than elsewhere. The building-and-loan association was an integral part of the East European immigrant neighborhood, for Chicago Czechs as well as Poles and Lithuanians. A society usually grew out of meetings held in a church or saloon where group members obtained home-buying information and organized a co-operative organization. Normally a member bought shares of the society regularly, at $ .25 per week in 1886 to about $2.50 in 1910, for about six years. At the end of that time contributions and the accumulated interest could be withdrawn. If extra funds were required to purchase a home, they could be borrowed in an amount up to two-thirds the value of the real estate. The building-and-loan association was a democratically run body which chose its own officers and met one evening every month. Occasionally there were lively sessions during which members criticized the directors.[23]

[22] Bureau of the Census, *Twelfth Census of the United States, 1900, Population,* Part I (Washington, 1900), I: 751; Edith Abbot, *The Tenements of Chicago* (Chicago, 1936), 367–372, 378–380.

[23] From the files of the Pulaski Savings and Loan Association, 1886–1903, Chicago, and interviews with Joseph Walczyk, July 8, 1967, and John P. Grzemski, July 13, 1967, in Chicago. See also *Ksiązka Protokolowa Ligi Polskiego Towarzystwo Budowniczo-Pozyczkowych Kas Oszczędności w Stanie Illinois* (Chicago, 1911), 24, in the possession of Mr. Grzemski and the comment in *Polska Przegłąd Emigracyny,* May 25, 1908, Kórnik Library, Poznan, Poland.

The Polish and Lithuanian societies performed well because the members took a vital interest in their operation. Table 5 compares the growth of group associations with those of the city and state as a whole.[24]

TABLE 5: Growth of Building and Loan
Associations, 1894–1905

Years	Illinois Assets	Polish Assets	Polish Percentage	Chicago Assets	Polish Percentage	Lithuanian Percentage
1894	$81,796,350	$1,158,766	1.4%			
1895	82,639,258	1,096,269	1.3			
1896	80,105,574	1,475,056	1.8			
1897	73,399,193	1,070,750	1.5			
1898	63,451,758	992,252	1.6			
1899	54,104,602	858,007	1.6	$22,492,800	3.8	
1900	44,896,148	903,295	2.0	18,524,126	4.8	
1901	43,684,290	963,299	2.1	15,464,928	6.2	.2
1902	40,303,852	1,110,315	2.8	13,061,080	8.5	.3
1903	39,432,282	1,264,237	3.2	12,320,721	10.3	.4
1904	40,975,601	1,479,671	3.6	12,422,203	11.9	.5
1905	42,897,267	1,739,586	4.1	12,345,829	14.1	.7

These figures were taken from Illinois state reports which began extensive records in 1894. Lithuanians often utilized the facilities of Polish societies just as some Poles used Czech societies, but despite these statistical reservations the conclusion is clear: these building-and-loan associations performed consistently better than other societies in Illinois and especially in Chicago. Moreover these agencies had an outstanding comparative durability. Of the twenty-eight Polish associations listed in the reports from 1892 to 1905, only one went into receivership; statewide 320 did, though none were Lithuanian.[25]

The Illinois auditor of public accounts, himself apparently aware of the preceding reports, recognized the significance of the building and loans among Chicago's Eastern European im-

---

[24] Illinois, *Reports of the Auditor of Public Accounts, 1892–1905.*
[25] Two Polish societies were "liquidated" and two "dissolved." Illinois, *Reports, 1892–1905;* interview with Joseph Walczyk; *Lietuva,* June 8, 1895; March 10, 1899; February 8, 1900; January 18, 1901; March 8, 1904, *FLPS.*

migrant groups. He marveled at their primitive though successful home-buying technique:[26]

> [With] simple and economic business methods (occasionally quite crude), . . . steady and general success, . . . the great majority [of immigrant building and loan societies] operate in the territory bounded by Twelfth Street and Halsted Street on the east, embracing the great stockyards district. . . . Some of the significant features of their methods are that the books in many cases are kept in the foreign language, all payments of dues and interest are weekly, moneys are received only on meeting nights, no regular office quarters are maintained, officers' salaries are minimal, economy seems to be the watchword and among the membership a fraternal feeling is cultivated.

He continued, expounding in 1904, on the impressive performance of the Polish and Czech associations and its meaning:

> [The] list comprises 81 associations with $6,200,000 in assets, 220,000 shares in force, and an approximate membership of 28,000. Of the above number, all but seven show an increase in assets during the year [1904]—a remarkable exhibit. The industry, thrift and ambition to own a home prevalent to such a marked degree among the classes, is responsible for the standing and splendid record of these institutions. The people, believing and trusting in them, deposit therein their savings and hundreds of homes have been and will continue to be acquired through the popular agency.

The significance of the immigrant financial institution apparently went beyond being an important part of their own society. According to a present-day official of the Illinois Savings and Loan League, a large part of the growth of the idea in "Illinois, and particularly Cook County during the early part of the century was due to . . . the various nationalities. . . . It was only natural that these new citizens of Polish, Bohemian, and Lithuanian extraction who came to America to achieve their dream

---

[26] Report of J. S. McCullough in Illinois, *13th Annual Report of the Auditor of Public Accounts . . . 1904* (Springfield, 1905), viii; *18th Annual Report of the Auditor of Public Accounts . . . 1909,* iv. See also *Polskie Przegląd Emigracyjny* (May 25, 1908), 11.

of owning a home should give added impetus to the . . . movement."[27]

Albert Wachowski, the Chicago Pole who knew most about the co-operative principle in home buying, explained the reason for its popularity among his countrymen and perceptively designated its source in the immigrants' experience. The "Father of the Polish Building and Loan Associations" personally organized six societies in the Chicago area and founded the Polish American League in 1911. He specifically related the quest for real estate to the peasants' land consciousness: "The Polish arrivals quickly comprehended the necessity of land ownership, knowing from past experience that . . . the man without his own land and home had always been a serf, a slave." Having had some European experience in co-operation in Prussian Poland, the immigrants, beginning about 1881, "rapidly organized building and loan associations." With that assistance they "started on a rapid and successful march for home ownership and possession."[28] The persistence of the agrarian mentality was again evidenced in the gardens and livestock which home-owning Poles and Lithuanians maintained in Chicago.[29]

An accurate but little-known observation early in the history of Chicago Polonia correctly noted the objectives of the strange arrivals. While the foreigners appeared poor and destitute, an astute newspaper reporter in 1886 cautioned his readers not to mistake the immigrants' simple lifestyle with indigence: "The Pole is not a spendthrift . . . and his helpmate . . ." was "nearly always a hard-headed practical economist." They wanted "a

[27] An address by E. T. Boynton, August 26, 1954, at the League's headquarters in Springfield on the occasion of its diamond jubilee. See also the comment of Bodfish, ed., *History of Building and Loan,* 376–377, and *Financial Review and American Building Association News,* 30: 50, (February, 1910).

[28] His speech at the thirty-fourth meeting of the Illinois League, Springfield, October 23, 1913, in the Wachowski Scrapbook, at Wachowski Savings and Loan Association, Chicago. Compare the speech of M. S. Szymczak, in *Proceedings of the Forty-fifth Annual Meeting of the Building and Loan League . . . 1924* (Chicago, 1924), 68–69.

[29] Hunter, *Tenement Conditions,* 141; Breckinridge and Abbot, "South Chicago," 173–174; Chałasinski, "Parafja," 637; Balch, *Slavic Fellow-Citizens,* 333; Hughes, "Lithuanians," 303.

comfortable wallet" before "decoration." Their first goal was
"to make enough money to buy a home in the city or a farm in
Minnesota [or] Dakota." The fact was that "Poles . . . are prospering and getting rich"; almost half already owned their own
homes by means of their self-help societies, and "very many are
comparatively wealthy." All were "making money, saving it,
and investing in homes and real estate."[30] The ex-peasant was
quickly becoming an American homeowner.[31]

The Polish and Lithuanian immigrants were well on their way
to accomplishing one of their major goals in coming to Chicago:
earning capital to purchase land. Their other objective was to
re-establish their primary community, the parish. To do so at
the outset, they would have had to depend upon society at large,
especially the Roman Catholic nationalities with whom they
were most familiar.

A general review of the emergence of the two groups' Catholic parishes indicates an essentially pacific relationship, hardly
the sort which pitted Pole as Pole or Lithuanian as Lithuanian
against Americans, Czechs, or Germans. There was no contact
comparable to the traditionally hostile Irish-Italian confrontation. By the twentieth century, ethnic neighborhoods had
evolved with little residual animosity. The far greater trauma in
becoming aware of ethnicity came from within. This survey
covers the Chicago parishes which began before 1900, for by
then incoming members did not have to confront outsiders in
getting established. Few incoming Poles after 1900 needed to
suffer cultural shock in this city where over 150,000 of them
lived in the so-called "American Warsaw."

The first Polish settlement, St. Stanislaus on the north side,
became the largest and most important in Chicago. By the
1890's this church was serving almost half the group in the city.
Its origins show how a related nationality, the Germans, generally received the Slavs with assistance, not resistance. This initial

[30] *Chicago Tribune,* March 14, 1886, *FLPS.*
[31] Note the consensus of Ozog, "Polish Home Ownership," 52–53, 57, 136–
137; Cressey, "Succession of Cultural Groups," 187; Mary F. Bruton, "A
Study of Tenement Ownership Among Immigrant Workmen in Chicago"
(M.A. thesis, University of Chicago, 1924), 9; and Abbot, *Tenements,* 379–
380.

Polish colony formed about 1850 within the German St. Michael's Church; a short time later another began to attend the Bohemian St. Wenceslaus. The remaining unorganized Poles attended the other two north-side German parishes, St. Peter's and St. Joseph's. Nearly all these Polish pioneers came from the Prussian borderlands of Silesia, West Prussia, and Poznania. Most knew German and were acquainted with that culture; in fact one regional element known as Kashubes were a kind of unique German-Polish hybrid. [32]

This early acquaintance with an "old immigrant" nationality is important in assessing Polish-American adjustment in Chicago, for until the end of the last century the familiarity of the "new immigrant" with German was rather pronounced. In 1886 almost three-quarters of the Poles of Chicago, and as late as 1900 half, came from the land of the Kaiser. [33]

While the Polish pioneers minimized cultural shock by gravitating toward the nationality whose language they knew, the largest nucleus later grew into a parish, also with a minimum of disorientation. Again, related nationalities and Church officials were especially helpful. Poles planned for their separate ethnic church at the grocery of Anton Schermann, a countryman in spite of his non-Slavic name. Schermann and Peter Kiołbassa organized the St. Stanislaus Kostka Society in 1866, and the little Polonia of about a hundred families began to seek a pastor of its own. [34]

---

[32]Arthur Waldo, *Sokolstwo* (3 vols., Pittsburgh, 1953, 1956, 1972), 1: 287–289, offers the undocumented theory that German American persecution forced the Polish "founder" of the famous north side, Anton Schermann, to change his original Slavic name to an altered Germanic form of his wife's, Schermer. It is more likely that he chose the form and kept it for his own business advantage. Note the photograph in *ibid.*, 290. For the unusual ethnographical case of the Kashubes, see Kruszka, *Historya*, 8: 142; *Dziennik Chicagoski*, November 21, 1945, part 6, p. 2; Fr. Lorentz *et al.*, *The Cassubian Civilization* (London, 1935), vi–vii; *Illinois Staats-Zeitung*, January 20, 1879, FLPS.

[33] *Chicago Tribune*, March 14, 1886, FLPS. The 1900 breakdown is 32,995 from Germany; 9,499 from Austria; 15,026 from Russia; and 2,193 origin unknown. *Twelfth Census of the United States*, 798.

[34] The society actually had started in 1864 when Kiolbassa first visited the city. It disbanded probably due to Kiolbassa's two-year absence. Reverend John Iwicki, *The First Hundred Years* (Rome, Italy, 1966), 46–47.

Up to this time Church authorities had not only not opposed the Polish church organization, but had also attended to their ethnic needs. The Polish pastor of the Bohemian St. Wenceslaus and his Czech successor, Father Joseph Molitor, gave masses in their language in St. Joseph's German church.[35] A nearby Polish Jesuit, Father Francis Szulak, was the most likely pastor of the new St. Stanislaus parish, but because he knew Czech he was first put in charge at St. Wenceslaus. Later, due to the national shortage of Polish priests, he became a missionary to countrymen as far away as Pennsylvania.

In the next two years, 1867–1869, the Catholic bishop helped the Poles seek their first pastor. He asked the head of the Resurrectionists, a European order recently brought to America, to send one of his community to Chicago.[36] Resurrectionists, then located in a few American parishes, replied that they could not spare anyone then for a permanent position. An 1869 letter from Kiołbassa to the Resurrectionist head suggests that the delay in obtaining a priest was due more to the shortage of nationality clerics than the opposition of Germans, Bohemians, or the Chicago bishop. In fact both the German Benedictines in a parish near the Poles and the diocese itself encouraged the order to take control.[37] The bishop finally located an ethnic pastor late in 1869.

Apparently not all Polish communicants responded enthusiastically to having their own religious leader, suggesting a considerable lack of interest in the ethnic issue. For example, the nearest German parish, St. Boniface, had a pastor who ministered to Slavs as well. Polish names appeared frequently in the baptismal register all through the 1870's and 1880's.[38] The Kashubes of St. Stanislaus in the mid-1870's actually fre-

---

[35] Wachtl, "Dzieje Parafji . . . ," 9–10; Archdiocese of Chicago, *Antecedents and Development* (Des Plaines, 1920), 355–379.

[36] Paulo Smolikowski, *Cenni Stovici Sui Lavori del Padri Eugenio Funcken . . . della Congregazione della Resurrezione* (n.p., 1908), chapter XVI; Iwicki, *First Hundred Years*, 48n.

[37] Quoted in Iwicki, *First Hundred Years*, 49–50.

[38] St. Boniface Parish Records; Rev. F. C. Kalvelage, comp., *The Annals of St. Boniface Parish, 1862–1926* (Chicago, 1926), 27. Some of the "Slavs" listed may have been Czechs, but certainly not all.

quented the German Catholic churches more than their own.[39]

There was little Polish-Czech friction on the north side in the early years. The St. Stanislaus pastor commented in mid-1873 on the particularly amicable contact of Poles with other Slavs.[40] An outstanding example of the harmony was the joyous 1873 Polish-Bohemian outing to celebrate the completion of their jointly financed cemetery.[41] The Poles recorded their appreciation for Bohemian assistance in starting home building-and-loan associations down to the end of the century.[42] Relations between Poles and their neighbors were not universally harmonious, but at least the outside groups did not try systematically to suppress Polish attempts to reconstruct their culture.

In addition to the minimal ethnic hostility at St. Stanislaus, the origins of virtually all of the other Chicago Polish parishes until the end of the century demonstrated little intergroup friction. St. Stanislaus itself, the Resurrectionist Order which supplied its pastors, and the enormous financial and political assistance given by its pastor, the Reverend Vincent Barzynski, gave birth to new parishes, not to inter-ethnic Catholic animosities. Table 6 lists most of the group's nineteenth-century parishes and the reasons for their establishment.[43] The time lag between the parishioners' request and diocesan approval is included to assess possible dissatisfaction. The longest delay (St. Michael's) was three years; most took one year or less. Only at St. Joseph's did the older nationality, the Germans, clearly oppose the request of the Poles for their own house of worship. For every other Slavic church the delay in getting started was probably caused by organizational problems, not Irish or Ger-

---

[39] Letter of Reverend Wincenty Barzynski, the Polish pastor, September 19, 1874, and his "Report of the Polish Mission," September 7, 1875, in *Listy z Ameryki,* on microfilm at Weber High School, Chicago (hereinafter WHS).

[40] Reverend Adolph Bakanowski, "Report of the Mission to Rome, July, 1873," in *Relatio de Statu Domus Canadensissive Americanae . . . 1873,* WHS.

[41] Reverend John Wollowski to Reverend Louis [Funcken?], August 11, 1873, in John Wollowski, *Listy z Ameryki, 1864–1880,* WHS.

[42] *Księga Protokolowa . . . ,* 24; *Dziennik Chicagoski,* January 9, 1911, in the Wachowski Scrapbook, Wachowski Savings and Loan Association, Chicago.

[43] From parish albums and Kruszka, *Historya, passim.*

TABLE 6: The Rise of Polish Parishes in Chicago, 1872–1899

Parish	Request	Begun	Location	Reasons for Establishment
Holy Trinity	1872	1872	north side	To relieve St. Stanislaus overcrowding; first pastor a Resurrectionist.
St. Adalbert	1871	1873	west side	First pastor a Resurrectionist.
Immaculate Conception	1881	1882	south side	First pastor a Resurrectionist at Rev. Barzynski's request.
St. Mary of Perpetual Help	?	1882	west side (Bridgeport)	First pastor a Resurrectionist.
St. Josephat	1882	1884	north side	Barzynski loan, and begun after his application to Bishop; Resurrectionist held first mass.
St. Joseph	1886	1886	west side (Back of the Yards)	St. Adalbert request to Bishop.
St. Hedwig	1887	1888	north side	St. Stanislaus overflow; Barzynski loan; First pastor Resurrectionist, Barzynski's brother.
St. Casimir	?	1890	west side	No information.
St. Michael	1889	1892	south side	Application to Barzynski with resultant St. Stanislaus loan; Resurrectionist aid with some diocesan hesitation.
St. John Canty	1892	1893	north side	St. Stanislaus overflow; Barzynski loan; first pastor a Resurrectionist.
St. Stanislaus Bishop & Martyr	1893	1893	north side	Barzynski aid; first pastor a Resurrectionist.
St. Hyacinth	1893	1894	north side	Barzynski loan to forestall independents; first pastor a Resurrectionist.
St. Jacka (Avondale)	1894	1894	north side	Barzynski loan to forestall independents.
St. Peter and Paul	1894	1895	west side (Stockyards)	Not Resurrectionist.
St. Mary of Angels	1898?	1899	north side	St. Stanislaus overflow; first pastor a Resurrectionist.

man animosity. The founders of the west-side "mother," St. Adalbert's, in fact commended the Bohemian Reverend Molitor for his guidance.[44] National self-identification for Lithuanians was more complex than for Poles. Many had been Polonized in the nineteenth century, and it is difficult to distinguish them from the Slavs. Some Lithuanian writers broadly stress anti-Polishness as the basis for immigrant group consciousness. Even reliable Chicago sources mention some Polish-Lithuanian friction when the smaller group first settled at St. Stanislaus in the 1870's. But the quarrel may not have been clearly between the two nationalities. Certainly the Lithuanians did not suffer cultural shock, for most early arrivals in Chicago were *Zemaičiai* (Lowlanders) who knew Polish and some German.[45] Polish-Lithuanian relations on the north side were generally friendly. The first and largest Lithuanian parish began to the south in 1892 at St. George's in Bridgeport, an area which showed no Polish hostility. All Bridgeport Lithuanians then were deeply involved with serious internal divisions.[46] One Chicago Lithuanian priest who claimed Polish abuse of his people had to admit that the "oppressors" did render his group aid, shelter, and even wives and husbands.[47]

[44] Archdiocese of Chicago, *Antecedents*, 433. The St. Joseph story is in *1887–1937, Złota Księga . . . 50-cia Lecie Św. Jozefa* (Chicago, 1937), 9–11, and Town of Lake *Journal*, 1–2. All jubilee albums used in compiling the above table are in the Polish Museum. See also Iwicki, *First Hundred Years*, 68, 72, 73, 75, 76, 79, 100; and Kruszka, *Historya*, 10: *passim*.

[45] Joseph Roucek, "American Lithuanians," in *Baltic and Scandinavian Countries*, 4: 348 (September, 1938); M. Birziska, "Chicagos Lietuviai," in *Lietuviškoju Enciklopedija* (Kaunas, 1937), 5: 270–271.

[46] See below, Chapter VIII. The Polish-Lithuanian relations are discussed in *1877–1927, Album Złotego Jubileuszu Parafju Św. Jadwiga w South Bend, Ind.* (South Bend, 1927), 27, 54; and Aleksas Ambrose, *Chicagos Lietuviu Istoria, 1869–1959* (Chicago, 1967), 17–19. Note also the Record Book of St. George's Parish; *Katalikas* (Chicago), April 23, 1909; *Lietuva*, June 10, 1891; March 22, 1893; July 23, August 20, September 17, October 10, 1909, in *FLPS; Šv. Mykolo Archangelo Parapijos . . .* (Chicago, 1929), 8, 79–80; *Dziennik Chicagoski*, June 10, 1891, September 10, 1895, in *FLPS; Dziennik Chicagoski*, January 9, 1911, June 13, 1914, at offices of *Dziennik Chicagoski*, Chicago; and "Start of A. Wachowski Loan and Savings," in Wachowski Savings and Loan Association. It would be impossible to determine relations through marriage statistics if Alfred Senn, *The Emergence of Modern Lithuania* (New York, 1959), 7–8, is correct.

[47] Garsva, *Negestanti Šviesa*, 50.

This brief survey of East European economic and social adjustment is not intended to "prove" that universally amicable relations existed among Chicago nationalities before 1900. For that assessment a more detailed sociopsychological examination would be necessary. But clearly the Chicago experience for Poles and Lithuanians conforms to the adjustment of the groups nationally. While group friction occurred occasionally, the normal contact between Germans, Czechs, Poles, and Lithuanians was one of widespread social and cultural coexistence, even occasional intimacy. The traditional thesis that Anglo-American discrimination and Old World enmities produced ethnic group consciousness in the New World is faulty when applied to the early experience of East European immigrants in Chicago. The Poles and Lithuanians were well on their way to achieving their goals in Chicago—and likely elsewhere—by the end of the century. They were earning, saving, buying property, and building homes and churches with a minimum of outside resistance.

During this very time of intergroup peace, however, intragroup friction had begun, and intensified. The hostilities originated among certain group leaders who dealt with the sensitive issue of ethnic control of parish wealth. The tension soon affected all group members who had carried over vital spiritual and material desires, and, in the process, educated them to the issue of ethnicity and Roman Catholicism. From the inception of Polish and Lithuanian America, two elite elements in each group arose and clashed in a bitter struggle over what constituted their ethnic community and what were their group's goals. One, the "nationalists," passionately sought the establishment of an independent homeland, and thus placed nationality (or ethnicity) above faith in their group identification. The other, the "religionists," insisted that their faith (Roman Catholicism) and their nationality were synonymous and exclusive; any other view was godless and disloyal. The critical stage in this controversy, that is when *all* group members became involved, took place when the nationalists, professing to speak for all parishioners, demanded more ethnic control, even ownership of their local Catholic parish. To religionists, such a demand was anathma as it violated Catholic principles; so they responded by rejecting nationalists' claims. They loyally defended diocesan control, ownership and their pastor. The contest within the groups was upsetting and painful, even causing social conflict and violence. Gradually, because of their intense, traditional commitment to land and religion, most members of the Polish and Lithuanian communities heeded if they were not persuaded by the nationalists' argument. In any event, in the long run the ordeal affected everyone, the factions as well as the rank and file. As a result of this experience all group members came to see more clearly than ever before that they were not merely immigrants nor a people from Eastern Europe but rather a part of the Polish and Lithuanian nation.

FOUR

God and Country on Chicago's North Side, 1866–1893

THE CLASH between those who supported the ethnic-national position and those supporting the religious position within the Polish-American community grew out of an apparently insignificant disagreement on Chicago's north side in the 1860's. But the initial factionalism was insignificant only in scope, not in its later ramifications, for the matter was ultimately to involve all of Polish and Lithuanian America.

Several features of the group division must be kept in mind in order to discern how the bitter exchange enlightened the most inarticulate and naïve members of the rank and file, thus bringing them to a more advanced level of ethnic consciousness. The first noteworthy characteristic of the conflict was its timing. It began precisely when group organizers decided to establish their first ethnic parish, the "mother" community for the hosts of later-coming countrymen. Thus, when they had the first opportunity and means for reconstructing their basic group institution in America, the parish, Polish leaders already disagreed as to its constitution. The quarrel arose at the very beginning of the Chicago Polonia, and Pole fought Pole over the very organization of the colony.

Another important aspect of this conflict which raised Polish ethnic consciousness was its duration. The specific issue between ethnic and clerical factions in the north-side neighborhood continued unresolved for three decades. Even after the Catholic hierarchy solved the local issue in 1893, the deeper struggle between Polish factions continued in Chicago, and throughout the entire American community, for another fifteen years.

The third feature, and most significant, was the pervasive impact of the dispute. Although only two small groups, a mere handful of the nationality membership, fought verbally over the issue of parish control, a third, massive element, the nonparticipant parishioners, also became involved. When the debate became physically violent and when occasionally the bishop closed one of the two north-side churches, it affected the entire rank and file. The initial conflict among the articulate soon became a neighborhood conflict among all parishioners. Everyone, even the most apathetic, had at least to confront the issue of ethnic identification. The slightly more sophisticated Poles who had been aware of their ethnic difference now realized with the others that that difference had a particular purpose—either to help bring about a Polish state or to help perpetuate Polish Roman Catholicism. This greater awareness for all originated in north-side Chicago during the mid-1860's.

The two camps, "religionists" on the one hand and "nationalists" on the other, contended over the objectives of Polonia. Nationalists, numerically the smaller faction, but highly articulate lay writers, argued that the primary goal of the total group membership was to work for restoration of the homeland. Thus, as the work of the nationality was mainly political, a member's religion was of secondary importance; a Pole could be Jew, Protestant, Greek Catholic, or Roman Catholic. While nationalists recognized the predominance of the latter faith among the group, and respected Catholicism as an important part of the nationality, they felt that nationality and faith were divisible. The larger faction, religionists, was led by the clerics. The religionists insisted that a Pole could be only Roman Catholic, and that the primary function of the community in America was to maintain that identity. They agreed with their protagonists that an independent homeland was a desirable goal for immigrants, but for them it was a secondary objective; keeping the Pole Roman Catholic came first. By their definition, a non-Catholic, even if he was a Polish nationalist, was not a Pole.

The conflict was far more than a war of words; it was a war of deeds which interfered with the daily operation and administration of the local parish. Because many felt that as church-goers they should determine the distribution of parish wealth, the conflict made *all* parishioners begin to think of themselves more deeply as Poles. The Polish cleric found himself in an awkward position in this interminable battle. On the one hand he was a servant of a non-Polish bishop, who claimed the parish property as his; on the other, he was the representative of his property-conscious parishioners, who rejected the claims of outsiders to parish ownership. The cleric had to decide whether his primary loyalty was to his superior or to some of his congregation. When he chose his bishop, as the cleric usually did, the nationalists aroused parishioners to a more substantive ethnic consciousness by charging the priest with ethnic disloyalty for "misusing" parish wealth.

All the features of this neighborhood tension were evident in the rise of Chicago's Polish north side. There were verbal battles in which nationalists castigated priests as "autocrats" and "traitors" and religionists berated the patriots as "atheists" and "masons." The verbal disagreement begun just after mid-century soon gave way to physical assault and riot and disorder took place within the churches into the early 1900's. The first manifestation of this escalating tension was the birth of the city's second Polish parish, Holy Trinity, in 1871—a contentious "birth" that only the Vatican itself could resolve some years later.

A comprehension of the mounting polarization in the Polonia capital and ultimately throughout all Polish America requires a detailed account of the initial divisions between clericalists and some of the laity. Of particular importance in these early years is the character of the latter faction—the nationalists who typified patriot leadership throughout the country in the later years of the century. The members of this group were well-educated, highly literate spokesmen, mostly writers and journalists, a few of whom were even refugees of the abortive 1863 Polish Insurrection in Russia.

While the rebellion itself had failed, its consequences did

broaden the effort's geographical support. As thousands of emigrés fled to sanctuaries all over the West—Geneva, Paris, London, New York, and even Chicago—Polish freedom became more of an international movement. The Polish base in Switzerland soon established itself as the headquarters of a worldwide communications network. Despite the great distance between the "cells" of the new movement, Polish nationalists kept in contact with one another regularly and worked for homeland independence. The Chicago section of the network, organized under the name of Gmina Polska, began functioning in 1866. While its membership was very small, numbering just ten members at that time, this cell, like the others in Philadelphia, Buffalo, New York and elsewhere, was made up of an elite. The nationalist rosters in these cities for the rest of the century consisted of articulate journalists, writers, and professional people, as Władysław Dyniewicz, Antoni Małlek, and Franciszek Jablonski of Chicago; editor Ignacy Wendzinski and publisher Michael Kruszka of Milwaukee; and chemist-manufacturer Julian Andrzejkowski and emigré Julian Lipiński of Philadelphia.[1]

From the very outset the nationalist notables in Chicago encountered group resistance when they tried to arouse their immigrant countrymen. The Gmina complained early that the larger, religious St. Stanislaus Kostka Society, also founded in 1866 (to establish a parish), was unpatriotic. For example, the cell wrote to its fellow nationalists in 1868 that the society rejected its exhortations: "We have tried already several times to influence and arouse in them the idea of nationalism. We have invited them to each national celebration, but our work has been in vain."[2]

The relationship between the two groups was rather strained, for the next year Peter Kiołbassa, the lay leader of the society,

[1] Kruszka, *Historia,* 3: 139–141; Mieczysław Szawleski, *Wychodźtwo Polskie w Stanach Zjednoczonych Ameryki* (Lwów, 1924), 89, 97. The recent, standard work is Jerzy Borejsza, *Emigracya Polska Po Powstania Styczniowym* (Warszawa, 1966). See also Krystyna Murzynowska, "Henryk Korwin-Kałussowski," in *Problemy Polonii Zagranicznej* (Warszawa, 1964–1965), 4: 118–128, and Arthur L. Waldo, *Sokolstwo* (3 vols., Pittsburgh, 1953, 1956, 1972), 1: 299ff.

[2] Quoted in Borejsza, *Emigracya,* 87.

wrote to a priest that the Gmina had begun calling his members "stupid peasants and overly pious [*Głupami, chłopami i bigotami*]." He added that the nationalist goals were chimerical in their insistence that "we can begin a nation without God [*możemy zączać ras bez Bogo*]."[3] It is likely that the Gmina's willingness to accept Jews, Lutherans, and Greek Catholics influenced Kiołbassa's charge that the nest was without religion. The point at issue was more than a differing ideological interpretation of the ethnic group, and it soon led to a conflict over the establishment of the St. Stanislaus parish itself. The nationalists, then and afterward, also had a religious policy which upset the entire neighborhood; they insisted that parish property ought to be essentially ethnic, not diocesan. When parishioners acquired land for the church at the corner of Noble and Bradley, nationalists, led by Władysław Dyniewicz, had the deed include the phrase, "The church is to be for the use of Poles."[4] Kiołbassa and his religionists balked at such assertive ethnic feeling, fearing the bishop would reject the entire application.

The nationalist demand for official recognition of nationality groups reopened an issue which had plagued the Church in America ever since the 1790's. "Trusteeism" had arisen when Catholic ethnic communities occasionally demanded autonomous administration of their local parishes. The Curia, with the formal approval of American bishops, had decided in 1866 that where state laws permitted, the diocese was to be the proprietor of its local units and that the bishop must possess the legal ability to hold and convey real estate under the title "corporation sole." Illinois had already given those wide property-holding powers to its bishops in 1861.[5]

Thus armed with both state and ecclesiastical support, and

---

[3] Kiołbassa to Reverend Jelowicki, June 15, 1869, quoted in X. Pawel Smolikowski, *Historia Zgromadzenia Zmartwychwstania Panskiego, 1836–1886* (Albano, Italy, 1908), in manuscript, Book IX, 39. Note the suggestion that the Gmina was elitist. Joseph J. Parot, "The American Faith and the Persistence of Chicago Polonia, 1870–1910" (Ph.D. dissertation, Northern Illinois University, 1971).

[4] Quoted in Helen Busyn, "Peter Kiołbassa," in *Polish American Studies,* 8: 75 (July–December, 1951).

[5] *Chicago Record Herald,* August 25, 1907. The best summaries are Rev. Patrick J. Dignan, "A History of the Legal Incorporation of Catholic Property

possibly fearing lay interference with diocesan authority, the bishop, with the support of the Kiołbassa camp, denied the restrictive wording of the deed, although he approved the request for an ethnic parish. The Poles did erect the city's first Polish Catholic structure in 1869, but because of the dispute over precise ownership the church opened for worship without the bishop's blessing. He did not consecrate the structure until 1871, when the title was clearly in his hands.[6]

Not only was the constitutional question of parish title a bone of contention between the two Polish factions; the role of the first pastor was equally divisive. Nationalists, then and in later cases, might have accepted the bishop's holding legal title to the property if the pastor would have administered the church practically in the interests of his countrymen—that is to say "ethnically" rather in his own interest or in that of the non-Polish bishop. However at St. Stanislaus, as would occur so often in the future, the first religious leader conducted his church affairs autocratically, causing the nationalists to attack him and eventually to establish a parish of their own.

With the beginning of St. Stanislaus parish, Peter Kiołbassa asked for a cleric from the Resurrectionists, a Polish order with whom he had been familiar in Texas. Due to a lapse in communication, the bishop instead selected the Reverend Joseph Juszkiewicz, a diocesan priest who assumed his pastoral duties late in 1869. The appointment was not propitious, for almost immediately some parishioners, probably nationalists, criticized the cleric's arbitrary handling of funds. He had taken in $1,600 per year, almost twice as much as the people had stipulated, and he spent even more than that without suitably accounting for it. Further, his encumbrance with an attractive "cousin"—a female "relative"—provoked the economy-minded parishioners.[7] A

---

in the United States, 1784–1932" (Ph.D. dissertation, Catholic University, 1933), and V. J. Feehan, S.V.D., *A Study of the Movement for German National Parishes in Philadelphia and Baltimore* (Rome, 1955).

[6] Busyn, "Kiołbassa," 75; X. Hieronim Kajsiewicz, *Rozprawy, Listy z Podroży* (Krakow), 1872), Tom III: 344, 346; Iwicki, *Hundred Years*, 55. Parot, "The American Faith," 14–16, has additional details on the matter.

[7] *Illinois Staats-Zeitung*, January 20, 1879, FLPS. Reverend Adolph Bakanowski to Reverend General of the Resurrectionists in Rome, August 18, 1870, WHS.

collision was sure to come, because the nationalists also objected that Juszkiewicz was Lithuanian, not Polish.[8]

The crowning incident took place in mid-summer of 1869. Six masked gunmen assaulted the Reverend Father in the rectory. They knocked him down, covered him with a sheet, and beat him with rubber rods. As the battered but conscious priest lay on the floor, his attackers threatened to kill him if he continued his tyrannical parish policies.[9]

The beating convinced the bishop that a new pastor was necessary, and he asked the Reverend Adolph Bakanowski, a Resurrectionist then passing through the city, to run the parish temporarily.[10] The priest did so willingly.[11] He became immediately popular—a "beautiful" cleric "of bodily perfection" with a sonorous voice. With widespread support he ended the title dispute by convincing his parishioners to yield to the bishop without restrictions.[12] In return for the pastor's success and his loyalty, Bishop Thomas Foley gave the church to Bakanowski's Resurrectionist Order for ninety-nine years. The formal dedication of St. Stanislaus in June, 1871, attended by both the bishop and the head of the order, symbolized complete diocesan and Resurrectionist control.[13] Thus the religionists had won a solid victory, and the "mother" Polish parish in Chicago was firmly Roman Catholic.

Not all members of the Polish community celebrated Bakanowski's accomplishments. In fact the two opposing camps continued to debate nationalism and religionism, and the increasingly bitter contest entered a new arena, the press. When the struggle for parish control reached the pages of the first ethnic group newspaper in America, *Orzeł Polski* (Polish Eagle), published near St. Louis, it exposed the issue to all

---

[8] A valid charge. *Orzeł Polski*, August 4, 1870, Polish National Alliance Library, Chicago.

[9] According to the account of a contemporary, the Reverend Adolph Bakanowski, *Moje Wspomnienia* (Lwów, 1913), 74.

[10] *Ibid.*, 75–76.

[11] Actually the cleric's presence might have been more than a coincidence since Bakanowski had been Kiołbassa's pastor in Texas and the two may have managed his appointment.

[12] *Illinois Staats-Zeitung*, January 20, 1879, *FLPS*.

[13] Kajsiewicz, *Rozprawy, Listy z Podróży*, Tom III: 325, 344, 346.

Polish-American settlements.[14] In the summer of 1871, as Bishop Foley was blessing St. Stanislaus, *Orzeł Polski* broadcast the parish conflict nationwide.

Over a two-month period, a pro-religionist writer calling himself "Silesian [*Szlązak*]" and a nationalist supporter of the Gmina exchanged viewpoints—and epithets—in a fashion which typified the whole controversy. The debate produced much invective and *ad hominem* argument. "Silesian" denigrated the influence of the Gmina because of its small membership and commended the St. Stanislaus Society for its popularity. The defender of Gmina replied that size was not significant as the true representative of the Polish people, for there were many weaklings who used religious societies to heal their spiritual suffering. "Silesian" countered that no objective observer could ever report the exact number of Gmina members because their meetings were secret and deviousness was their hallmark. He advised them to "abandon shifty talk" and "go the way of a man." The nationalist answered that he did not respond to slander with his pen, only with a stick [*hijem*] or a club [*obciasem*], and that Gmina meetings were not held in secret. To say so was to blind the readers "with mud [*z błotem*]." He pointedly questioned "Silesian's" personal secrecy, why he kept his own anonymity.

The final exchanges spoke to the basic philosophical differences between the contending factions, specifically, whether a Pole had to be a Catholic. To an apparent charge that the Gmina was an unholy mixture of Catholics, Orthodox, and Jews, the nationalist reminded the clericalist spokesman that he ought to use Christian principles in speaking of other faiths. More importantly, the nationalist argued that by stressing religious differences among Poles, Poland itself would be lost. The true problem of the group, according to the patriot, "has its beginning at the corner of Noble and Bradley [the location of St. Stanislaus] not at the 'Gmina'."

"Silesian" finally withdrew his charge that Polish nationalists were non-Catholics, but concluded that the so-called patriots

<hr>

[14] Technically the first Polish paper was *Echo z Polski (Voice of Poland)* of New York, but it printed only Polish, not Polish-American news.

were really atheists who exacerbated divisions among the Catholic Poles. He warned his respondent "in the future do not go poking your nose among the cracks [the divisions among Poles]."[15]

Clearly nationalist members at St. Stanislaus were critical of their own ethnic clerics, who now ran a church which was legally in the hands of the bishop. Their efforts to arouse Poles to ethnic consciousness were not stilled; they had lost a battle, not the war. Through the columns of *Orzeł Polski* all Polonia became aware of the issue; and, more importantly for the group in Chicago, the nationalists quickly devised and applied a new strategy to further their cause. The ethnic patriots' new campaign—to establish their own Roman Catholic parish, Holy Trinity Church—intensified ethnic consciousness throughout the city. The battle for control lasted nearly two decades, but in the end the patriots humbled clericalists at St. Stanislaus, especially the powerful Father Barzynski. Admittedly their victory was not complete, for the nationalists had to surrender title to the bishop; but in their new parish they had a strong ethnically conscious pastor who was less subservient to the diocese.

The opportunity to renew the clericalist-nationalist struggle came with the increasing, religious demands of the burgeoning Polish north side. By 1871 the little frame church of St. Stanislaus was inadequate for the hundreds of Polish families it served, so a parishioners' meeting decided to construct a second church nearby. The building of this new house of worship was certain to lead to conflict, because Reverend Bakanowski and Bishop Foley imposed restrictions on the undertaking. They insisted that the new parish be under the control of St. Stanislaus. Holy Trinity was thus to be a wing of the religionist mother church, not a completely autonomous unit. The choice of the St. Joseph Society at St. Stanislaus to oversee the new structure was a mistake for the religionists. The men of St. Joseph's were "young and energetic" nationalists, who aimed at erecting a more ethnic religious center.[16]

[15] The full exchange is in *Orzeł Polski,* July 20, August 3, 17, 31, September 7, 14, 28, 1871 at Polish National Alliance Library, Chicago.

[16] *Pamiętniki, 1893–1918, Parafii Świetej Trójcy* . . . (Chicago, 1918), 6.

The men of St. Joseph's proceeded to make their colony more nationalist and administratively independent. After receiving funds from St. Stanislaus parishioners, the society quickly bought lots and erected the new church in the fall of 1873. The speed and implications of the deed alarmed the members of St. Stanislaus, who had been unaware of nationalist objectives. The St. Joseph members had bought an immense tract of land on the very same street, only three blocks away. This implied not simple relief for the overcrowded mother church but real competition for members. The true nationalist goals for the new parish became clear when the St. Joseph Society drew up the deed in its own name, not that of the Bishop of Chicago, and immediately began seeking a pastor. Holy Trinity not only violated diocesan regulation by not affiliating with St. Stanislaus, it also reopened the dispute over title. Nationalists again declared for Polish, not diocesan, ownership of church property.[17] The new pastor of St. Stanislaus, the Reverend Felix Zwiardowski, who supported the diocesan position, further charged the already tense neighborhood atmosphere by leading services in the new church late in 1874. The bishop, meanwhile, withheld his official blessing of the building until the dispute over affiliation and title was settled. A Polish conflict appeared imminent. The patriots at Holy Trinity girded for battle and appointed a special committee to safeguard their parish.[18] The confrontation was delayed because Zwiardowski asked to be relieved of his pastoral duties at St. Stanislaus due to his "poor health." Apparently he did not have the heart for struggle.[19] The Reverend Vincent Michael Barzynski, his successor, did.

Reverend Barzynski's appearance in Chicago in 1874 raised the dispute to a new level, for more than any other man in America until his death a quarter-century later, he personified Polish Roman Catholicism. Biographers have described the

[17] The details of the creation of Holy Trinity are in *Chicago Tribune,* January 5, 1891; Smolikowski, *Historya Zgromadzenia Zmartwychwstania Panskiego,* 61–62; Kruszka, *Historya,* 10: 4–13; *Pamiętniki . . . Świetej Trójcy . . . ,* 6–9.
[18] The emerging strategy is in Kruszka, *Historya,* 10: 11–14.
[19] Letters of Bishop Foley and Zwiardowski, April 7, July 25, 1874, Polish Museum, Chicago.

famous priest as a man of immense influence and imposing character. He was the unrivaled architect of Polish Chicago, if not Polish America itself. He was "the most commanding figure" among his nationality, according to a 1911 Catholic scholar, and "like Gregory VII, a man of an iron strength of will," according to the group's major historian.[20] In Barzynski, religionists acquired a formidable leader around whom they could rally in their struggle with the nationalists.

Barzynski provided the administrative vitality for the clericalist camp. He had the foresight to envision the enormous increase in the numbers of his people in Chicago, to plan for it, and in the process to benefit both his Resurrectionist Order and St. Stanislaus parish by the influx. To provide for the needs of his countrymen and to build power, he needed money. Almost immediately upon his assuming command at St. Stanislaus, Father Barzynski established a parish bank where parishioners could deposit funds and earn interest. Immigrants found some advantage in the service because they hesitated to keep their monies in non-group institutions. Father Barzynski used it as a ready source of funds to aid the many parishes and religious institutions which arose in Chicago, and to fund colonization enterprises. But he managed the bank poorly, and by 1897 owed over $400,000 to depositors.[21]

Growth figures of the St. Stanislaus congregation and its wealth testify to Barzynski's influence in the American Polonia between 1874 and his death in 1899. Church membership expanded from about 2,500 to more than 40,000, likely the largest Roman Catholic parish in the world. His personal income at the end of his life was $5,200 per year; the assets of his church exceeded $500,000.[22] By the start of the twentieth century St.

[20] Felix Seroczynski, "Poles in the United States," in *Catholic Encyclopedia* (1911), 12: 207; Kruszka, *Historya*, 9: 84. See also Karol Wachtl, *Polonja w Ameryce* (Philadelphia, 1944), 66–67, and other histories of Poles in America.

[21] Kwiatowski, *Historia*, 340, 362, 374, 389.

[22] *Report of St. Stanislaus Parish, May 31, 1877;* "Sprawozdanie ze stanu ... Missyi Chicagoski, 1874–1892," in Letters of Barzynski, WHS; Reverend J. Kasprzycki, C. R. *Rendiconto della Missione di Chicago, Ill.,* June 10, 1901, WHS; *Dziennik Chicagoski*, August 9, 1899; *Chicago Tribune*, February 23, 1877.

Stanislaus was really a double house of worship, containing an upper and a lower church, with a combined yearly income of $60,000.[23] To assert that Father Barzynski personally constructed Polish Roman Catholicism in the group's American center is not to say that he was not a patriot. He had suffered much at the hands of the Russians. He grew up in Russian Poland, participated in the January Insurrection of 1863, and ultimately had to flee his homeland. He later lived in the emigré Polish colony in Paris before settling in Texas in 1866. It was there that he began to urge Rome to appoint a Polish-American bishop. Finally, he did occasionally support patriotic anti-German and anti-Russian demonstrations in Chicago.[24] However, as a loyal religionist he supported a nationalism that was integral with faith. Just as his friend Kiołbassa had remarked in the 1860's in his condemnation of the Gmina, Barzynski believed that to seek an independent Poland without a Roman Catholic God was false patriotism, against which he would fight.[25]

Such a commanding figure as Barzynski, with his vision of building a Polish-American capital in Chicago, generated ethnic consciousness by his role as a forceful protagonist in the nationalist-religionist struggle. His domineering personality and determined religionism agitated his patriot opponents for the next quarter-century, everywhere hardening group divisions.

His uncompromising strategy became clear in his first steps on the north side in 1874. Barzynski decided to build a larger St. Stanislaus parish under his control and, with the help of the Holy Trinity treasury, to obliterate that church's identity for good. After the nationalists at Holy Trinity refused to surrender their money and Barzynski unsuccessfully tried to invalidate their title, the patriarch consulted Bishop Foley. The bishop,

---

[23] Emil Dunikowski, *Wśród Polonii w Ameryce* (Lwów, 1893), 66. The parish in 1891 would often have fifty christenings and two funerals per day, and ten weddings on Sunday. Rev. Henry Malak, O.F.M., *Apostle of Mercy of Chicago* (London, 1961), 45.

[24] For his nationalist activities see *Dziennik Chicagoski*, January 26, 27, 1892, March 20, 1893, *FLPS;* Smolikowski, *Historya*, 56–57; Kruszka, *Historya*, 2: 60; 9: 245–247.

[25] See the worshipful Ks. Stanisław Siatka, *Krotkie Wspomnienie o Zycie i Działalność Ks. M. Wincenty Barzynskiego, C.R.* (Chicago, 1901), 29, 32, 59.

following Barzynski's wishes, closed the second parish in 1875 and declared it would reopen only when consolidated under St. Stanislaus.[26] The outlines of the struggle assumed the classic pattern that would appear in the 1890's around the country: a religionist Polish pastor, loyal to his bishop, attacking the ethnic trustees of a Polish parish.

Once again the nationalists lost a battle with the hierarchy, but, as before, they maintained the struggle for their ethnic parish. Despite the diocesan ban, members of Holy Trinity held services in their church with the help of a newly arrived secular priest, the Reverend Wojciech Mielczusny.[27] The trustees assured the cleric that there would be no trouble, and he agreed to become pastor. Some of his parishioners applied again to the bishop for his blessing, but the prelate rejected their petition: "I do not know Rev. Mielczusny and I do not wish to know him." The bishop would give his approval only when the parish submitted to Barzynski's control.[28]

Apparently Father Mielczusny himself assumed some leadership at Holy Trinity, for about this time he decided to take the whole issue to the higher authority of the Vatican itself. Apparently without consulting diocesan authorities, Rome gave him permission to open the church, and the pastor finally held a sanctioned mass on March 24, 1877. The matter became even more complex when Bishop Foley proceeded to a radical solution and excommunicated the new pastor of Holy Trinity.

Although misunderstanding and bitterness grew between group leaders, both clerical and lay, the effects of the warfare upon the laity as a whole were more important. Hostility increased between all ordinary parishioners on the north side. Barzynski wrote to his superior in his 1877 annual report that he had had to battle a great variety of opponents, who possessed an "acid mixture" of liberalism and American effrontery. The

[26] The series of events are in Kruszka, *Historya*, 10: 15–22; *Chicago Tribune*, January 5, 1891.

[27] His background is in J. Mierzynski *et al.*, *Polacy w New York* (New York, 1908), 46, 48.

[28] Quoted in Kruszka, *Historya*, 10: 24. See also F. Niklewicz, *Historya Polaków w Stanie Illinois* (Green Bay, Wisconsin, 1938), 13.

enemy used systematic "free mason tactics." He lamented that "our people are divided into two churches," really "two camps"; at the head of one was "a clique of unbelieving saloon-keepers . . . and barflies . . . whose tool is the unfortunate Mielczusny."[29] The rank and file at St. Stanislaus supported their pastor's vilification of their antagonists. Mielczusny, himself, complained of widespread harassment by parishioners of the north side "mother" church. In 1878 and 1879 he wrote to Barzynski's superior in Rome that Polish school children frequently abused him, adults threw rocks at him, and one St. Stanislaus woman spat on his parishioners. An English-language newspaper put the situation simply but concisely: the feeling between the two parishes was "very bitter."[30] The animosity and suspicion between the two Polish neighborhoods on the north side were so pervasive that when Mielczusny died unexpectedly in 1881, a group from Holy Trinity demonstrated in the streets, charging that some parishioners from St. Stanislaus had murdered him.[31]

As intense as the conflict was by the early 1880's, this parish unrest still may have appeared minor to observers. But the basic issue was deeper than simple competition between the parishes of St. Stanislaus and Holy Trinity or a conspiracy of schismatics and freemasons. The division was inherent in the religionist-nationalist struggle for control of Polonia. As the Reverend Leopold Moczygęba, a friend of Barzynski's, told Rome in 1880, his religionists condemned their opponents as pseudo-nationalists, and "Presently we are forced to defend the Polish people from the infections of Jews and freemasons, who *under the cloak of patriotism* want to obtain the power of directing the Polish people [emphasis added]."[32]

Later incidents in the controversy further illustrate that the

[29] "Report of the Polish Mission in Chicago, Apr. 10, 1877," "Parish Report, May 31, 1877," both in WHS.
[30] Kruszka, *Historya,* 10:33; Smolikowski, *Historya,* 69; *Chicago Tribune,* November 4, 1878.
[31] Some years later they also charged that they had stolen costly altar pieces. *Ibid.,* January 5, 1891.
[32] Quoted in Kruszka, *Historya,* 10: 35.

conflict was more than a political contest between rival parishes, and that it was also a philosophical contest over ethnic identity. After a new archbishop, Patrick Feehan, had replaced Bishop Foley, in 1880 Holy Trinity parishioners again attempted to win hierarchical sanction for their church. But Bishop Feehan, like his predecessor, steadfastly refused until he had clear title and the parishioners submitted to Resurrectionist control. A typical exchange took place in April, 1884, when a diocesan representative laid out Feehan's terms. The parishioners rejected the proposal unanimously, and the archbishop's emissary left the hall with the Holy Trinity church choir's rendition of a Polish national hymn, "Poland Will Never Die," ringing in his ears.[33]

The Polish north side continued in factionalism and turmoil. With no pastor, Holy Trinity remained closed after Father Mielczusny's death in 1881 until March, 1889, when it appeared as if the dispute were about to end. Archbishop Feehan and the parishioners did reach a settlement. The trustees of Holy Trinity allowed the appointment of a Resurrectionist, the Reverend Szymon Kobrzynski, as their religious leader, and placed the parish title in the name of St. Stanislaus parish.[34] However, the arrangement failed when the parish committee refused to yield church funds to others and adamantly insisted that the property belonged to the parishioners, the Polish people.

Almost as soon as Father Kobrzynski assumed his position, the jealous parish committee sharply constrained his administrative function. Even though he showed the people that the archbishop had designated him as pastor, they refused to support him fully. Frustrated, he repeatedly tried to disband the trustees.[35] As he told his superior, he knew who his antagonists were and what their fundamental objections were; they were rooted in anti-Catholic, unholy Polish patriotism. The trustees, he said, sought disloyal priests like Mielczusny "who have yielded their entire soul and sold out to nationalists. These nationalists educate the people without religion, lead them to impracticality and drunkenness and hold picnics on Saturday

---

[33] *Ibid.*, 41.
[34] *Ibid.*, 42; Kobrzynski to Feehan, September 4, 1889, WHS; Holy Trinity Marriage Records for 1889, Holy Trinity Church, Chicago.
[35] Kobrzynski to Feehan, September 4, 1889, WHS.

and dances on Sunday against the most explicit order of the Baltimore Council."[36]

His last days at the church verified his assessment of his opponents' position. In early September, Kobrzynski held a parish meeting in which he tried to convince his parishioners of their Roman Catholic obligation to allow him to handle their collections and the treasury. When most of those assembled shouted down his appeal by crying "Long live Poland" and singing the national anthem, "God Bless Poland," the pastor retired to the sacristy. Shortly thereafter Kobrzynski decided to surrender his post and return to St. Stanislaus. As trophies of his brief encounter, he took with him the Holy Trinity account book and the keys to the parish cash box.[37] Archbishop Feehan completed the affair by declaring the parish closed, only six months after he had reopened it.

Obviously this diocesan action did not end the issue for the nationalists. As before, they believed that higher authority would sustain their position and that in the end their persistence would prove them correct. The members of Holy Trinity again sent two well-known trustees with a petition to the Apostolic Delegate, Monsignor Francis Satolli, in Baltimore. At first Satolli replied that he had no jurisdiction over the matter, but after the complainants sent a mission to Rome itself and made a second application, the Papal representative agreed in 1893 to resolve the issue on a forthcoming visit to Chicago. Succeeding events proved a setback for the Barzynski religionist faction at St. Stanislaus. Leaning heavily on the advice of Francis Jabloński, a nationalist at Holy Trinity, Satolli conducted hearings on the two-parish dispute in early June. After listening to both sides, especially to Barzynski and his St. Stanislaus delegation, he ordered the reopening of Holy Trinity under the Holy Cross Fathers of Notre Dame, Indiana, with the Reverend Kazimir Sztuczko as pastor.[38]

While the outcome was not a total victory for either camp,

---

[36] *Idem.*

[37] *Idem;* Kruszka, *Historya,* 10: 48.

[38] The arrival of Satolli and subsequent events are in Kruszka, *Historya,* 10: 57; *Zgoda,* June 7, 1893; and *Ksiązka Jubileuszowa Parafii Św. Trójcy, 1893–1943* (Chicago, 1943), 23.

the nationalists were the major beneficiaries. Holy Trinity maintained its independence and its ethnocentrism. It was probably more Polish than Roman Catholic, because the new pastor, Sztuczko, had been a fellow seminarian of the Holy Trinity leader, Jabloński. They were friends because of each other's spirited Polish nationalism. Sztuczko later showed himself as one of the most nationalistic of all Polish priests, the very kind of cleric that Holy Trinity parishioners would support. To him, Roman Catholicism was ethnically pluralistic. He did not believe in the more homogeneous and centralized model of the Church that most of his Polish colleagues favored.

Sztuczko's later policies justified the delight of Holy Trinity parishioners in his appointment. He was conspicuous at the frequent local demonstrations of national heritage. For example, religionists criticized his close association with the Polish National Alliance.[39] Yet at the same time he showed his loyalty to his universal faith. Father Kazimir often led parades during the national holidays, but throughout his career no serious criticism of his being a Catholic ever arose. Probably the real test of his acceptance generally, and his achievement at being both patriot and priest, was his half-century of service at this leading nationalist parish.[40]

While in 1893 only a few at Holy Trinity knew Sztuczko on the basis of his personal qualities, he personified for them their satisfying victory in winning independence from St. Stanislaus. After a generation the Church, in effect, had sanctioned their nationalist parish once and for all. They were clearly no longer an appendage of the Resurrectionists nor under the St. Stanislaus pastor, Barzynski. While Monsignor Satolli's decision brought joy to Holy Trinity, it brought gloom to St. Stanislaus. Father Vincent himself charged that Satolli had acted, "high handedly" in defense of "blasphemers [*bluznierc ów*]" and

---

[39] Note his controversial blessing of the new Polish National Alliance home in 1896. *Pamiątki Złotego . . . Ks. . . . Sztuczko* (Chicago, 1941), 33, 38; *Ksiązka Jubileuszowa Parafii Św. Trójcy, 1893–1943* (Chicago, 1943), 24, 108.

[40] Szczesny Zahajkiewicz, *Księza i Parafie Polskie w Stanach Zjednoczonych w P.A.* (Chicago, 1897), 41.

"slanders [*oszerców*]." Embittered by the resolution of the matter, he left on a trip to Canada. Other Resurrectionists at the corner of Noble and Bradley put the best face on their defeat, insisting that it was not a complete disaster. Admittedly the new pastor was not of their order, but he was still a regular Catholic and not a hated secular. Some felt the nationalist parish would hardly compete with St. Stanislaus. It would be poor, draining all Polonia of its "dregs *(hołota)*."[41]

The office of Archbishop Feehan was silent. It had bet on the losers. Throughout the long struggle both Foley and Feehan had consistently upheld the Resurrectionist position. In fact, Bishop Feehan "constantly fell back on Barzynski's judgment whenever problems arose."[42] Thus it was no surprise at the hearings that Feehan had specifically pleaded the religionist case with Satolli. On the other hand, the outcome probably did not disturb the diocesan leader seriously, for it still recognized his office, not the parish trustees, as legal owner of Holy Trinity. Whoever managed the parish—regular, secular, or lay leaders —was always less important to the archbishop than who actually owned it. He was satisfied as long as his name was on the deed, in accordance with Catholic conciliar stipulation.[43]

The long conflict which had beset and divided the major Polish section on Chicago's north side, pitting neighbor against neighbor, had thus come to a close. Or had it? The problem had arisen from the continual efforts of one church to exist independently of another. Monsignor Satolli settled that dispute by granting autonomy to Holy Trinity. The controversy, however, was far more than a drive for a completely separate parish. Underlying the conflict was the more basic issue of the relative places of ethnicity and faith in the Polish-American community. The Papal representative neglected to resolve that disagreement, which every parishioner of both churches had to confront, and therefore for over twenty years the issue interfered with the

---

[41] The Resurrectionist reaction is in Kruszka, *Historya*, 10: 60–62.

[42] Quoted in Parot, "American Faith," 53.

[43] *Dziennik Chicagoski*, June 13, 1893, *FLPS*. Feehan recognized Satolli's decision officially by visiting Holy Trinity the following May. *Książka . . . Św. Trójcy*, 26.

parishioners' profound agrarian-religious heritage and their everyday life. Ethnic consciousness—the recognition by masses of ordinary people that they were Poles—developed here.

The dimensions of the problem were far wider than Chicago's north side. Almost at the very moment of the "peace treaty" between St. Stanislaus and Holy Trinity, the rest of the Poles of that city, as well as across America, were encountering the same disagreements within Polonia that had arisen on the north side. This local conflict between two Polish parishes over the place of ethnicity was really a prelude to strife that soon affected all of Polish America. The battle between Polish Catholics and Catholic Poles over which group ought to be paramount would be carried to all parishioners in every major settlement.

The two-parish struggle in Chicago was really the same contest over group definition that dated back to the Gmina activity of the 1860's, and which would continue to agitate and educate parish members elsewhere. Later, more serious intragroup disputes would occur. Unlike the Holy Trinity parishioners in 1893, some elements would not be willing to yield any ethnic authority to their bishops, insisting even upon keeping parish title in the hands of the congregation to assure its ethnic character. Much less accommodating to religionists and ecclesiastical authorities, they would go to the extremity of setting up "independent" ethnic parishes and of establishing an entirely new denomination, Polish National Catholicism. The nationalist practice of striving for more Catholic recognition of a parish's ethnic character was to continue into the 1890's, further spreading and heightening ethnic consciousness.

FIVE

God and Country on the National Scene, 1866–1893

THE ENORMOUS IMPACT of the religionist-nationalist controversy throughout Polonia was reflected by the rise of Polish-American societies in the late nineteenth century. The differing points of view were in fact the philosophical inspiration for the organization of Polish-American fraternalism. Ideas about religion over nationality and nationality above religion motivated not only local branches and parishes, as on Chicago's north side; the contending notions also provided the organizational rationale for the two leading, nationwide fraternal associations of the nineteenth century, the Polish National Alliance (PNA) and the Polish Roman Catholic Union (PRCU).

The roots of both societies were in the St. Stanislaus neighborhood. The PNA and PRCU flourished there, and were headquartered only a few blocks apart on the north side of Chicago during most of the period. The two organizations spoke to all Polonia in their journals; each competed for the immigrants' loyalty; each labeled its opponents irreligious or unpatriotic.[1] The continual debate disturbed many Polish-Americans, who knew not which body they ought to support.

This acrimonious, high-level exchange took place simultaneously with the St. Stanislaus-Holy Trinity warfare, from the

---

[1] After spending its early years in other cities, the PNA located in Chicago in the 1880's.

1870's to the 1890's. The intensity of this parallel conflict generally fluctuated with the level of the local parish dispute. The two warring national societies maintained their opposing ethnic and religious positions on the matter of national identity. The disagreement was over who was a part of the Polish nation, and it increased the tension for Poles across the country.

The institutional home of the nationalist camp was the Polish National Alliance. The organization officially began in 1880, though its antecedent was that same small group which had worked for the ethnic parish on Chicago's north side, Gmina Polska of 1866.[2] The goals of its leaders, especially Michael Majewski and Władysław Dyniewicz, were to propagate national awareness among their fellows and work for the resurrection of an independent homeland. They looked toward the formation of a national body in America for that purpose. A group of New York emigrés had attempted unsuccessfully to create such a national organization in the later 1860's. By 1873 Chicago, with three nationalist societies and *Gazeta Polska,* a paper which Dyniewicz had begun, had taken the lead.

Early in its existence the *Gazeta* dealt with role of the Catholic religion in the incipient patriot movement. It articulated the nationalist position on ethnic identity that would last through the century. The true member of the Polish nation was not an atheist; he never neglected God or prayer, "but he also does not condemn other faiths either [*ale tez przy tem nie potępia i innych wyzńan*]." The nationalist view was progressive and liberal toward other religions; the paper reminded its readers that Poland historically had been a tolerant nation.[3]

Although they agreed with this enlightened view of Polish nationalism, the New York and Chicago centers could not at first form a united organization. After several failures in the 1870's, success came in 1880. Agaton Giller, a Polish refugee in Switzerland, had exhorted his American compatriots in 1879

---

[2] The *matka* (mother) of nationalist societies in America according to Kruszka, *Historya,* 3: 140–141.

[3] Quoted in Stanisław Osada, *Historia Związku Narodowego Polskiego* (Chicago, 1905), 63. See also *ibid.,* vii–viii, 3, 49, 50.

to form a dynamic patriot association in the United States so that the unenlightened Polish immigrant, "a plain man formerly ignorant and passive for the national cause, will become an individual consciously and actively serving the idea which rests upon nationality."[4] This overseas appeal galvanized supporters, especially Dyniewicz, to demand a national society. A Philadelphia cell invited the other nationalist branches to meet there in 1880, and the Polish National Alliance was born. On the sensitive subject of Catholicism and Catholic societies, the fledgling fraternal organization decided to accept local religious branches, even priests, but to offer them no special privileges.

While it did not seem so from the outset, the principal adversary of the PNA was to be the Polish Roman Catholic Union. Reverend Theodore Gieryk, a Detroit priest, had conceived of the society as a liberal organization. He began the PRCU in 1873 as a broadly inclusive national body for mutual aid that would accept any Poles regardless of faith. A number of strongly nationalist clerics, including Mielczusny of Holy Trinity and the Reverend Dominic Majer of St. Paul, discerned no antinationalist aims in the PRCU in the early years. But after the Union met at St. Stanislaus in 1874 and came under the Reverend Vincent Barzynski's iron domination, it became more purely Catholic. It adopted the *Gazeta Katolicka,* run by Barzynski's brother, as its newspaper and moved its headquarters to Chicago. Barzynski, the apostle of religionism, defined the goal of the PRCU as the maintenance of the Roman faith. Founder Gieryk left the society over the issue in 1875.[5]

In the 1870's, even before the Polish National Alliance had officially been formed, the religionists and Barzynski clashed with the nationalists over the subject of Polish identity. For the most part the battle was waged in the appropriately named

---

[4] Quoted in Robert E. Park and Herbert A. Miller, *Old World Traits Transplanted* (New York, 1921), 135. See also Osada, *Historya,* 97–98.

[5] *1867–1917, Złoty Jubileusz . . . Świetego Stanisława Kostki w Chicago* (Chicago, 1917), 15–16; Kruszka, *Historya,* 3: 143ff; Osada, *Historya,* 241, 255; Casimir Stec, "The National Orientation of the Poles in the United States, 1608–1935" (M.A. thesis, Marquette University, 1940), 57–58.

Gazeta Katolicka (Catholic Gazette) and *Gazeta Polska (Polish Gazette)*. The religionists' opening salvo was fired during the 1873 Chicago celebration of the October Insurrection. St. Stanislaus' pastor, the Reverend Felix Zwiardowski, characterized the observance as excessively secular, and asserted that in regard to the resurrection of the homeland, "Not men but miracles will deliver Poland." On the other hand Dyniewicz called for Poles to work as well as pray for an independent homeland, "since prayers without deeds are dead."[6] From then on the exchanges between the two camps resounded in the press, at times assuming "scandalous form, never quieting down completely."[7] It was during this debate that *Gazeta Katolicka* labeled the Dyniewicz newspaper "masonic," an epithet that religionists would hurl at their opponents often in later years.[8]

By the mid-1870's the outlines of this journalistic war over Polish-American objectives were clear. The religionists were usually the aggressors, denouncing nationalist societies not only for subordinating Roman Catholicism but for attacking it. In response, the nationalists assumed a more congregational and a more democratic posture. Patriots implied that the clerics were autocratic toward their people, that they were more interested in subjecting the masses to their control than in teaching them pride in their national traditions.

A characteristic exchange took place at the founding of the Polish National Alliance in 1880, and again in 1881. Barzynski's paper offered a portentous prediction about the organization's future among the Poles: "As a great fraternal founded on masonic principles, the Polish people without doubt in their accustomed manner will turn their back on it."[9] In 1881 the nationalists countered in the very first issue of *Zgoda*, the PNA newspaper, with the standard patriot rebuttal: clerics were an obstacle to the enlightened nationalism which the downtrodden Polish people so badly need. The new nationalist publication issued a clarion call to all patriots. It urged readers to join the

---

[6] The exchange is in Kruszka, *Historya,* 4: 14.
[7] Osada, *Historya,* 63.
[8] *Ibid.,* 63.
[9] Quoted *ibid.,* 135.

Alliance and proposed to raise all Polonia to national consciousness and respected status in America:[10]

> We can be sure of one thing, that if our emigrants continue to
> submit, as they have done until now, to the influence of [cleri-
> cal] obscurantism, the influence of those who for centuries have
> kept the people in blindness, they will never rise above the level
> of the Irish (the most downtrodden European people) and the
> Polish name will never shine in any light in this country.

Verbal warfare opened in the 1870's, and a more heated debate characterized the next decade. The more intense conflict
was partly the result of more general journalistic involvement.
By 1887 the religionists had more papers with which to chide
nationalists. *Wiara i Ojczyzna* (the official PRCU paper), the
Kropidło, the *Wiarus* of Winona, Minnesota, and others joined
Zgoda in expressing the nationalist position. By the end of the
1880's, the field of battle expanded beyond Chicago to Buffalo
—the second-ranking Polish city—to Milwaukee, and elsewhere.

In addition to the multiplication of participants, by 1890 the
dispute had reached new levels of invective. As one authority
wrote, the two camps by that time were involved in a "press
struggle . . . so bitter that it nearly reached the courts." In a
satirical rhyming couplet, an Old World Russian journal of
1890 enumerated the astonishing variety of names that each
side had called the other.[11]

By the early 1890's the intensity of the disagreement between
the two camps must have bewildered ordinary Polish immigrants everywhere in America as they read their newspapers.
Their two leading voluntary societies, which represented their
collective aspirations and ideals were locked in heated argument over community objectives. The Polish layman's sensitivity
toward nationality matters, and thus his consciousness of self

---

[10] Quoted in Thomas and Znaniecki, *Polish Peasant*, 2: 1630–1631.
[11] There were at least thirty epithets, including scoundrel, knave, villain,
rogue, thief, drunkard, rake, swindler, dunce, fool, imbecile, ass, dumb ox,
sprinkler (meaning clerics), souse, buffoon, and "lightning-struck." Quoted in
Haiman, *Zjednoczenie*, 82–83, who also describes the animosity.

and nationhood, was surely raised as the leading institutions were discussing and disagreeing about the meaning of *Polskość* (Polishness).

The Polish media had awakened or heightened the newcomers' sense of group identity, but if they lived outside of Chicago's north side, the ordinary immigrants as yet had no personal involvement in the debate. In a few years, however, they would experience a more immediate disruption of their own neighborhoods first hand. Soon a schismatic parish would compete for their loyalty, too, on nationalist principles.

Another development of nationwide significance which contributed, albeit briefly, to the raising of ethnic consciousness of thousands of Polish Americans was the holding of the World's Columbian Exposition in Chicago in 1893. At the Polish Day observance at the fair, the conflict between religionists and nationalists was briefly submerged in a harmonious moment of ethnic pride and unity. Well before the great exposition opened, the Polish religionists laid the groundwork for reducing factional tensions. They urged widespread ethnic group participation in the fair, thus liberalizing their position slightly. About 1890 the clerical camp began to emphasize the ethnic as well as the religious quality of the philosophy of *Polskość*. In no sense did this newly expressed definition of Polishness in America signify a capitulation to their nationalist opponents. But rather than stressing the negative, antireligious features of their opponents, the religionists simply increased the ethnic content of their own outlook: the Polish Catholic could indeed be Polish as well as Catholic. Ethnic characteristics had never been denied in religionist philosophy, but merely subordinated to faith. Clericalists now discussed the subsidiary quality that made up a Pole in America, demonstrating their ethnic loyalty more conspicuously than before.

This shift to a more encompassing definition of a Pole was evident in the editorials of *Dziennik Chicagoski* late in 1891 and early in 1892. The religionist organ still attacked the PNA and its hated mouthpiece, *Zgoda,* not for being "masonic," but for being superficially ethnic and even insufficiently nationalist. The best defense against assimilation and denationalization, it said, was not the Polish National Alliance but the Catholic priesthood. By being antireligious, *Zgoda* was "retrograding" and being really "anti-nationalistic." As proof, *Dziennik* added that the patriot paper was written in poor Polish.[12]

The Resurrectionist organ's new task included news of clerics' patriotic activity. Father Barzynski, who had fled the repression which followed the 1863 insurrection in Russia, had recently organized a committee to protest the barbarous treatment of his countrymen by the Russians. The journal thus concluded that supporters of the PNA had no monopoly on patriotic expression. The nationalists' insistence that priests confine themselves to strictly religious work was wrong.[13]

The two camps continued to fight one another into 1892, but on new ground: nationalism. This common basis could eventually supply the elements of harmony. Co-operation between the Alliance and the Union was close at hand. Such a joint effort almost took place on May 3, 1891, on the hundredth anniversary of the Polish Constitution. Representatives of Catholic societies and of the Polish National Alliance met to plan for a combined observance of the event at St. Stanislaus parish; but when nationalists refused to agree to the religionist demand that non-Catholics be excluded—the old point of difference—the preparations broke down. Both groups decided to hold separate observances.[14] Despite the failure, however, the two factions had established a precedent for a joint venture, which materialized in Polish Day at the Chicago world's fair.

The Columbian Exposition of 1893 was the symbol of the age, a huge spectacle where a recently industrialized America displayed its cultural and economic wares for visitors from all over the world. In addition there were countless exhibits from other countries, and, on different days during the summer of 1893, salutes to specific American nationalities. The sponsors selected October 7 for the Poles and asked the Chicago Polish community to help plan for a celebration. Conscious of the

---

[12] *Dziennik Chicagoski,* December 15, 1891, February 24, 25, March 1, 3, 1892, *FLPS.*

[13] *Ibid.,* January 26–27, August 12, 1892.

[14] Haiman, *Zjednoczenie,* 110–113; Osada, *Historya,* 310–317.

status that fair officials granted them as a separate and distinct nationality, the Polish-American leaders and societies responded with enthusiasm and unity. Contrary to all previous Polish-American history, leaders evinced national consciousness not by combat but by unified action, broadcasting their ethnicity to Chicago and the world.

Planning began with an organizational meeting of Polish business and fraternal representatives at St. Stanislaus Church Hall on August 16, 1893. The indomitable Father Barzynski reiterated the altered ethnic posture of religionists and spoke of the necessity of making Polish Day a sincere expression of national feeling. With considerable relief, *Dziennik Chicagoski* reported that the old animosities seemed to be absent: "What is more important, it was agreed that the Poles will unite for this occasion without regard to partisanship."[15] But despite growing support for a harmonious demonstration, it was evident that the old enmities might yet ruin the opportunity for demonstrating Polishness. *Polak w Ameryce*, the major clerical paper in Buffalo, urged that the day's observance be renamed "Polish Catholic Day." The nationalist Milwaukee *Kuryer* best expressed the hopes and fears of moderates: "The idea is to show that we exist as Poles, that we have not forgotten our homeland and past, and finally that we already constitute something of a power in the United States. . . . But the greatest obstacle remains, [one] that is well nigh insurmountable—the lack of unity amongst the American Poles, the misunderstandings and jealousies, which . . . will never permit all of the Poles . . . to gather together and go forward hand in hand."[16] The paper concluded that all Poles still ought to work for the success of the event.

As it turned out, Polish Day was successful. Unity and enthusiasm bloomed among the nationality. One reason for increased ethnic pride was the action of fair officials who defended, and thus encouraged, ethnic consciousness among Poles. They insisted, over the objections of both the German and Austrian governments, that designated Polish works of art were

[15] *Dziennik Chicagoski*, August 17, 1892.
[16] *Ibid.*, July 18, 1892.

admissible to the competition on the grounds that the Poles *did* constitute a separate nation.[17] In this atmosphere of widespread Polish involvement and American recognition, the *Dziennik Chicagoski* wrote ecstatically in late August that the forthcoming day would be a memorable one: "Members of Chicago Polonia from various neighborhoods and camps have joined hands. . . . This beautiful work, so promisingly begun in fraternal harmony, will end beautifully also. 'Polish Day' will announce to the world that 'Poland is not yet lost' [the title of a national hymn] nor ever will be!"[18] The affair was more than a local expression of unity, for more than 100 societies of various interests from as far away as Buffalo participated. The Polish National Alliance was officially represented by two of its members on the planning committee, and it made a formal contribution of $400.

Polish Day itself, October 7, was as satisfying to most Poles as the anticipation and preparation for it. The event affected both Polish and American consciousness. Even the weather was helpful. Rain had ruined Irish Day the previous Saturday and it had poured on the sixth, but the morning of the seventh dawned bright and clear.[19] Participants started from the mother churches on the north and west sides, near St. Stanislaus and St. Adalbert's. Preparations at the latter place included two huge triumphal arches through which the marching columns proceeded. The main demonstration filed down the city's main thoroughfare, Michigan Avenue, to Van Buren Street. The marchers and celebrants later gathered in Festival Hall on the Exposition grounds to listen to addresses by important personalities.

The color of the spectacle and enthusiasm of the participants impressed onlookers. Uniformed Polish policemen sixteen abreast, leading the parade in the brilliant sun, made an "imposing appearance." They were followed by equally colorful participants—Grand Marshal Peter Kiołbassa, Mayor Carter

---

17 *Ibid.,* July 26, 28, August 11, 1892.
18 *Ibid.,* August 28, 1892.
19 *Ibid.,* October 10, 1892; *Chicago Daily News,* October 7, 1892.

Harrison alone in his carriage, girls in white shirts and red stockings (the national colors), and men of the military societies in blue, red, and gold uniforms with shiny helmets and flags on their bayonets. The long file ended with sixteen floats decked out with flowers and Polish and American bunting, children in bright peasant costume, horseman in red and white sashes, and a number of politicians and fraternal representatives. The climax of this display of Polish and American nationalism was the ringing of a "Liberty Bell" replica by the oldest Pole in the city, a gentleman of 104 years named Adamski.

Amid more red-and-white bunting and Polish coats-of-arms, the speakers at Festival Hall that afternoon maintained the atmosphere of Polish pride with speeches on the anti-Polish injustices of European despots. Mayor Harrison, giving one of the main addresses, complimented the nearly 10,000 gathered in the hall for their impressive parade, which surpassed those of the previous German, Bohemian, and Irish Days. He reminded his listeners that such expressions of ethnic pride were possible only in the free land of America. Polish Day undoubtedly raised the level of national consciousness of the ordinary Poles who participated in and attended the ceremonies. The large number present suggested its significance: about 50,000 people marched in the parade, and twice that number watched. As the mayor observed, the event had a pervasive impact, particularly when the Polish activities were compared with those of older American nationalities, such as the Irish and Germans.

The fact that Polish Day came off without the usual rancor between Poles further stimulated the nationalist fervor, even among religionists. As a result of this experience, some Polish spokesman predicted an end to the clericalist-nationalist division. The leading religionist paper, *Dziennik Chicagoski,* dwelt on what it regarded as the most encouraging aspect of the event, a united Polonia. "It was a pleasure to see national and church societies marching side by side, hatreds and rivalries forgotten, a tear of emotion in each eye, joy and brotherhood in each heart." Several months later the paper still recalled the spectacle as a hopeful dawn of a new era. Polonia was now one. "We marched side by side . . . even though the day before we had been enemies. . . . We learned how to group together in one rank. Pax Dei, peace of God is descending on the Polish people in America. Let this peace last forever."[20]

Several other nationalist projects benefited, at least temporarily, from the heightened ethnic consciousness of 1893. One was a plan to raise money to construct a statue of Thaddeus Kościuszko in Chicago, the Polish hero who had fought with Washington. Another was to encourage Polish-American participation at a nationalist exposition to be held in 1894 in Lwów in Austrian Poland. Most importantly, to co-ordinate all these nationalist campaigns, clericalists and nationalists joined in 1896 to organize a new society, the Liga Polska (Polish League.)

The demonstrations of ethnic loyalty resulting from Polish Day were short-lived, however, and soon the historic conflict of God and Country resumed. By 1896 the Kościuszko monument fund was still so small that critics urged that the money collected be used for some other purpose; the Lwów contributions fell far short of anticipated expenses; and the Polish League died within a year because of the feuding between patriot and clerical elements.[21]

The brief manifestation of Polish ethnic pride and unity in the early 1890's was an unusual contribution to the propagation of ethnic consciousness. In Chicago, for the first time, Poles acted as one body on a particular occasion to display their national heritage—to outsiders as well as to themselves. Polish-American leaders wanted to demonstrate that their group was on a par with other American immigrant nationalities. They were successful at the Columbian Exposition, but this unified effort was exceptional and of brief duration. In spite of its avowed success, and the good will it engendered, Polish Day was only a minor agent in the spread of national consciousness.

---

[20] *Dziennik Chicagoski,* January 2, 1894, and quoted in Haiman, *Zjednoczenie,* 129.

[21] See *Dziennik Chicagoski,* August 22, 1892; July 10, October 9, 1894; February 11, March 6, 1896, *FLPS,* February 3, 1894; Haiman, *Zjednoczenie,* 139–146; Osada, *Historya,* 387–390. See also the list of Lwów Exposition contributors in Victor Bardonski file, March, 1895, in the Polish Museum, Chicago.

In these very years, especially 1894, a far more profound, internal development affected—one might say afflicted—the Polish community. The conflict between religious and nationalist Poles, evident already in the 1860's, blossomed in the 1890's as the result of new, differing interpretations. The rise of an entirely separate denomination, National Catholicism, became a unique and more dangerous threat to Polonia. The issue arose over the ownership of the ethnic parish. Certain lay leaders insisted, as they had on the north side of Chicago during the previous decade, that the parishioners ought to hold title to their religious property. In the subsequent atmosphere of disorder and riot, the "congregationalists" were able to obtain the leadership of a few clerics, which gave historic, ecclesiastical sanction to their cause. They formed so-called "independent" parishes without diocesan blessing, in fact sometimes under excommunication, and eventually they erected their own Polish National Catholic Church in America. It was this critical development— the growth of schism and its attendant group friction and trauma —in the decade of the 1890's that was the major factor in producing a deeper group consciousness among Polish-Americans.

The Roman Catholic Church had resolved the earlier dissatisfaction over hierarchical ownership of property at Holy Trinity by appointing a patriot priest who could mediate the potentially explosive religious-nationalist conflict between his followers; but similar unrest in other cities plagued Polonia for many years. The source of the trouble was the strong reaffirmation of parish ownership enunciated by the Third Plenary Council of the Catholic Church in Baltimore in 1884. This religious body decreed that all such wealth was the possession of the bishop.[22] Approximately 12 per cent of their total income was going to the Church, and some Polish laity, especially the more nationalistic ones, simply refused to accept that decree; parish wealth had to be theirs.[23] They argued with other parishioners that

[22] Reverend Francis Hodur, later head of the Polish National Catholic Church, called this decree "the bugle call that awakened the Polish People in America"; See "Polish National Catholic Church History" (typescript, 1923), 32, in the Polish Museum.

[23] The figure is the estimate of Jozef Miąso, *Dzieje Oświaty Polonijnej w St. Zj.* (Warszawa, 1970), 51–53.

Polish clerics who defended diocesan control of their property were unrepresentative, autocratic administrators who were insufficiently nationalistic. While the pressure on the Polish clergy intensified from both above and below, several other factors affected Polonia as a whole and brought the community to the crisis of 1894 and 1895. Beginning in 1892, the nationalist wing forcefully articulated its position on the administration of parish wealth. In February, possibly due to the burgeoning Holy Trinity problem, the Polish National Alliance organ *Zgoda* explained its position in detail. It accepted the priest as collector of funds in the parish, but asserted that such financial activities were to be conducted with the guidance of the parish committee, especially its secretary and treasurer. Both the pastor and the parish secretary were to maintain records of income and expenses, and were to publish a financial statement twice a year. The funds themselves, even those received for such priestly duties as administering the sacraments, belonged to the parish treasury.[24] The nationalist paper, then, carefully delimited the role of the cleric in financial administration, forcing him to share income management with the congregation. (Of course most Polish pastors, up to and after 1894, disregarded the nationalist position and followed diocesan practice by answering only to their superiors about financial administration.)

The aggressive patriot attack on the pastors' fiscal control focused on the activities of Polonia's most powerful cleric, the Reverend Vincent Barzynski. The concentration upon the old patriarch of St. Stanislaus was due not only to his stature as the pre-eminent Polish religionist leader but also to his extensive but little-publicized financial dealings. Barzynski was more than the independent manager of a huge parish treasury; he was also a "banker." Ever since 1875 he had manipulated the St. Stanislaus monies as assets in a financial institution. The "bank" accepted deposits of parishioners, paid interest, and loaned money, particularly to Chicago Polish groups anxious to establish their own parish. By 1893 the bank's assets had grown to

24 See also "Slavic Catholics in the United States," in *The Ecclesiastical Review* (November, 1903), 505–506.

$135,000, and Barzynski had loaned five Chicago parishes just under $50,000.[25]

Besides the campaign which demanded that priests share church property with their parishioners, a second cause for neighborhood disorder was the unusual combination of demographic and economic conditions which affected the city in the few years preceding the 1894 unrest. An influx of immigrants in the late 1880's overburdened some of the old parishes and resulted in the establishment of new ones, thus dividing the financial resources of the Polish community. The Panic of 1893 and the ensuing depression made hard-pressed churchgoers more sensitive to the pastor's handling of church collections. A third and most immediate catalyst for schism was the existence of spiritual leadership for the discontented. A few popular, congregationally oriented Polish priests appeared in the front ranks of the "independent" movement. Some were ordained by the regular Church and could claim valid ecclesiastical sanction for their involvement. These religious leaders more responded to congregational and nationalist sentiment than initiated it, for independentism was essentially induced by the Polish laity.

Ecclesiastical support for these parish disorders came from the odd, dissenting denomination known as Old Catholicism, particularly the bizarre activities of its eccentric bishop in America, Joseph Rene Vilatte. Old Catholicism had developed in 1871 in certain western European countries as a liberal reaction against the announced doctrine of Papal Infallibility. Vilatte was a remarkable opportunist who encouraged and profited from any dissatisfaction among American Roman Catholics. Born within the Church in France, he obtained a Presbyterian congregation in northern Wisconsin. Later, with Episcopalian assistance, he was ordained an Old Catholic priest in Switzerland in 1886. Aspiring for a more elevated ecclesiastical office, he applied to the Jacobite Archbishop of Ceylon, who granted him a bishop's mitre in 1892.[26] Despite his questionable

[25] From the *1893 Report of Finances,* quoted in Kwiatkowski, *Historia,* 347.
[26] Vilatte's absorbing biography is in Rev. Walter H. de Voil, "The Origin and History of the Old Catholic Group of Churches . . ." (Ph.D. dissertation, University of Edinburgh, 1936?), 64, 88, 97; "Recent Schismatic Movements

credentials, Vilatte considered himself the Old Catholic leader in the United States, and upon returning to America, "whenever he heard of dissatisfaction about [Roman Catholic] Church relations . . . , he was sure to turn up . . . , urging the people to throw off the yoke of Rome."[27]

Through 1893 Vilatte found no religious dissension, and, his funds exhausted, he made overtures to the Roman Catholic Church to accept him again. The following year Polish-American dissatisfaction over parish administration came to his attention. Thereupon Vilatte "found an asylum among the schismatic Poles," as well as lieutenants for his movement among their apostate clerics.[28]

The year 1894 was ripe for a major upheaval among the Poles in America, one which would ultimately help to deepen the Polish laity's understanding of their ethnic group. Given deteriorating economic conditions prodding them to scrutinize parish income, an active nationalist effort to safeguard congregational autonomy, and an alternative ecclesiastical legitimization of the Old Catholic movement led by Vilatte, the Poles of America were about to enter a period more turbulent than any yet experienced by loyal Catholics. No compromise similar to that at Holy Trinity could contain the forthcoming dissatisfaction. The virus of apostasy and nationalism produced "independent" parishes. The new movement was noticeable in outlying settlements first, but it soon affected profoundly the core of Polonia, particularly Chicago, Buffalo, and the anthracite coal-mining districts of Pennsylvania.

. . . ," in *American Ecclesiastical Review*, 21: 1–8 (July, 1899); and Rev. William S. Shea, "The Polish Independent Catholic Church Movement . . ." (Ph.D. dissertation, Boston College, 1934), 103–128.

[27] Peter F. Anson, *Bishops at Large* (New York, 1964), 111. Vilatte's Episcopalian mentor later reversed his enthusiasm for his protégé, calling him "morally rotten . . . a swindling adventurer [with] exceptional gifts as an imposter [and] no religious principles." *Ibid.*, 117–118.

[28] The quotation is allegedly that of Bishop Messmer of Milwaukee; *ibid.*, 112.

SIX

The Rise of Independentism, 1894–1900

IN THE LAST DECADE of the nineteenth century, the major concern of Polish America was the matter of accommodating ethnicity with religion. A new religious movement, "independentism," arose among the Poles in 1894 and 1895, producing a schism that eventually induced some to separate from their ancestral Church. The number of Poles who actually left Roman Catholicism was small, to be sure, and it may well have been true (as the conservative religionists asserted) that only a small, selfish minority of clerics supported the schism. Nevertheless, the issues raised, and the heat of the arguments on both sides, held the attention and interest of a great many Poles who were not directly involved. To these immigrant laymen, fragmentation and disorganization were anathema, and the extent to which "independentism" wracked Polish America was a measure of their concern. The tension between ethnic identity and religious tradition, which had eased during the euphoria of the Columbian Exposition, once again drew taut around Polonia.

The question arose in the mid-1890's, as it had in the mother parish of St. Stanislaus in the 1860's, over who was to control parish resources. Most Polish pastors believed that they and their non-Polish superiors ought properly to control the local church property; some Polish laymen, especially the more nationalistic, insisted that the ethnic congregation ought to have authority over parish wealth. As before, the outcome was widespread dissatisfaction among the laity with their pastors management of church resources. The issue nettled many ordinary parishioners—former peasants who were very sensitive about real estate title—who were gradually awakened to a clearer vision of both the religious and the ethnic aspects of their Roman Catholic faith. Some of the more dissatisfied rank and file formed independent parishes, though they still claimed to be loyal Catholics. Ultimately, with the advice, counsel, and encouragement of orthodox Polish priests, the Church excommunicated the leaders of the new parishes, including the occasional cleric who sided with them. The entire matter affected everyone deeply—independents, loyal parishioners, and even the most Roman Catholic of clerics, who themselves felt constrained to demand greater hierarchical recognition of their ethnic group, too. Rising ethnic consciousness was like a virus, and no one seemed immune.

The leaders of the independent parishes, many of whom became National Catholic later, were the more assertively ethnic, secular figures. It is sufficient to describe these strong-willed laymen as "enlightened" Poles who felt that Church wealth and property ought to be congregationally, that is, ethnically controlled. These critics of Church policy were really not hostile to religion, nor even to Roman Catholicism; they were not schismatics, as some charged, for they sought, until the end, to remain within the fold. Independentism was not a conspiracy of a few religious malcontents, but a new byproduct of the old God-and-Country controversy.

It is difficult to determine the date of the first independent parish. Certainly the first of a series spawned by disagreements with pastors over financial administration began early in 1894. In Omaha some parishioners forced their priest to leave the church because of his mishandling of funds, though the local bishop insisted that the accounts were in order and ordered the trustees to pay the cleric what was owed him. At about the same time in Baltimore some "insurrectionists" at St. Mary's sued the church for the right to own pews, rather than have the priest rent them. Describing a similar disturbance at Mill Creek, Pennsylvania, the religionist *Dziennik Chicagoski* warned, "The participation in parish disorders is not only a sin in the presence of God but it is also a crime against national solidarity."[1] The spirited harmony of the 1893 Polish Day had ended.

A more serious and perhaps more representative disorder, which clearly reflected the nationalists' demands, took place in Cleveland, where Polish dissenters had found clerical sympathy and ecclesiastical sanction in the person of the Reverend Francis Kołaszewski. The precise cause of the unrest is not clear, but the dissatisfied element was decidedly more ethnically sensitive than the others. As in the parish troubles elsewhere, a group demanded that the bishop remove the Polish pastor at St. Stanislaus because of his monetary mismanagement. A local Polish newspaper editor assumed partial direction of the unrest and urged the anti-pastoral forces to form their own parish and join the Old Catholics. The dissenters ignored this suggestion and applied to the Apostolic Delegate to consider their grievances. A nationalistic faction of laymen who directed the early stages of unrest in Cleveland formed a new society of their own and applied for admission to the Polish National Alliance.[2]

Father Kołaszewski became active when he declared the opening of his new independent parish at the end of the summer —followed shortly by his excommunication. When the apostate priest brought in the peripatetic Bishop Vilatte to bless his new church and ordain him as an official in the Old Catholic Church, the ceremony caused a riot between Polish Roman Catholics and Kołaszewski's followers in which two people were seriously injured and several arrested. Later, representatives of independent factions in Detroit, Buffalo, Winona, the Pennsylvania anthracite districts, Chicago, Omaha, Pittsburgh, and Milwaukee gathered at Kołaszewski's church in something of a synod. The Polish-American press reaction to the new Kołaszewski faction showed the effects of the nationalist-religionist controversy. The *Ameryka* of Toledo praised Kołaszewski as a man of high ideals and as one who stimulated the heart of every Polish patriot, but the loyal Catholic *Polak w Ameryce* of

[1] *Dziennik Chicagoski,* January 19, 1894.
[2] *Ibid.,* March 27, June 12, 1894.

Buffalo retorted, "Judas Iscariot likely sent Kołaszewski a telegram of congratulations from Hell."[3] Through the late summer and early fall of 1894 discontent over the clergy's financial administration of the several parishes continued, frequently producing independent parishes. One example was Winona, Minnesota, where several hundred Polish parishioners succeeded in persuading the bishop to remove their priest. Later the prelate refused to accept the laymen's nominee for the pastorate, and some parishioners began to plan a separate church. In Omaha, when the Polish pastor had the parish treasurer arrested in mid-October for interfering with his administration of the church, the opposing group of laymen obtained court approval of their title to church property with the help of an independent cleric.[4]

The largest independent movement took place in the capital of Polish America, Chicago. It showed the salient features of the earlier unrest elsewhere: widespread dissatisfaction with the priest's financial administration; an attempt by leading parishioners to win Papal support of lay control of their church; opposition by established Polish clerics; the creation of a separate independent house of worship under a priest who claimed he was still Roman Catholic; excommunication of the priest; and, most importantly, the nationalistic character of the dissenters as well as the profound impact the whole experience had on the ethnic community. The unique aspect of the independent movement in Chicago was the outstanding administrative ability of its leader, the Reverend Antoni Kozłowski. By 1907 his "church" had between 75,000 and 100,000 Polish communicants in twenty-three parishes from New Jersey to Manitoba.[5] Kozłowski's efforts heightened ethnic group consciousness for many Polish parishioners, both within and without his church.

---

[3] Quoted in *ibid.*, August 28, September 7, 1894; *Niedziela* (Detroit), August 12, August 26, 1894.

[4] *Dziennik Chicagoski,* July 25, August 17, October 15, 1894.

[5] The estimate is from *Chicago Record-Herald,* January 15, 1907; Anson, *Bishops,* 524; deVoil, "Origin and History," 101; *Philadelphia North American,* October 5, 1902; *The Living Churchman* (September 27, 1902), 713–715.

This largest, independent movement started at St. Hedwig Roman Catholic Church on the city's well-known Polish battle-ground, the north side. There, as he did so often, the Reverend Vincent Barzynski had helped the neighborhood organize a local house of worship by granting a loan to the lay leaders in 1888. He then continued to play a major role in the development of St. Hedwig. In 1889 the Resurrectionist leader had the bishop appoint his brother, Joseph, pastor; the choice was regrettable, for the cleric had an unattractive, abrasive personality. Soon after he assumed his position, some parish leaders objected to the way he handled church accounts. Father Joseph's normally cold and withdrawn manner intensified the growing disaffection, and when he defended his policies on the grounds that he was simply acting in the name of his superior, the archbishop, many parishioners termed his administration excessively autocratic.[6]

The arrival of the Reverend Antoni Kozłowski as Father Joseph's assistant in the summer of 1894 was a catalyst for action by the anti-pastor faction. Young, personable, and sympathetic to the parishioners' criticism of Barzynski, the new cleric acquired a large following, especially among the women. Quite likely due to his own jealousy and his assistant's apparent lack of loyalty, Father Joseph removed Kozłowski in December of 1894. By that time the malcontents of St. Hedwig had already received a visit from emissaries of the Cleveland independents and had tried unsuccessfully to start their own parish.[7]

Unquestionably the forced departure of Kozłowski increased the animosity of some parishioners toward their pastor, the Reverend Joseph Barzynski. They went to Archbishop Feehan to petition his removal, but even under this pressure the pastor refused either to resign or confront his opponents. Violence broke out at one of Barzynski's Sunday masses in January, 1895. Afterward *Dziennik Chicagoski* pleaded with the St. Hedwig people to come to their senses because the widespread group divisions were disgracing all Poles. Barzynski's brother, the powerful Father Vincent, begged them to remain loyal

[6] *Chicago Daily News,* March 16, 1896.
[7] *Dziennik Chicagoski,* October 23, 1894.

Catholics: "Return to the true path, the peaceful path, and respect Church laws."[8]

As a result of the disorder and the continuing hostility of embittered parishioners, Father Joseph finally submitted his resignation, but Archbishop Feehan at first refused to accept it. On the third and again on the eighth of February angry mobs, composed mostly of women, stormed St. Hedwig Church in near zero-degree weather to attack Barzynski. A police guard blocked their advance and several persons were injured. The frightened pastor took refuge in his brother's church, leaving his assistant, the Reverend Joseph Gieburowski, in charge at St. Hedwig.[9]

It appeared that the anticlerical faction had won a victory by forcing the archdiocese to discharge their pastor, but their success was not complete. Archbishop Feehan, very likely basing his action on Father Vincent's advice, appointed the Reverend Eugene Sedlacek, another Resurrectionist cleric, as St. Hedwig's religious leader.[10] Some parishioners took their case to the Apostolic Delegate in Washington to get his approval of their financial grievances and his support of Kozłowski as pastor.[11] The dissenters also raised a more fundamental objection to diocesan control of the parish when they insisted that, as contributors to St. Hedwig's coffers, they, not the bishop, were the owners of the property.[12] However, unlike the recent appeal to Satolli by lay leaders of Holy Trinity parish, these pleas were in vain.

From the moment Father Sedlacek entered the parish, he encountered determined opposition. Critics saw him as a representative of the Resurrectionist Order, a religionist, and a lackey of the archdiocesan head, despite the fact that he was

---

[8] Quoted in *Dziennik Chicagoski,* January 19, 1895; see also January 17, 1895.

[9] The best accounts of the incident are in *Kuryer Polski* (Milwaukee), February 5, 9, 1895, and *Chicago Inter-Ocean,* February 9, 1895.

[10] *Niedziela,* February 14, 1895.

[11] He ultimately refused to intervene; *ibid.,* February 21, 1895; *Kuryer Polski,* February 21, 1895. Parot, "An American Faith," 69–70, has further details.

[12] *Kuryer Polski,* February 12, 1895.

willing to negotiate congregational participation in parish government. The dissenting party refused to discuss the matter, and three times before mid-June Archbishop Feehan had to close the church because of unyielding lay attitudes. The anti-pastor hostility even led to the establishment of a second parish committee, parallel to the more "loyal" one recognized by the pastor.

In March the unrecognized committee of trustees refused to honor Sedlacek's appointment. On the fourteenth several hundred angry Poles met in the parish to protest Sedlacek's appearance and to resolve that if he did come, they would forcibly expel him. A spokesman for the anti-pastor faction described their hostility as not anti-Catholic in general but rather directed specifically against the Barzynski camp, which had urged compliance with diocesan rules. He went on to express forcefully the feeling of most parish dissenters:[13]

> In every case of these troubles . . . it is the same order of Resurrectionists that is at the bottom of it all. We are tired of them. They propose to own us entirely—our money, our thoughts, our political beliefs, our bodies and souls—we will have no more of it. We want secular priests and while I will not say there is a concerted action yet everywhere, we Poles have recognized that these Resurrectionists are dangerous enemies we must crush. And we will.

He also warned that the St. Hedwig conflict might produce bloodshed:

> Shall we go armed tomorrow? . . . I say frankly if this affair is not settled definitely before Sunday and these people [Sedlacek's supporters] persist in trying to hold that church, blood will be shed and men will lose their lives. It will not take much more to drive these people to utter desperation.

The next day, March 15, a crowd made up mostly of Polish women, led by a man named Lewandowski and armed with pepper to throw in the eyes of the police who were guarding the church, marched on the parish. Some dissidents entered the

---

[13] *Chicago Daily News*, March 15, 1895; *Chicago Chronicle*, September 30, 1895.

church, but police reinforcements soon forced them out. A woman and her two sons who hurled rocks at the police were arrested and the crowd was soon dispersed.[14]

The final scene of the confrontation took place the following evening at a neighborhood meeting place, Khulap's Hall. Father Sedlacek, who had earnestly hoped that some amicable agreement could be reached, willingly accepted the opportunity to talk to his dissenting parishioners. The atmosphere at the meeting was tense, due in part to the emotional fervor with which the issue of parish control was discussed and in part to the overflow crowd of 700 persons, twice the capacity of the hall. Sedlacek tried to convince his listeners that he was sincerely their representative, in spite of his being in the Barzynski Resurrectionist Order. He emphasized that he, too, was a patriotic Pole, and he reminded his audience that, unlike his predecessor, he was not related to the pastor of St. Stanislaus. He admitted that they had some valid complaints about the former pastor's administration of parish finances, and that he, their new cleric, wanted to work with the trustees at all times and would allow anyone to inspect the account books when they wished. Upon the completion of his statement, the parishioners voted unanimously against accepting him as their pastor, although they did promise to discontinue violent opposition. Father Sedlacek left the hall in tears.[15] Bishop Feehan shortly thereafter closed the parish for the second time.

During the three months that St. Hedwig remained closed, the efforts of the pro-Sedlacek faction to reopen it were blocked by the dissidents. In turn, the dissenters' petition for a court injunction to keep the church closed until a judge could rule on ownership was refused, thereby leaving the archbishop with both control and title.[16]

The dissidents now turned to their only alternative: forming

[14] *Chicago Daily News,* March 16, 1895; *Niedziela,* March 21, 1895.

[15] The dramatic session is in *Chicago Daily News,* March 16, 1895. Apparently Sedlacek was partially in sympathy with his parish critics. See Reverend W. Barzynski to the Resurrectionist Superior, Chicago, October 16, 1896, in the Barzynski Letters, WHS.

[16] *New World* (Chicago diocesan paper), June 22, 1895; Iwicki, *First Hundred Years,* 89–90. St. Hedwig did reopen June 24 with a Resurrectionist replacement for Sedlacek.

a separate parish and campaigning for ecclesiastical sanction from some authority in the Roman Catholic hierarchy. These independents already had grouped around Kozłowski in May, just after he reappeared in the city, and All Saints, their new church, opened for its first mass as soon as the court ruled on St. Hedwig.

It was later said that this emerging group with its nationality consciousness resulted from the machinations of a disaffected priest, Reverend Kozłowski, not from the efforts of a dissident congregation. Although it is difficult to determine precisely the origin of the parish's discontent, the preponderance of evidence suggests that Kozłowski was an important catalyst in the independent movement, but not its initiator. Independentism in Chicago was a general lay reaction to a religious issue, not a conspiracy of clerical malcontents. Kozłowski was a beneficiary of the movement, not its founder. The evidence is clear. Apparently Kozłowski was not present on the north side during the period of parish meetings and occasional violence in the early months of 1895, and no lay leader of the discontented faction even referred to him. In the five-month period from his removal from St. Hedwig in December to his agitation for a new parish in May, he was probably on a long trip through the South. While Kozłowski had been popular at St. Hedwig, the outspoken dissenters sought any secular priest who would lead them. Furthermore, he was an exceedingly modest and cautious rebel, who consistently urged his ardent followers to exhaust all avenues of appeal within the Roman Catholic Church. Kozłowski's activities and counsel were simply not those of a determined revolutionary.[17]

The groundswell of support for the anti-pastor faction was impressive, and indicated its strong grassroots character. When Kozłowski opened All Saints in June, he took about 1,000 of the St. Hedwig's 1,300 families with him.[18] Support for Koz-

---

[17] *Philadelphia North American*, October 5, 1902; *The Living Churchman*, September 27, 1902, and the somewhat biased Kruszka, *Historya*, 10: 138–140.

[18] *Dziennik Chicagoski*, April 9, 1906. Three thousand persons attended the opening mass; *Chicago Chronicle*, June 17, 1895.

łowski and the paucity of "loyal" Polish Catholics were more likely due to an abiding hostility to the established Church administration than to the persuasiveness of the independent cleric; Polish animosity in Chicago was not yet anti-Roman Catholic.

The lay dissent at St. Hedwig was basically conservative, and it therefore drew widespread support for independentism. Even years after the opening of All Saints, the dissidents still did not consider their activities schismatic. They believed that their view of congregational parish government was within the Roman Catholic tradition, until the Pope himself excommunicated Kozłowski in 1898. When Archbishop Feehan had so condemned the priest in September, 1897, the independents had believed their prelate was mistaken. Kozłowski promised his people that he would go to Rome to obtain the Holy Father's blessing as bishop of the emerging movement. Though he may have deceived his congregation by going to Switzerland to be consecrated as an Old Catholic bishop in November, 1897, rather than to Rome, the important consideration is that for almost three years the independents regarded themselves independent of the Resurrectionists, the religionists, and the Roman Catholic archbishops—not of the Pope.[19]

That the parish unrest had spread to other Chicago parishes as well as elsewhere in the country by 1898 is the most conclusive proof of widespread Polish-American dissatisfaction and the extensive impact of the issues. Even though only a minority of the Polish community joined the dissenters, the independent movement was a problem of national dimensions. For example, a similar disorder erupted at St. Joseph on Chicago's west side in August, 1895, and there, just as in the Polish neighborhood

---

[19] The account of Kozłowski's trip are in *Chicago Chronicle*, December 20, 1897, and de Voil, "Origin and History," 103. Vilatte, who had claimed Kozłowski's position and who had encouraged the Chicago cleric in 1895, now of course became his rival. Ernest C. Margrander, "Joseph Rene Vilatte," in *The New Schaff-Harzog Encyclopedia*, edited by S. M. Jackson (12 vols., New York, 1951–1953), 12: 188. The distinction of whom the independents were separate from was obtained from "A Close Observer," "Recent Schismatic Movements," 11–12; Kruszka, *Historya*, 10: 143–144; and Reverend M. J. Madaj, "A Study of the Polish National Church," in manuscript, especially 25.

to the north, some parishioners condemned the arbitrary management of church funds by the pastor, the Reverend Michael Pyplatz. The immediate result was the beginnings of another independent church.[20] Also at that very time and for a year afterward independents at nearby St. Adalbert sought and obtained funds for their separate parish.[21] The congregational insurgency extended even to the bastion of Polish Roman Catholicism, St. Stanislaus itself, early in 1895, when, in a rare and dramatic scene, several lay trustees had the temerity to question Father Barzynski about his handling of accounts. The group patriarch had to show them the books and orally account for his financial responsibility.[22]

Even prior to the Chicago disorders, several outlying Polish centers had indicated the nature of forthcoming parish disturbances. By 1898—at Omaha once again, at Buffalo, and at Scranton, the birthplace of National Catholicism—particularly bitter parish divisions erupted between lay leaders and priests, whom their critics felt were too loyal to their superiors at the expense of their parishioners.

The violent and rancorous conclusion to the Omaha trouble was a good example. Some parishioners succeeded in wresting legal title of St. Paul Church from the designated Polish pastor and bringing in a cleric from Cleveland, the Reverend Stephen Kaminski, whom Bishop Vilatte had ordained. However, a civil court declared that Church rules were valid in this case and that the bishop had title. On March 13, 1898, a group of Polish "loyalists" marched on the church to claim the key from Father Kaminski. A pitched gun battle resulted in the wounding of two men, extensive damage to the building, and the arrest of Father Kaminski for shooting one of his attackers. Later another judge clouded the issue of ownership by finding for the Kaminski camp. Here, as elsewhere, it was lay leadership among the dis-

---

[20] *Dziennik Chicagoski,* August 26, November 14, 1895, *FLPS; Chicago Chronicle,* August 25, November 19, 1895.

[21] They probably also fought over financial control; see *Chicago Daily News,* June 8, 1890; *Dziennik Chicagoski,* March 1, 17, 21, November 13, 1897, *FLPS; ibid.,* December 9, 13, 1897.

[22] *Chicago Record,* February 11, 18, 1897.

senters, rather than the Old Catholic cleric, who agitated the issue.[23] Contemporaneously with the trouble in Omaha, the Polonia of Buffalo experienced a similar internecine contest between Polish defenders and critics of diocesan authority. The disorders resembled those in Chicago. The rise of Buffalo's congregational movement was in response to its leading priest. The Polish community in Buffalo had grown enormously since the 1870's under the authority of the Reverend John Pitass, a priest who in many respects resembled Chicago's Father Barzynski. Like his Resurrectionist colleague and friend, Pitass nearly ruled the Polish community from his parish, which was coincidentally named St. Stanislaus and was the mother parish in the city. While not of the regular clergy like Barzynski, Pitass did resemble his Chicago counterpart in the great confidence and esteem in which his Irish superior held him. In fact Bishop Stephen Ryan officially honored his loyal Polish councilor in 1894 by designating him vicar forane, or dean, of all the Polish people in the diocese just before the outbreak of disorder.[24] So here, as elsewhere, when Polish separatists appeared, they leveled their major criticism at Pitass, rather than at the bishop.[25]

The origins and development of events concerning the emerging independents in Buffalo resembled those at St. Hedwig in Chicago. Some parishioners at Buffalo's second Polish church, St. Adalbert, began agitating in 1894 for the priest they had had in 1890, the Reverend Antoni Klawiter, whom, on Pitass' advice, the bishop had dismissed.[26] They charged that the current

[23] *Kuryer Polski*, March 11, 1897, has the best account of the disturbance. Joseph Inda appeared to be the leading independent; see *Dziennik Chicagoski*, March 13, 1897.

[24] Polski Spolki Wydawnicznej, *Album Pamiątkowe . . . Buffalo* (Buffalo, 1906), 51–58. Ryan's official diocesan letter appointing Pitass is quoted in Kruszka, *Historya*, 13: 12–13, 16. Ryan's successor confirmed Pitass' position by designating him "irremovable rector." *Ibid.*, 16–17.

[25] See the interview of a parish committeeman in the *Buffalo Express* in Madaj, "Study," 33–34.

[26] Mieczysław Haiman, "Historya Parafji Św. Stanislaus . . ." in *Księga Pamiątkowe . . . w Buffalo, New York, 1873–1923* (Buffalo, 1923), 323.

pastor, the Reverend Thomas Flaczek, Pitass' former assistant and nominee for the position, was exploiting parish funds. They insisted that the church title be in the name of the parish. After some violent exchange between the Flaczek and Klawiter factions, the dissidents began their own independent parish at an unusual open-air mass in August, 1895, with Father Klawiter officiating.[27] The new congregation invited the Reverend Stephen Kaminski to take charge of the parish in April, 1896, and the group prospered thereafter.[28] By 1905 Kaminski's following numbered about 6,000, and by 1911 the value of his parish was about $250,000.[29]

A third major insurrection of parishioners took place in the anthracite districts of Pennsylvania. The significance and peculiarity of this case was that the priest in charge of the disaffected faction, the Reverend Francis Hodur, was able to consolidate the Buffalo, Chicago, and other independents into his own Polish National Catholic Church by about 1912. The trouble in Pennsylvania originated at the mother parish for the region, again a church named St. Stanislaus, in Nanticoke, Pennsylvania. The Reverend Benevenuto Gramliewicz, the pastor, was, like Barzynski and Pitass, a strong Roman Catholic leader, "the patriarch of Polish priests" in eastern Pennsylvania.[30] A group of Polish patriots began a second parish, Holy Trinity, over the objections of Gramliewicz and the Irish bishop, William O'Hara, by getting the permission of Apostolic Delegate Satolli in 1894.[31] Bishop O'Hara accepted the establishment of the parish and appointed Hodur, then a young cleric,

---

[27] *Sixteenth Anniversary, 1895–1955, Holy Mother of Rosary Cathedral . . .* (Buffalo, 1955), in Immigration History Research Center, University of Minnesota.

[28] Vilatte later made Kaminski a bishop of his Church in 1898, just before the priest's excommunication. *Ibid;* Hodur, *Polish National Catholic Church,* 35.

[29] Kruszka, *Historya,* 1: 132.

[30] The nickname is that of Kruszka, *Historya,* 12: 110.

[31] *Ibid.,* 87–89; Reverend John Gallagher, *A Century of History* (Scranton, 1968), 163–166. Note especially the bishop's permissive ethnic policy, a " 'hands-off' approach," *ibid.,* 157.

as pastor. Possibly aware of the group conflict in Chicago, the bishop chose the more popular Hodur in order to avoid another struggle between the two hostile Nanticoke congregations.

Although the prelate was successful there, a Polish conflict occurred in his home city of Scranton in August, 1896, when a minority of parishioners at Sacred Heart demanded that the Reverend Richard Aust be removed for his arbitrary administration and his lack of knowledge of Polish (he was a German).[32] After some violence at the church in September and October, Bishop O'Hara acceded to the appeals of the parish committee and chose a more authentic Pole, the Reverend Bronislas Dembinski. The parish committee objected to the new pastor's attitude toward their money and again asked O'Hara for another priest; the bishop rejected their request. As in Chicago and elsewhere, it was the dissenters who were the active promoters of independentism, not the priest; it was laymen who convinced Father Hodur to take charge of Sacred Heart in March of 1897.[33]

At first Father Hodur behaved very much like Father Kozłowski in Chicago; he tried to avoid schism. But early in 1898 the new Scranton bishop, Michael J. Hoban, excommunicated him. Still seeking some compromise, Hodur went to Rome to plead his parishioners' financial and nationalistic demands.[34] Unsuccessful in his mission, Hodur returned to Pennsylvania, and by the end of 1899 he had brought five new parishes under his control in the anthracite region.[35] Only then did he try to obtain external ecclesiastical sanction for his movement, from the Old Catholic Church. Unfortunately he had to wait until 1907 to succeed Kozłowski as that Church's bishop in America. By shortly before World War I, Bishop Hodur had drawn into

---

[32] Hieronim Kubiak, *Polski Narodowy Kościół Katolicki w St. Zj . . . 1897–1965* (Kraków, 1970), 112–114.

[33] See Kruszka, *Historya*, 12: 96–97.

[34] These were, specifically, the lifting of Hodur's suspension, the retention of the deed of the church in parish hands, and congregational control of income and pastoral appointment; Gallagher, *Century*, 223; Hodur, *Polish National Catholic Church*, 95.

[35] Gallagher, *Century*, 230; Kruszka, *Historya*, 12: 110.

his Polish National Catholic Church widely scattered insurgencies in New Britain, Connecticut (1895); Bay City, Michigan (1896); Baltimore, Maryland (1896); Bayonne, New Jersey (1897); and Buffalo.[36]

In this ever-widening pattern of disturbances in the mid-1890's Polish-Americans confronted firsthand the conflict within their community, and in the process of resolving the disputes a new sense of group membership spread throughout the laity. The impact of this experience was broad and deep within the American Polonia. In settlements from Nebraska to New England, Minnesota to Maryland, a few aggressive, ethnically sensitive parishioners began to assert a congregational, really a national, authority over both pastors and church property; and other group members defended the American Catholic administration.

In an unusual council held at Buffalo in October, 1895, all the apostate leaders—Kozłowski, Kołaszewski, Kaminski, and Klawiter—singled out their own religionist countrymen as their opponents, not the non-Polish-American Catholic hierarchy. Their movement was a reaction against "diocesan pastors, [like] Pitass, Rosinski . . . , Barzynski, Wincenty, and Jozef, Lange, Nawrocki . . . and the Resurrectionists in general."[37]

The pro- and anti-independent forces pitted one Pole against another at a time when the Polish people were struggling by means of mutual aid to attain economic and cultural viability in a strange environment. The flurry of excommunications of

---

[36] Authorities judge that by then he had thirty-four churches and just under 30,000 communicants. The relatively small numbers are not an indication of the significance of independentism earlier, for there were undoubtedly many who returned to the Roman Catholic Church after initial dissatisfaction. Compare Kruszka, *Historya,* 1: 93, 121, 125, 126, 132–137; Kubiak, *Historia,* 134–135; and U.S., Department of Commerce, Bureau of the Census, *Religious Bodies,* 1916, Part I (Washington, 1919), 547. The descriptions of disorders in these locations are in *Dziennik Chicagoski,* September 5, 1895, February 9, May 18, 21, June 6, 22, October 27, 1896; *1903–1953, Golden Jubilee . . . Heart of Jesus National Catholic Church . . .* (Bayonne, New Jersey, 1953); and Daniel Buczek, *Immigrant Pastor* (Waterbury, Connecticut, 1974), 7–8, 10–21.

[37] *Dziennik Chicagoski,* October 29, 1896, *FLPS.*

popular clerics in the late 1890's, actions which Polish Catholic leaders supported, forced each church-going group member to ponder which of the three wings of the nationality—Catholic, nationalist, or independent—was the proper one for a Pole. The issue of parish control which had stirred Chicago's north side since the 1860's and divided Polish institutions into nationalist and religionist camps in the early 1890's now came to the immediate attention of all Polish-Americans. The immigrant could not attend mass comfortably, for his countrymen, his friends, perhaps even his relatives, were hostile to the priest and might go to the extreme of assaulting him and interfering with religious services.

The leading clericalist paper, *Dziennik Chicagoski,* expressed the intimate, personal consequences of the controversy, calling the troubles the scandalous excesses of a minority. At the opening of Kozłowski's All Saints parish in mid-1895, the paper condemned "schismatics" who in a number of cases assaulted "loyal" parishioners with eggs, rocks, and sand. Later it asserted that the antagonisms had even affected family relations. In an exchange between a brother and an "independent" sister who had repented, the paper quoted her as stating, "Brother, . . . you can be sure that the schism will not last a long time." The brother answered, "Thank God that the rest of our family holds." As another example of the destructive influence of independentism on the family, the paper used the case of a man who attended Kozłowski's All Saints parish and separated from his wife because she refused to leave St. Hedwig.[38] The disorder on the north side continued into 1896, when the religionist paper condemned a number of schismatic "hoodlums" who by means of a series of assaults were intimidating citizens and bringing "untold misery."[39]

The neighborhood was in a quandary as to how to stop the social disorder. Early in 1896, in an attempt to pacify the in-

---

[38] *Ibid.,* June 18, 20, November 20, 1895, August 7, 1896, *FLPS.*
[39] *Ibid.,* May 11, 1896, *FLPS.* Kruszka refers to another rock-throwing incident in 1898; see *Historya,* 9: 241.

flamed factions on the north side, the editor of *Dziennik Chicagoski* urged his readers to renew their dedication to Catholic principles:[40]

> Our lack of unity stand[s] in our way . . . a thousand roads [lie] before us. . . . There is not one leading star. . . . There are only will-of-wisps rising from stinking swamps. They [the independents] tempt one to approach false roads. How much longer will we be lost in the desert. . . . Let the one guiding star shine for us . . . the star of salvation. . . . In the cross lies our salvation.

A short time later a Polish cleric, who must have experienced the troubles firsthand, anathematized the schismatics for nearly destroying the very social fabric of the community by their demands for autonomy: "O, weighty, weighty Judgment, and punishment awaits those who separate man from wife, son from mother, father from daughter, [a situation] which causes schism to arise and blood to flow. . . . These unfortunates [apostates] have forgotten that the Lord says that it is better to hang yourself with a millstone than scandalize [our] immigrants."[41]

A "sincere Pole" addressed himself also to the disastrous, fratricidal effects of parish unrest and the

> terrible . . . consequences of these fatal disorders in the parishes. Today suspiciously brother eyes brother; there is no catching a glimpse of a sincere smile on a face, one lies in wait for the other prepared almost to emplant a stiletto in the chest of another; neighbor shuns neighbor; relative throws out his kin; your children that wonderful progeny in the presence of such examples accustom themselves to these scandalous affairs; [with the closing of churches by the bishop] Polish hymns become silent in the sanctuary; the House of God remains idle and empty, waiting for harmony and love, but in vain!

He concluded with the appropriate appeal, defining Polishness for all: "Brothers, remember your heritage . . . abandon strife

[40] *Dziennik Chicagoski,* January 30, 1896, *FLPS.*
[41] Szczesny Zahajkiewicz, *Księża i Parafie Polskie w St. Zj. w. P.A.* (Chicago, 1897), 61.

The Reverend Vincent Michael Barzynski, C.R., of St. Stanislaus parish, Chicago, who for the last quarter of the nineteenth century personified Polish Roman Catholicism.

Above, Polish and Slovak immigrant women, about 1900; below, a Polish man in Cracow.

Above left, Peter Kiołbassa, a prominent layman who supported Barzynski and the religionists; right,Władysław Dyniewicz, publisher of the Gazeta Polska Narodowa *and critic of the religionists. Below, Stanisław Slominski of Chicago, standing in front of the store where he sold religious and patriotic regalia in the late nineteenth century.*

Polish Museum

Rev. Paul Rhode, center, the first Polish-American bishop, during a procession in his honor on July 29, 1908. Archbishop James Michael Quigley is the older man to the right.

St. Stanislaus church, hall, convent, and school in Chicago, about 1915. This Polish parish had more than 40,000 members when Barzynski died in 1899, and was probably the largest Roman Catholic parish in the world.

Left, Rev. Matas Kraučiūnas, the most powerful Lithuanian immigrant priest in Chicago; right, probably Rev. Michael Krušas, his assistant at St. George's.

Rev. Alexander Burba of Penn-sylvania, who established the first purely Lithuanian parish in the United States.

Antoni Olszewski of Chicago, the publisher of Lietuva *and a strong supporter of the national-ists among the Lithuanians.*

Left, Dr. Jonas Šliūpas, who fought Roman Catholic restric-tions on Lithuanian nationalism in America, and, right, Dr. Jonas Basanavičius, often called the "Father of Lithuanian National-ism."

Above, a Lithuanian-American picnic, St. George's Church, Chicago, about 1900; below, a Lithuanian-American wedding in Chicago, 1914.

Above, a Lithuanian-American band from the Town of Lake, Illinois, 1914; below, delegates
the convention of the nationalist-controlled Lithuanian National Alliance held in Baltimore
1911.

... call in one voice 'God was and is, God and Country, Down with discord.' "[42]

Anxious Roman Catholic leaders voiced their anguish and grief over the imminent breakup and possible disappearance of the group. The disorders weakend the very foundations of Polish society in America. However, though religionists wrung their hands in despair and appealed for unity, few of them searched deeply for causes. Their analysis of the troubles was shallow and simplistic. These outbreaks of parish strife were more than a conspiracy of greedy clerics, a dispute between trustees and pastors, or even a demand for enlarged popular influence in church affairs. The troubles at St. Hedwig in Chicago, St. Adalbert in Buffalo, and Sacred Heart in Scranton represented a growing ethnic awakening of parishioners which had begun to affect all of Polish America.

Obviously such a perceptible change in the traditionally apathetic rank and file encouraged the old-time nationalists. The members and supporters of the Polish National Alliance were delighted at developments, and assisted the budding independent movement. They did not create the divisions between pastor and parishioners; those had started with the clash over Church rules by the property-conscious Poles. But once independentism aroused the masses to national consciousness, the more enthusiastic patriots flirted with the schismatics. A slight modification of the historic struggle between religionists and nationalists occurred in the mid-1890's, and a new camp emerged, an independent-nationalist coalition.

The independents advanced ethnic consciousness both by adopting Polishness as a cause and by simply raising Polishness as an issue. Throughout, their complaint over parish control was far less a criticism of Irish bishops than of their own clerical leaders, who, they protested, were not sensitive enough to the people's demands for greater congregational autonomy. Priests, especially the Resurrectionist regulars, were exploiting their very own people for their own as well as their bishop's advan-

[42] *Dziennik Chicagoski,* March 21, 1896.

tage. In this sense independentism was also a populist and nationalist phenomenon. Feeling themselves more now as Poles, they would not allow church property to be turned over to a non-Polish authority.

A number of contemporary sources explicitly referred to the spirited ethnic quality and consequences of independentism. A Polish Roman Catholic paper in Buffalo in 1895 recognized the claims of the schismatics, and, by rejecting them, defined the issue as one that concerned nationality recognition: "The 'Independent' churches are the greatest evil that befell the Poles in America and if the Polish schism last a long time, that will be the most consequential agent in [their] denationalization. For he who asserts that the Polish schism takes its start from patriotic sentiments, that is an outright lie."[43]

The strategy of *Dziennik Chicagoski* was to "unmask" the independents as pseudo-nationalists: Roman Catholicism was the one true faith and Polishness had to be integral with religion; the dissenters therefore were misleading their followers, for they were not true Poles. It took pride in exposing the Cleveland independent leader, Kołaszewski, as actually a Polish-speaking German named Rademacher.[44] About the same time it insisted that those who attacked Polish priests were directly opposed to the cause of the nationality, and since they were not true Roman Catholics and therefore without religion, they could not be Polish patriots. The success of these schismatics would mean the obliteration of Polishness. Religion, meaning Roman Catholicism, was its core; those who attacked clerics wished not for Polish fulfillment but for Polish extinction:[45]

> This fight against priests—a struggle without cause nor compromise against everything without exception [and] which is savage and fierce—will lead directly to the removal of the religious basis of our people and further to the disturbance of church and school. Then what will happen to us? . . . Dissen-

---

[43] From *Polak w Ameryce* in *Dziennik Chicagoski*, August 30, 1896.
[44] The allegation was probably accurate. See Rev. Francis Bolek, ed., *Who's Who in Polish America* (New York, 1943), 212; and the section in *Prawda* (Detroit), quoted in *Dziennik Chicagoski*, August 21, 1895.
[45] *Ibid.*, April 23, 1895.

sion. We are annihilated without a trace in the Anglo-Saxon sea. . . . Those who say down with the priests might as well say down with religion. Our people ought to understand this.

The movement stirred ethnic consciousness even in the patriotic response of religionists to it.

A pro-independent newspaper later reiterated the strongly nationalistic content of the issue and saw the dissidents as enthusiastic patriots. All true Poles ought to support the emerging movement: "We sympathize with the 'independent church' . . . as the first means for the training of Polish nationality in our people and as the most productive defense here against the Americanization of Poles by the Roman Catholic Church."[46]

The independents' claim that they were a nationalistic movement drew them close to the nationalists and the Polish National Alliance. Holy Trinity in Chicago, the leading nationalist parish, became so sympathetic that its pastor, the Reverend Casimir Sztuczko, had to call a special church meeting during the height of the north side disorder to forbid any of his people to attend the dedication of Kozłowski's All Saints chapel.[47] Despite this prohibition, the Free Polish Cavalry, a parish society, participated in the ceremonies along with two Polish National Alliance branches, and some of Father Sztuczko's people left his parish for good.[48]

The Polish National Alliance soon gave the independents formal, organizational sanction, and while its annual convention in 1895 still barred them from membership, in reality the anti-independent provision was not enforced. It admitted a Cleveland branch headed by Kołaszewski, an action that drew fire from *Dziennik Chicagoski,* which commented that if it were Kołaszewski today, tomorrow it would be Kozłowski and Klawiter.[49]

[46] *Gazeta Pittsburgska,* quoted in *Dziennik Chicagoski,* December 6, 1895.
[47] Quoted in *Dziennik Chicagoski,* November 11, 1895; see also *Pamiętnik 1893–1918 Parafii Świetej Trójcy . . . ,* 24.
[48] *Pamiętnik 1893–1918; Dziennik Chicagoski,* November 12, 1895; and especially *Chicago Chronicle,* November 11, 1985; *Ksiązka Jubileuszowa Parafii Św. Trócy 1893–1943* (Chicago, 1943), 27.
[49] See Kruszka, *Historya,* 4: 23–24; *Dziennik Chicagoski,* September 9, November 7, 1895.

The clericalist organ went on to describe in detail the most incriminating example of nationalist support for the Kozłowski movement, the testimonial given in his honor for his being appointed Old Catholic bishop. The affair was an evening banquet at All Saints, held in 1897 to welcome the apostate priest, just back from his elevation to prelate in Europe. The scene was a joyous one; independents and nationalists from all over the city came to praise him. *Dziennik Chicagoski* condemned one speaker who "represented the National Alliance, the only Polish organization having the same aims as those of the Polish Independent Church." The religionist paper growled, "The Alliance ought to go from there with Independents hand in hand." It noted also that later in the evening an "independent" troubador concluded the bacchanalian orgy by leading the hall in an enthusiastic finale: "Long live the Polish Bishop, Antoni Kozłowski, and our National Alliance."[50]

The PNA replied to the mounting criticisms of religionists that nationalist-independent fraternization was abetting schismatics as it had in previous encounters with clericalists. It recognized the primacy of Roman Catholicism among Poles, but it wanted to heighten ethnic consciousness among group members whatever their faith.[51]

In these final years of the 1890's another journalistic war engulfed Polonia. The old Catholic warhorses—*Dziennik Chicagoski, Polak w Ameryce* (Buffalo), *Gazeta Katolicka*—and newer ones—*Polonia* of both Cleveland and Baltimore, and *Naród Polski*—again exchanged broadsides with the nationalist and independent sheets—*Zgoda, Kropidło, Jutrzenka, Dziennik Polski* (Detroit), and others—to rekindle the issue of ethnic identity. However, this time the dispute over clericalism and patriotism was more meaningful to all, for it followed the lines

---

50 The hero of the evening left hurriedly to avert any overenthusiastic activity; *Dziennik Chicagoski*, December 21, 1895. Other evidence of the strong nationalist-independent tie is *ibid.*, July 25, 1896, and the secret report edited by Zbigniew Klein, "Policia Pruska . . ." in *Problemy Polonii Zagranicznej* (1962–1963), 3: 159.

51 *Zgoda*, July 16, August 6, December 17, 24, 1896.

of a devastating social cleavage in which some members had been ejected totally from the Roman Catholic community.[52] Obviously the enlarged nationalist opposition worried the Polish Roman Catholic camp. It was not simply an argument with the old patriot element; some independents of the new order were religious separatists who existed as a potential threat to Roman Catholic parishes, and whose apostasy undermined the very integrity of Polish America. Since independentism was almost immediately such a massive danger, clericalists had to devise a strategy to combat the menace. A hostile nationalist movement stimulated a correspondingly more energetic Roman Catholic campaign. The result was the convening of general Polish Catholic congresses. The average Polish parishioner, who was heretofore unaffected, suddenly was confronted with an even more serious issue of ethnic definition.

[52] See especially the Polish press reviews in *Dziennik Chicagoski*, August 14, 17, 21, October 25, 29, 1895.

SEVEN

Równouprawnienie:
God Yields to Country, 1896–1908

WHEN Polish Roman Catholics viewed Polonia in 1896, they found an unprecedented and deeply troublesome situation, a new crisis in factionalism. In the decades preceding 1894, loyal members of the faith had managed to contain ethnic sentiment within the confines of Roman Catholicism. The masterful diplomacy of Monsignor Satolli and the appearance of patriot-priests such as Sztuczko in Chicago and, before 1898, Hodur in Nanticoke had made ethnic enthusiasts content to remain within the fold. The Church itself was willing enough to allow the establishment of ethnic religious institutions in order that old, loyal patriarchs like Barzynski, Pitass, and Gramliewicz could uphold diocesan authority. But 1894 and 1895 brought such upsetting changes in Polish America that clericalists could not confine the groundswell of ethnic feeling within the traditional ecclesiastical structures. Some dissatisfied parishioners sought expanded congregational recognition, and when the established Polish religious leaders (as distinguished from non-Polish prelates) refused to accept their demands, the dissidents fashioned an extra-diocesan, ultimately non-Roman-Catholic movement to attain their objectives.

To respond to and deal with this "schism" (the term of the loyalists, not of the independents, who still thought of themselves as Roman Catholic), religionists decided to call a national meeting to devise ways to maintain Polish allegiance to the

Church and, if possible, to destroy the now more aggressive nationalist and independent movement. The tactics decided upon at the first congress were traditional ones, that is, to continue the verbal battle with "excessive" patriots. However, the later congresses in 1901 and 1904 decided on new mechanisms, which, ironically, were less a means of attacking independentism and more a means of working for ethnic reform within Roman Catholicism itself. At these later meetings, and as a result of other developments down to 1908, an ever-increasing number of loyal Polish Roman Catholics turned to their own religious superiors to bring about changes in the Church hierarchy in order to save Polonia from further schism. The remedy urged—delicately in 1896, more forcefully after 1901—was *równouprawnienie* (equality), which could be achieved by the appointment of a Polish-speaking bishop in America. Thus, during the late 1890's, ethnic consciousness spread noticeably from the nationalist camp and the independent parishes to the religionists themselves.

This transformation of the Polish Catholic position was not easily accomplished, for not all clericalists welcomed this effort to seek greater ethnic recognition in the Church. Decided differences of opinion among clericalists became rather marked through most of the period down to 1908. By the turn of the century the center of Polish group controversy had definitely shifted from a nationalist-religionist dichotomy to divisions within the religionist camp. But whatever the scene of conflict or the views of its combatants, the impact of the struggle continued to educate the ethnic rank and file to its Polishness.

Serious disagreements developed, particularly in 1905 and 1906, over how much pressure loyal Polish Catholics ought to exert on superiors to bring about *równouprawnienie*. Conservatives were content to accept the hierarchical determination of when it would come; critics, led by the irrepressible Reverend Wacław Kruszka and supported by patriots, wanted equality immediately. This fresh division among clerics brought new verbal exchanges within Polonia, leading to disorder and legal suits. So, with the possible exception of the few years after 1900, the average Pole experienced another period of tension over the question of identity. The continued exacerbation of the issue by nationalists, independents, and priests kept the ordinary immigrant in the dilemma of ethnic consciousness that had been building over the last quarter-century. Fortunately a solution to the problem came in 1908, when the Church appointed a Polish bishop. Poles no longer had to labor over reconciling God and Country. American Catholicism had Polishness (*Polskość*) in its highest councils.

In the earliest discussions concerning a Catholic conference, all religionist spokesmen agreed upon the need for a national meeting to stop further defections, but they disagreed over what, specifically, that meeting was to do. Most saw the proposed Polish Catholic congress as a national forum to propagandize against and anathematize independents. A few advised that the conference should also urge some sort of Church reform which would give Polish-American Catholics added recognition. For example, in February, 1895, *Dziennik Chicagoski* took what might be called a sampling of clerical opinion on the form of the meeting.[1] The strongest sentiment favored demonstrating and maintaining Polish Church loyalty by using the sessions to condemn the anti-Catholic "masons," "apostates," and "liberals," especially their outspoken journals. A few advised the discussion be more deliberate, internal action, presenting the problem of defections to the Pope. They even suggested, somewhat timidly, urging the appointment of a Pole to the American Catholic hierarchy.

Actually this latter proposal was not new. The Reverend Vincent Barzynski himself, and occasionally other priests, had suggested such an action in the late 1880's and early 1890's, but without much real determination.[2] While supporting a Polish Congress, the major clericalist organ quickly reassured American Catholics in 1895 that the group was not dissatisfied with the American hierarchy. It cautioned those Polish-Americans who advanced *równouprawnienie* that "a Polish bishop,

---

[1] *Dziennik Chicagoski,* February 25, 1895.
[2] Rev. I. Barszcz file in Polish Museum; Swastek, "Formative Years," in *Sacred Millenium,* 129–130.

exclusively for Poles, is something we cannot expect because this would be contrary to the organization of the Catholic Church, especially in the United States." Such a proposal meant "anarchy." It advised abandoning the idea, although it did favor a Polish advisor to the Apostolic Delegate in Washington.[3] The opening proceedings and concluding resolutions of the 1896 congress further demonstrated the continued factionalism in Polonia, not only between those present (Catholics) and those absent (nationalists), but even among the participants themselves. The clericalists at the congress used the sessions as they had planned, castigating other, nationalist Poles, especially apostate priests, whom they called "irreligious" and "unscrupulous." The conservative tone of the proceedings predominated in several ways. First, the twin clerical patriarchs, John Pitass of Buffalo and Vincent Barzynski of Chicago, sat on the organizing executive committee of the congress, which consisted of twice as many priests as laymen. Further, Father Pitass controlled the credentials committee which barred any Polish National Alliance member from attending the sessions. In addition, the formal proclamation of the meeting indicted the independent Poles: "It has come to this, that Poles in America, thanks to the inspiration of evil, discontented people, have divided us into two camps and these camps [are] bringing to us such hatred that can take place only between the greatest of enemies." It further commented on the seriousness of the division: "We do not know who sent those evil people, but we assert . . . that such a struggle is raging . . . in every settlement and Polish parish, in fact [there is] civil war among all our brothers."[4]

The opening ceremonies of the congress were an aggressive, loyalist criticism of other Poles, not of the Church. The gathering met in Buffalo with "Dziekan" John Pitass as sponsor and host. The first event was a parade on September 22 to the Pitass' St. Stanislaus Parish Hall under a banner depicting His Apostolic Holiness, Pope Leo XIII. When the several hundred dele-

---

[3] *Dziennik Chicagoski,* February 27, 1895.
[4] *Sprawozdanie z Pierwszego Polsko-Katolickiego Kongresu . . . Buffalo* (Buffalo, 1897), 8.

gates from all over the country had settled in their seats, Pitass welcomed them by proclaiming the symbolic motto of ethnic identity with his religionist bias: "God first, *then* country." The remainder of his greeting was a spirited attack on group traitors and a restatement of group identity as understood by loyal Polish Catholics. He considered the congress itself a victory over independents:[5]

> We have [already] won a victory over intrigues and ill will, . . . over bad people who wished by all means that this Congress should not meet. . . . Who are the people who thus calumniated us? No one else but their own brethren. [They] calumniated us . . . that we raised the standard and that at this Congress we wished to announce that first is God and then country . . . may God and country be our war cry. Let us follow right and then we shall raise high the standard of the Catholic Church, and with this standard we shall also raise our national standard. May God bless our labors.

The Polish cleric who followed Pitass expanded on the primacy of religion over nationality. The speaker, a German Pole who had come to help the loyalists as a Papal advisor from Rome, stressed that a strong Catholic faith was a far better prerequisite to national independence than an aggressive, secular nationalism. "Poland's independence [he said] cannot be joined by use of arms, but by faith in God who alone is able to bring back Poland free and independent." He reserved his harshest words for the Polish schismatics who fostered a "radicalism" which "is leading astray the unwary from the [true] religion." Such an evil appeal was making the people 'cosmopolitan" without any real national loyalty or "faith in the existence of any Supreme Being."[6]

After these two statements on the religionist character of Polishness, the delegates formed committees to consider a number of subjects: the relationship with the independents and the

---

[5] Quoted in Dr. Francis Fronczak Scrapbook, vol. II, 1892–1898, Buffalo Historical Society.

[6] *Ibid.*, quoted from *Buffalo Evening News*.

Polish National Alliance, the role of the press, and Polish Catholic equality in the Church.

The most lively and heated exchange occurred in the discussions over the condemnation of the PNA, and exposed the disunity of even staunch Catholics on the nationalist issue. Father Pitass, "interrupted by cheers," introduced the hostile conservative draft, which stated that no Polish Catholic could be a member of the society. When a few defenders of the Alliance attempted to respond to his proposal, near pandemonium broke loose in the room. Amidst shouting and general confusion, the committee had difficulty taking a vote on a modified resolution. The final statement was a barely acceptable compromise which condemned the PNA leadership and urged members to quit if they could not remove the most anticlerical officers.[7]

The other discussions were only slightly less spirited. No one objected to the general indictment of the independents, but the question of *równouprawnienie* required extended discussion. The members of the committee on equality all accepted the idea of seeking help from higher Church circles, but disagreed on the tone of the application; most wanted a request, not a demand. The resolution which was ultimately approved was the modest motion proposed by Father Barzynski. After a long statement upholding the authority of the bishops, the appeal suggested the appointment of a Polish-American advisor to the Apostolic Delegate in Washington. Barzynski included in his resolution no mention of a Polish-American bishop.

Other actions of the congress showed the loyalists' lack of interest over the question of equality. The priest who was assigned to present the congress' motion on an advisor was a conservative who had recently termed *równouprawnienie* a "fantasy [*mzonka*]."[8] So, of course, his mission failed.[9] The final action of the convention was another attempt to assuage any

7 *Sprawozdanie*, 38–40; "Bedlam Reigned," Fronczak Scrapbook, vol. II.
8 *Album Jubileuszowa . . . Św. Michała . . . South Chicago, Ill., 1892–1917* (Chicago, 1917).
9 Haiman, *Zjednoczenie*, 168; Kruszka, *Historya*, 2: 66.

hierarchical concern that the congress was critical of American Church leadership. A resolution, proposed by Barzynski, expressed "thanks to the American bishops for their protection of the Polish clergy" and ended with the cheer, "Long Live the Bishops of the United States!"[10] The delegates went home basically satisfied with having tackled the delicate problem of condemning other Poles while still remaining loyal Catholics themselves.

Instead of forging group unity in those troubled times, the Buffalo congress actually exposed deeper divisions, further dramatizing ethnic consciousness for the Polish rank and file. Not only did a more vigorous nationalist wing of the clericalists come to light at the congress, but the meeting also renewed the war on the nationalist camp. In condemning the Polish National Alliance as antireligious, the congress reopened the historic controversy and heightened the tension that had been brewing in Polonia for a quarter-century. *Zgoda,* the nationalist organ, had known that the congress would attack the PNA even when the meeting was still an idea, and therefore condemned the proposed sessions. Guessing that the promoters would exclude PNA membership, it described the meeting succinctly with the Polish term *farsa.* In an editorial in October the paper criticized the congress as undemocratically convened and unrepresentative even of Polish Catholicism.[11] The response of the nationalist organ showed that that camp, too, had renewed its verbal warfare. One large PNA branch responded directly to the congress' demand that Alliance members overthrow their officials by deliberately passing a ringing endorsement of its leadership. It defended particularly the Catholic loyalty of Francis Jabloński, the editor of *Zgoda* who had brought peace to their church in 1893:[12]

We members of branch 122, who belong to Holy Trinity

---

[10] *Sprawozdanie,* 42, 44.

[11] *Zgoda,* October 1, 1895. The charge of limited numerical and geographic representation was only partially valid. See the list of delegates in *Sprawozdanie,* 20.

[12] *Zgoda,* October 29, 1895.

Church and were its parishioners, know that Jabloński as a parish delegate to Rome and afterward to Cardinal Satolli asked the opening of [our] church and therefore gave witness that he is not an enemy of Catholicism; he did not seek to abandon the holy faith for the establishment of the independent church—but he was faithful to the entrusted matter to the end. . . . Long Live the Central Administration of the PNA.

It is unlikely that the appeal of the congress had any serious effect on membership. Although the rate of expansion of the PNA did decline markedly after 1896, its major competitor, the Polish Roman Catholic Union, fared worse.

TABLE 7: PNA and PRCU Membership and Assets, 1894–1899[13]

Year	Membership		Assets	
	PNA	PRCU	PNA	PRCU
1894	6,107	9,969	$23,673	$ 5,270
1895	7,515	8,782	28,182	4,051
1896	11,077	N.A.	30,407	4,154
1897	12,231	8,546	39,419	1,336
1898	13,513	8,111	54,733	9,821
1899	15,288	8,566	96,529	15,287

From 1897 to about 1899 the crossfire between the clericalist and nationalist-independent camps continued. Defections of Catholics to Kozłowski's church in Chicago and Hodur's in Pennsylvania fired the clericalists' hostility toward schismatics. The Church itself assisted Polish loyalists by excommunicating the independent leaders in 1898.

Oddly enough, at the turn of the century the nationalist-clericalist warfare began to decline, and the sides even moved toward unity. Probably most instrumental in this reduction of ill-will was the death, in 1899, of the leading Catholic loyalist, Father Vincent Barzynski of Chicago. For nearly a quarter of a century this powerful priest had led the largest Polish parish in the American city with the most Poles. He had been the personification of the clericalist faction. His demise left a vacuum in

13 From Osada, *Historya*, 618, and Haiman, *Zjednoczenie*, 541, 549.

Catholic circles, and, as his opponents themselves admitted, was a loss to all Polish-Americans. Five hundred carriages and nearly 10,000 persons made up his funeral procession; even the Polish National Alliance sent official representatives.[14] Barzynski was replaced by the Reverend John Kasprzycki and later by the Reverend Francis Gordon. Both tried to assume the role of their predecessor in maintaining the hostility to the nationalists and independents, but they were unable to command the loyal Polish Catholic forces in the way that Barzynski had, and more religionists, even clerics, began to move toward an active nationalist position. The small, more nationalistic faction among clericalist forces continued to grow.

Besides the loss of Barzynski, two other factors about 1900 accounted for the movement of Polish Catholic leaders to *równouprawnienie* and another Catholic congress. One was unified resistance to the anti-Polish efforts of several German Catholic bishops—a rare example of outside opposition contributing to Polish ethnic expression; the other was the Reverend Wacław Kruszka's fervent crusade for equality. Throughout, Polish leadership still was not entirely unified, as the early twentieth-century controversy over Kruszka's behavior revealed, and so the average Polish immigrant had to endure further arguments over Polishness.

Late in 1900, as a part of a general Americanization campaign by the Church, two Catholic bishops, Frederick Eis of Marquette, Michigan, and Sebastian Messmer of Green Bay, Wisconsin, ordered all their parishes to expand the instruction of English in their schools and religious services. For the first time the non-Polish Church hierarchy enunciated a position that threatened *Polskość,* and did so at a time when ethnic consciousness was already developing among the most loyal Polish Roman Catholic leaders. This diocesan action, while not deliberately anti-Polish, still tended to drive the feuding Polish factions together. The Polish National Alliance and the Polish Roman Catholic Union, the religionist fraternal society, in December, 1900, and January, 1901, passed similar resolutions opposing the decrees. The Union even renewed the 1896 call by

---

[14] Siatka, *Krótki Wspomnienie* (Chicago, 1901), 53–56.

the first Polish Catholic congress for a Polish-American representative at the highest level.[15] Further, some leading Polish clergy decided to convene another congress at Buffalo to consider the Church's new policy and, more seriously, to discuss *równouprawnienie*. In the flush of ethnic enthusiasm, even the PNA agreed to participate.

The unanimity of the Polish response to the Church's assimilationist campaign was more apparent than real. While the conservative *Dziennik Chicagoski* agreed to another national convention, it again urged caution. The religionist paper advised that no action ought to be taken on issues until all Polish Catholic clergymen presented their views, and, in any event, the new congress must condemn Polish superpatriots.[16] The PNA decided not to attend the new congress after the convention committee refused to allow any Alliance representatives who were members of independent churches. The nationalists thereupon termed that meeting as unrepresentative of Polonia as its predecessor.[17]

Nonetheless, whatever disagreement existed within Polonia, by the opening of the second congress the nationalist and clericalist factions had moved somewhat closer together. By 1901 the religionists had accepted in principle the idea that ethnic representation in the Catholic hierarchy was a desirable subject for the meeting, thus setting these delegates apart from their predecessors five years before. Barzynski was gone, and in his place as the most influential figure was the Reverend Casimir Sztuczko, the well-known patriot-priest of Holy Trinity who had earlier blessed the Alliance headquarters. Now the main issue was not to be a reaffirmation of Catholic loyalty, along with tirades against the independent heresy and support for the American hierarchy. This congress was certain to seek Church reform—equality—more aggressively.

This second congress was again a compromise, but its results

[15] Osada, *Historya*, 516; Haiman, *Zjednoczenie*, 185.
[16] Osada, *Historya*, 517; *Dziennik Chicagoski*, October 21, 1901. A new nationalist organ had recently begun which may have agitated the Resurrectionists. See Helena C. Schreiber, *Dzieje Jednej Instytucji Wydawniczej* (Chicago, 1959), 46.
[17] Haiman, *Zjednoczenie*, 190.

were more nationalistic than the first. The lay representatives wanted to seek immediately Papal sanction for a Polish-American bishop, while clerical spokesmen urged application first to the American hierarchy; the delegates finally resolved to do both. They approved a mission to the Vatican in principle but appointed a permanent executive committee to proceed first through American Catholic channels. By choosing Sztuczko as the committee's first secretary, the Polish Catholics indicated their serious interest in equality and gave the Polish nationalist priests some institutional recognition of *równouprawnienie*. In November the committee sent a memorial to a meeting of American archbishops in Washington which requested that the Church leaders appoint a Polish advisor. Only a few responded, but even those who did did not feel the petition was important. They passed off the request saying that, as a body, they had no jurisdiction and that the subject of equality was really a local matter for each archbishop.[18] The essentially apathetic response of American diocesan superiors stimulated the more nationalistic Polish priests to further action. The Polish secular clergy, always expressing themselves as more enthusiastic patriots than the regulars, were aroused enough to form their own society in 1902 in Toledo, with their major objective being better Catholic representation. In addition many Polish Catholics urged the committee to implement the alternative that the Congress had resolved by sending someone to Rome. The man who went on that mission was the Reverend Wacław Kruszka.

Father Kruszka played a unique role in spreading Polish ethnic consciousness. He was chiefly responsible for having the Church ultimately appoint a Polish "prince" (bishop), and, even more significantly, he more than any other single man fueled the continuing controversy over *równouprawnienie*. Unquestionably Kruszka was the most conspicuous and controversial Polish Catholic patriot-priest of his day, and he struggled mightily in the early 1900's to have the Church extend further recognition of his nationality. The reasons for his prominence

---

[18] Wacław Kruszka, *Siedm Siedmiolecie Czyli Pół Zycia* (2 vols., Milwaukee, 1924), 1: 444–447; Kruszka, *Historya*, 2: 66–68.

were his youthful energy (he was in his mid-thirties at this time), his facile pen (he utilized his brother Michael's outspoken Milwaukee newspaper and publishing firm), and his independence (both clericalist and nationalist critics attacked him).

At this early date Kruszka held an unusually advanced philosophical position on the relationship between Polishness and American Catholicism—a position which few of his colleagues could agree with or comprehend. In brief, he believed that both ethnic and religious sentiments could exist within Catholicism, and that the Church in America should be pluralistic.

In his autobiography he tells how he arrived at such an understanding. While the anticlerical attacks of the Polish National Alliance were unacceptable to him in the mid-1890's, he still felt loyal to his Polish, his Catholic, and even his American identities. He saw, correctly, that the Church's assimilationist campaign was really not "Americanization" as claimed but "anglicization." Much in advance of his day, and in agreement with the German Catholic Cahenslyites, he was advocating the notion of ethnic pluralism in America, positing the view that the Roman Catholic Church was a microcosm of the larger society, a universal faith recognizing many nationalities. Therefore, Kruszka believed, the objective of the American Catholic Church was to defend broadly accepted religious principles while maintaining ethnic variation within the universal faith. This policy was not contradictory; in fact, not to pursue it would either denationalize the Catholic elements, and thus demoralize them, or else help the dreaded independent movement. In either case confusion, personal misunderstanding, and factional misery would ensue. To forestall the continued expansion of the well-established National Catholic movement, and in fact to further bind all its diverse groups to its principles, the Church had to give further recognition to ethnicity. For Kruszka this meant that the hierarchy must raise its Poles to the highest councils.

At first Kruszka advocated the more extreme notion of a separate diocese for each nationality. But by the time of the second Polish Catholic congress he had moderated his demand, merely urging the appointment of Polish bishops in American sees. He related his cause to the democratic principle in a 1901 article in the *American Ecclesiastic Review* by insisting that bishops existed to serve the diocese. Since the prelates and their offices were representatives of the people, they ought to be able to speak the language of the faithful, or at least the larger blocs of them.[19]

Unfortunately Kruszka's advocacy of broad Church sanction of ethnic diversity—that is, urging pluralism within a religious unity—won no adherents. Few understood his position. Kruszka's outspoken dedication to equality on the one hand, and his refusal to leave his faith on the other, bewildered associates in both the clericalist and the nationalist camps. In any event, the Wisconsin priest's vigorous articulation of his position actually contributed to sustaining ethnic group tension. His fellow priests especially condemned him, saying that his Catholic loyalty was a facade, that he was simply a Polish nationalist in clerical garb.

Father Kruszka realized early that the Buffalo congress' approval of his trip to the Pope was merely lip service, a necessary but insincere gesture given to *równouprawnienie*. This lack of clerical commitment caused a number of problems which delayed his departure. First he had to await the outcome of negotiations with the American prelates. Then, since no one gave him travel money, he had to solicit contributions. Finally, the congress saddled him with the old loyalist fellow traveler, Father John Pitass, who tried to delay the mission as long as possible.[20] Thus, because of continued allegiance to their American Catholic superiors, many Polish clerics, not the Church hierarchy, proved to be the greatest obstacles to his going on his mission.

The result of his efforts caused a renewed division within the Polish Catholic camp, a difference between loyalists and reformers that had surfaced in the previous Congress. The disagreement now was over whether a Polish priest ought to go to Rome unsanctioned by the American hierarchy. The powerful and still intensely loyalist Resurrectionist Order, which led the

---

[19] Kruszka, *Siedm*, 1: 321, 335, 385–391.
[20] *Ibid.*, 593.

conservatives, criticized particularly Kruszka's blaming the Church hierarchy for the schismatic movement. According to the head of the order, the Reverend Francis Gordon, the defections were due not to the non- and therefore anti-Polish bishops, but to iniquitous, greedy Polish clerics. An official Resurrectionist historian later maintained that:[21]

> Charges that many Poles defected from the Church because of Irish and German discrimination [are] not historically valid, since the independent movements were initiated by ambitious and unscrupulous priests who sought power and stature. In the main such clerical malcontents usually deceived the simple folk to think that there was no essential difference between the Roman and nationalist church. The whole question of Polish representation in the American hierarchy was of such serious consequence that any demagoguery or chauvinistic propaganda was entirely rejected by the Resurrectionists. The *Dziennik Chicagoski,* under Father Gordon's direction, pursued a policy of obedience to the American bishops in every phase of apostolic endeavor, pronouncements, and ecclesiastical discipline.

In addition, even some secular priests, including one of his closest colleagues, the Reverend Paul Rhode of Chicago, "mocked and scoffed at [Kruszka's] trip."[22] Despite the general trend of Polish Catholics toward seeking greater representation in the Church, the movement toward equality proceeded very slowly. Some group members still defended their superiors, implying that the problem was among themselves; some said that the Church need not make any reforms at all. As interested parishioners viewed the inner group controversy, the loyalists still placed God above country, faith above nationality.

Ironically, while his own ethnic colleagues hampered Father Kruszka's proposed trip to Rome, a few non-Polish American Church leaders actually encouraged him. A German- and an Irish-American prelate demonstrated support for nationalities. His superior, Archbishop Frederick Katzer of Milwaukee, visited Rome in 1902 and carried the Polish-American case to

---

21 Iwicki, *First Hundred Years,* 106–107; Kruska, *Siedm,* 1: 517.
22 Kruszka, *Siedm,* 1: 593.

the head of the Propaganda; but he returned unsuccessful. Both Katzer and Archbishop James Michael Quigley of Buffalo encouraged him to go to the Vatican. Archbishop Katzer even assisted his preparations.[23]

By the beginning of 1903, Kruszka might well have wondered what had happened to the enthusiasm for a Polish bishop that had animated the Buffalo congress a year and a half earlier. Second thoughts and hesitation were to some extent based on fear of hierarchical disapproval by loyalists. Kruszka finally did leave for Rome in June, almost two years after being authorized. A number of Polish priests and, surprisingly, even the leading clericalist fraternal, the Polish Roman Catholic Union, contributed to his trip. Unfortunately Pope Leo died soon after Kruszka arrived in the Vatican, and he had to wait another year to speak to his successor, Pius X. However, when he finally obtained an audience with the Pope and asked that a Polish bishop be appointed in America, the leader of world Catholicism replied: "The decision will be appropriate and according to your desires."[24] Overjoyed that the Pope had granted his request, the Wisconsin priest returned to America in May, 1904. He reported his success to the third Polish Catholic congress, which convened in Pittsburgh that September.

By the end of 1904 Kruszka had rallied even the most loyal Catholic Poles to support his mission, but his efforts were still not entirely successful. He had the Pope's word of a favorable decision, but as yet no action. In the period 1904 to 1908, in the course of steadily rising national feeling among Poles, Kruszka became involved in a further rift in Polonia. The specific issue was how much pressure the group ought to apply upon the American Church to realize *równouprawnienie,* now that the Pontiff had approved of it in principle. There were now more clerics on the nationalist side, but the conservative and more cautious Polish Catholic camp remained sensitive to the will of the American hierarchy. The final impetus to bring about

---

[23] *Ibid.,* 491, 554, 568.
[24] *Ibid.,* 803–805. One ought to recall that Bishop (then Reverend) Hodur had visited Rome on a similar mission in 1898 and was rejected. *Ibid.,* 2: 25.

the appointment of a Polish prince, and to realize equality, came not from Kruszka, nor, in fact, from any Pole. The source was an Irish-American cleric who had earlier encouraged Kruszka, Archbishop James Michael Quigley of Chicago.

The start of the last phase of attaining *równouprawnienie* was the 1904–1906 period, during which time two kinds of events continued to stimulate ethnic consciousness among Polish-Americans. First, several important external events occurred which heightened *Polskość* in Polonia: the close attention of the Polish-American press in supporting the Japanese in the Russo-Japanese War; the magnificent unveiling of the Kościuszko statute in Chicago in 1904; and the triumphal tour of group colonies by the Polish Archbishop Albin Symon in 1905.[25] Also, internal forces continued to divide old, contending factions within Polish America, further raising ethnic consciousness.

The proceedings of and reaction to the Third Polish congress in 1904 exposed the reasserted partisanship. A major participant, John Smulski of Chicago, reminded Polonia of the continuing threat of independents, those lost countrymen who had been "led astray" by pseudo-bishops and false clergy, charlatans and men of ill-will. He concluded that to safeguard his group the Church ought to appoint a Pole as bishop. *Dziennik Chicagoski* disagreed, and urged its readers not to agitate a delicate matter; recognition would come in good time.[26]

The congress also reopened deeper nationality divisions by designating a newly formed body, the Federation of Polish Catholics, as the spokesman for all Poles. When the nationalists disagreed, rejecting the new organization as unrepresentative, the issue of whether religion was synonymous with nationality arose again. In a ringing religionist address, one speaker still accused the Polish National Alliance of being antireligious, of making war on God. The *Zgoda* replied that the new Federation

25 Milkowski, *Opowiadanie*, 174; *Dziennik Chicagoski, Golden Anniversary Number*, November 21, 1945, part III, p. 40; *Dziennik Chicagoski*, August 1, 12, September 12, 1904; Osada, *Historya*, 569, 581–583; Haiman, *Zjednoczenie*, 206.
26 October 7, 10, 1904.

was not *the* Polish organization in America because it did not include the Alliance or its supporting nationalist bodies. It appealed to the religionists to maintain the spirit of ethnic solidarity that had been growing in recent years. In an editorial entitled "Who Represents the Poles," *Zgoda* asserted that no Polish organization could exclude non-Catholics. It urged its readers to "reject like an infection those [recent Catholic] statements which incite intrigue, plotting, slander. . . . [Disregard] anonymous letters in which there is no word of truth."[27] Thirteen branches of the Alliance had attended the Synod which had just consecrated Bishop Hodur of the new Polish National Catholic Church, and that surely placed an added strain on nationalist-clericalist relations.[28]

The next year the visit of Archbishop Albin Symon did help to harmonize rather than polarize the two major wings of the Polish community; but his appearance also revealed underlying factional suspicion. The Vatican sent the prelate to America to determine the condition of Polish Catholicism. He arrived in May and toured every major Polish colony, receiving a warm reception from the nationality; as a Pole, he symbolized equality at the highest level. Patriots, parishioners, and priests all welcomed him. The most enthusiastic reception came on his visits to Milwaukee and Chicago in June. With a fiery appeal to nationalism to which all Polonia could respond, he unveiled the Kościuszko statue in the capital of Polish Wisconsin.[29] The prelate followed this with a triumphal tour of Chicago group parishes.

Despite all this encouragement of nationalist feeling, the Polish National Alliance was still suspicious of Symon's visit. The PNA viewed his tour as a Church matter and carefully never recognized the prelate formally. Symon returned the feeling. When he was in Chicago, he granted PNA members an audience but refused to acknowledge the fraternal's existence

27 *Zgoda*, October 6, 1904.
28 Kubiak, *Historia*, 120; Kruszka, *Siedm*, 2: 25.
29 Kruszka, *Siedm*, 2: 115–118.

as a society.[30] As it turned out, however, he did recommend a Polish-American bishop to his superiors.

While the year following Kruszka's return included a continual struggle over the definition of "Pole," the two years beyond, that is from 1906 to 1908, was a time of even greater internal conflict on the subject, especially in the clericalist camp. One reason for this heightened tension was the growing impatience of Kruszka for the Church to act; another was a revival of independentist troubles.

Apparently Father Kruszka expected rapid implementation of the Pope's promise. He had welcomed Father Symon, but by the end of 1905 he grew unhappy over the delays, so he inaugurated a spirited campaign in the press, demanding that the American Church fulfill *równouprawnienie* and appoint a Polish bishop. This one-man crusade tended to polarize the clergy around the country. At this time he acquired considerable support in Wisconsin, but he alienated some colleagues and countrymen who defended the Church's deliberate policy.[31] By 1907 Kruszka's efforts brought Polonia to the brink of that disastrous factionalism it had experienced in the 1890's over the similar issue of nationality recognition by the Roman Catholic Church.

The source of this renewed conflict was a feud Kruszka began in his own Milwaukee diocese with the new archbishop, Sebastian Messmer. The sharply nationalistic articles that Kruszka published in *Kuryer Polski,* his brother's newspaper, caused Church authorities to sponsor a competing Polish journal, *Nowiny Polski,* edited, appropriately enough, by the city's leading Polish cleric. The fight between the two papers split the Milwaukee community, and much of Polonia, over Church policy.

By 1907 Kruszka had provoked a number of Polish institutions. The society of Polish Catholic secular priests, one of the

---

[30] See the criticism *ibid.,* 122, 131–132.

[31] See the resolution of forty-two Polish Catholic societies in the *Chicago Record Herald,* October 29, 1906.

nationalist leaders in 1902, and a leading Polish priest in South
Bend, Indiana, all criticized Kruszka's agitation for equality,
insisting that his campaign would lead to anarchy. Soon afterward the conservative papers—*Dziennik Chicagoski, Wiarus,*
and two Ohio journals—joined the priest's opponents and supported general American diocesan policy, even suggesting that
a little anglicization in the parochial schools (the teaching of
English was then at issue) was not inimical to ethnic nationalism.[32] On the other hand, by this time a number of Alliance
chapters, the PNA organ, *Zgoda, Dziennik Polski* of Detroit,
Rolnik of Stevens Point, Wisconsin, *Gazeta Buffaloska* of Buffalo, and *Wielkopolanin* of Pittsburgh joined in supporting
Kruszka. Thus the old nationalist-clericalist press battle raged
anew.[33] The controversial position that Kruszka occupied within the Catholic camp, and the intense opposition his nationalist
campaign engendered, are evident in *Nowiny's* estimate of
him:[34]

> Father Kruszka, the unfortunate renegade, not only does not
> recognize the American bishops as a higher authority in the
> Catholic Church, but also spits venomously upon our Polish
> Bishops and Archbishops in the Old Country because they do
> not brush loose from . . . the Holy Father in Rome. . . . Father
> Kruszka delivers patriotic sermons, but he rises against the
> Church because he despises the Pope, the Cardinals and the
> Bishops; therefore he is even worse and more dangerous than
> Hodur. . . . Father Kruszka is the foremost rebel in Christ's
> Church in these last times. There were . . . Kozłowskis, Hodurs,
> Rademachers [Kołaszewski] . . . and several other scoundrels in
> America . . . but all those rebels are even morally higher than
> Father Kruszka.

Since he still regarded himself a loyal Roman Catholic, Kruszka
initiated a libel suit against *Nowiny.* Independent Bishop Kozłowski, infirm and near death, knew of the storm of protest
raging about Kruszka's Polishness and invited him to join,

[32] See especially *Dziennik Chicagoski,* February 10, 1906.
[33] Kruszka, *Siedm,* 2: 419, 534, 578–580, 613.
[34] Quoted *ibid.,* 604–606.

possibly to lead, his Church; but characteristically the loyal cleric refused to desert his faith.

Besides Kruszka's rekindling of intragroup hostility, another ominous development occurred in 1906–1907: a renewed Polish Catholic defection to the independents. Parish unrest such as had broken out in the mid-1890's erupted again in two major centers, South Bend and St. Louis, over the same issue, congregational control.[35] Kruszka and Smulski's warnings that continued hierarchical delay in granting *równouprawnienie* would mean schism appeared to be borne out. In mid-1907 a group of Buffalo priests formally demanded that the American Church act. They sent a memorial to that effect to the Vatican for appropriate action. The Irish-American archbishop in Chicago made a final, direct plea for his Polish constituents.

Archbishop James Michael Quigley had gained an intimate understanding of the Poles by being the highest Church officer in two of their principal cities. He was head of all Buffalo Catholics when the Poles held their second Catholic congress there in 1901, and later he moved to Chicago. Sympathetic to *równouprawnienie*, he had encouraged Kruszka to apply to Rome at the end of the Buffalo meeting. In the summer of 1907, as a result of his sympathy, his desire to reunite the Polish factions, and for the general good of the Church, Archbishop Quigley decided to visit the Pope about the matter. He returned from Rome with instructions that his diocesan Polish priests nominate a candidate for auxiliary bishop, for Pius X had informed him that the next vacancy would be filled by a Pole. The caucus overwhelmingly voted for the Reverend Paul Rhode, a Chicago pastor little known outside the diocese.[36] Actually Archbishop Quigley may not have been solely responsible for

---

[35] *Ibid.*, 529; Frank Renkiewicz, "The Polish Settlement of St. Joseph County, Indiana" (doctoral dissertation, University of Notre Dame, 1967), 192, 194, 201; Reverend Joseph Swastek, "The Polish Settlement in South Bend" (master's thesis, University of Notre Dame, 1941), 57–60. See also *Dziennik Chicagoski*, August 21, 1907.

[36] *Ibid.*, June 20, 1908; *Wydania Pamiątkowe z okazji Srebnego Jubileusza Sakru Biskupiej J.E.Ks. Biskupa Pawła Rhodego, DD, Przegląd Katolicki*, 9: 32 (March–April, 1934).

the Vatican taking the necessary action; oddly enough, though probably to keep peace, Kruszka's superior, Messmer, the prelate whom he had been prodding to recognize the Poles, told the outspoken priest a short time later that he, too, would urge a Polish bishop for Chicago, Buffalo, or Milwaukee.[37] On May 17, 1908, the Pope officially approved Rhode's appointment as bishop under Archbishop Quigley in the Poles' largest center. At long last, the American Polonia had a"prince."

The first Polish-American bishop helped resolve the struggle between loyalists and reformist Polish Roman Catholics, and he also gave all Polish-Americans a conscious formula to make compatible formerly hostile elements of their group. The new Polish prince resolved an issue that had disturbed the Chicago Polonia since the 1860's, Polish leadership from the 1870's, and many American parishes in the 1890's. Nationalists and sympathetic parishioners demanded that Catholicism recognize their nationality. Their earliest desire was to make their house of worship their own—that is, Polish—regardless of the 1883 Church rule which prohibited congregational autonomy. In effect, in 1908 the American hierarchy finally made clear to its Polish constituency that one could be both Catholic and Polish. With Rhode as Chicago auxiliary, the parish wealth, which by Church law was the bishop's, was now Polish as well. Bishop Rhode signaled to American Polonia that Catholic Poles could also be Polish Catholics.

[37] Kruszka, *Siedm,* 2: 623.

EIGHT

Lithuanian Ethnic Consciousness, 1870–1914

THE PROCESS of heightening ethnic consciousness among Lithuanians followed the same pattern in general, though not in detail, as among the Poles. The Lithuanian emigrants who came to America also respected both land wealth and their Catholic traditions, and they likewise found it difficult to enter an American Church which required nongroup ownership of their parish. As with the Poles, the result was a deeply divided community leadership and an elite which debated the meaning of ethnic identity—specifically, how to accommodate both religion and ethnicity. This factionalism seeped downward to even the most naïve Lithuanian immigrants and gradually familiarized them with the nationalist issue.

The Lithuanian drama repeated the Polish. The combatants were religionists, who defined the faith of group members as Roman Catholic alone, and nationalists, who accepted members of any faith so long as they worked for an independent Lithuania. An independent movement emerged, ultimately becoming Lithuanian National Catholicism. The source of the parish disorders which ultimately spread ethnic consciousness widely was a controversy over the insistence of some parishioners for secular title to their own church.

The Lithuanian experience differed slightly from the Polish in two ways: the greater initial fragmentation and the conclusion of the conflict. As Lithuanian society arose in America, three, perhaps even four differing attitudes toward their group identity appeared. This multiple view quickly reduced itself to just two in the late 1880's, following the pattern of clericalist-nationalist dichotomy then current among Poles.

The religionist-nationalist dispute in the Lithuanian community was never fully resolved, because the Roman Catholic Church never granted it a Lithuanian bishop. Considerable ethnic-religious compatibility did emerge by World War I, as both Lithuanian camps united to work for an independent homeland. In effect, the entire Lithuanian Catholic camp, which had once stressed faith, by then supported nationalism with equal enthusiasm.

A factor complicating the growth of Lithuanian consciousness in America was their very intimate relations with the Poles. Any treatment of the two groups encounters the great difficulty of separating them.[1] Throughout history the two peoples had been connected geographically, sometimes politically, often socially. Intermarriage was common, as the large number of Polonized Lithuanians in the 1880's attested. Thus, as the Lithuanians began entering America in the late 1860's with no independent state of their own and frequently with Polish as their second language, they were indistinguishable in the Slavic colonies where most settled. This intimate relationship with the Poles in America tends to invalidate the standard interpretation of the Lithuanian-American rise to consciousness, namely that the Poles stimulated Lithuanian group awareness by stifling their non-Slavic culture.[2] One can never be entirely certain if the repression came from Poles or from Polonized Lithuanians; but one can be sure that anti-Polishness motivated only a limited number of early arrivals. The standard hypothesis does not explain why national consciousness among the Lithuanian-

[1] One Lithuanian scholar has stated that the only way to determine which of the two an individual belongs to is his own statement; see Senn, *Emergence of Modern Lithuania*, 7–8.

[2] F. Kamesis, "Ideologines Kovos Lietuviškoje Šiaures Amerikos Išeivijoje," in *Krikščionybė Lietuvoje* (Kaunas, 1938), 113, and Sister M. Timothy Audyjaitis, "Catholic Action of Lithuanians in the United States" (master's thesis, Loyola University, Chicago, 1958), 22, are typical examples of the prevailing view.

Americans became a mass phenomenon after 1890, when Polish repression was no longer a real issue among immigrants. Organized Lithuanian-American society began in two regions in the 1870's, first in the eastern Pennsylvania mining district and only slightly later in Chicago, which by the 1890's had become the nationality's major colony.

The first substantial Lithuanian settlement and separate group colony, at Shenandoah, Pennsylvania, harbored both intra- and intergroup hostilities. A strong-willed Polish pastor in a predominantly Polish parish begrudgingly granted a few Lithuanian demands for group recognition after 1877, but only after some of the minority prepared to sue him in civil court. When the cleric withdrew his concessions in 1889, the Lithuanians obtained permission from diocesan authorities to bring their own patriot-priest, the Reverend Alexander Burba, from Europe. The cleric arrived quickly, but after performing some religious duties in Shenandoah, he settled in Plymouth, Pennsylvania, where he replaced the Lithuanian pastor of another Polish-Lithuanian church. There, too, a violent conflict with Poles flared up, and Father Burba, apparently with hierarchical approval, established the first purely Lithuanian parish in America. He later visited other group colonies in the region and helped found Lithuanian parishes in eastern Pennsylvania and elsewhere.[3] The friction which existed here between the Polish and Lithuanian nationalities was used later by Lithuanian nationalists to influence later-arriving countrymen. These initial encounters with Poles did little to bring about the sweeping consciousness of the 1890's; in truth there was no unified Lithuanian reaction to Polish "oppression" in Pennsylvania or elsewhere.

At the time of Father Burba's first separate Lithuanian church, his countrymen held three or four distinct viewpoints about their ethnic identity. The simplest, most straightforward view—and one which left little or no record—was probably

[3] Fr. Jonas Žilius, *Kun. Alexandras Burba* (Plymouth, Pennsylvania, 1898), 19, probably the originator of the anti-Polish view of Lithuanian consciousness. S. Michelsonas, *Lietuvių Išeivija Amerikoje* (South Boston, Massachusetts, 1961), 31–34, lists other presumably anti-Polish "scandals" in the 1890's.

that held by Lithuanians who were virtually assimilated into Polish America and who, while keeping certain Lithuanian traditions, saw no necessity for supporting separate group institutions at all. A second group, somewhat less Polonized, formed separate Lithuanian organizations, but still did not wish to establish their own independent ethnic parish. Lithuanian writers have referred to these two attitudes as being held by *lenkberniszkos* (freely translated "Polonophiles"). A third view was held by the followers of Father Burba, who felt that the group was a distinct Catholic nationality and ought to have a separate religious life within its own parish network. A fourth and last faction agreed with the Burba camp on the need for ethnic separation from the Poles, but separate religious houses were not enough: the Lithuanian community ought to include all members, even those apathetic and hostile to Roman Catholicism. The major proponent of this fourth view was the lay patriot, Dr. Jonas Šliupas.

Often omitted from the standard chronicles of the Shenandoah and Plymouth disorders is the significant role played by active mediating figures, the Polonophile Lithuanians. Precise measurement of the *lenkberniszko* influence is difficult, but it is clear that certain outspoken Lithuanians were close to the Poles and felt that they either could retain their group traditions within the large Slavic community or remain on good relations with the larger nationality as a separate ethnic entity. At the outset Father Burba may well have fought the Polonized members of his own group more energetically than he did Polish "oppressors." Unfortunately the sources do not precisely identify Burba's early opposition; but clearly more than one Lithuanian faction was involved in the incidents. At Shenandoah the Polish pastor based much of his policy toward Lithuanians on the advice of Dominic Bačkauskas, his parish organist and head of a *lenkberniszko* faction in the region. This pro-Polish Lithuanian element was large and influential enough in 1889 to support two journals—*Saulė* and *Vienybė*—and a fraternal society based on Polonophile principles.[4] Even the outspoken

---

[4] Žilius, *Burba*, 19–23; Antanas Kučas, *Shenandoah, Lietuvių Šv. Parapija (1891–1966)*, (Brooklyn, 1968), 170, 175, 180, 196–197.

Burba camp quickly moderated its anti-Polish position. Almost immediately after the parish disturbances in 1890, the priest's followers joined the Bačkauskas group to form the religionist wing of the Lithuanian community.[5] This faction voiced the same definition of nationality as its Polish counterpart: Lithuanians had to be Roman Catholic. The new element grew in response to an emerging, fourth Lithuanian element, the secular patriots under Šliupas.

Jonas Šliupas had been an enthusiastic nationalist even before his arrival in New York in 1884. His patriotism originated under the influence of the so-called "Father of the Lithuanian Renaissance," Dr. Jonas Basanavičius, who, with his colony of emigré countrymen in Tilsit, East Prussia, published *Aušra* (Dawn). Thus the leading Lithuanian-American enthusiast like the Polish members of the Gmina in Chicago, brought his nationalism with him from Europe. Šliupas came to America to arouse his countrymen in the New World through the publication of a journal, *The Lithuanian Voice* (1885), and the founding of a fraternal society. Originally a friend and sponsor of Father Burba, encouraging him to go to Shenandoah in 1889, Šliupas soon drew away from his clerical associates. He came to view Lithuanian patriotism increasingly in anti-Catholic terms. Although the personal ties between Burba and Šliupas did not end formally until 1892, long before then outspoken laymen in the secular movement criticized their religious leaders for hampering the nationalist awakening.[6] A conflict, then, between religious and nationalist figures and their organizations was evident in the Lithuanian community by 1890. The following decade was to Lithuanians what the 1880's was to the Poles— a newspaper war between clericalists and nationalists over the predominant elements of their ethnic identity.

The struggle within Lithuanian America worsened by 1901 to the point that the major fraternal body, the Lithuanian Alli-

---

[5] Compare Michelsonas, *Lietuvių,* 33: "In spite of such scandalous events in mixed parishes, Lithuanian priests always tried to shore up the Lublin [pro-Polish] union."

[6] Kučas, *Shenandoah,* 175; *Varpas* (September, 1894), 94–95, at the Casimir Sisters Motherhouse, Chicago; Kazys Gineitis, *Amerika Ir Amerikos Lietuvių* (Kaunas, 1925), 276–279; Žilius, *Burba,* 20.

ance of America (abbreviated SLA from its Lithuanian title), which once had included all differing group viewpoints, could no longer do so. At the organization's Wilkes-Barre convention that year a floor fight broke out over whether members had to be Roman Catholic, causing a split in the SLA. In a bitter court suit the clericalists retained the organizational continuity as well as the old administration of the fraternal, but the seceding nationalists kept the name. The religionists appropriately retitled their society the Lithuanian Roman Catholic Alliance (SLRKA), and the combatants thereafter operated from separate, competing fraternal societies.[7] The newspaper battle continued between the nationalist *Tévyné* and the clericalist *Žvaigždé*, each criticizing the "false Lithuanianness" of the other in the early 1900's.[8]

With the emergence of the two antagonistic Lithuanian camps, what hostility there was toward the Poles seems nearly to have disappeared. The Polish-Lithuanian institutional connections in the period after 1890 were stable, compatible, even friendly. The reason for the Lithuanian clergy's improved relations with Poles was their mutually held definition of nationality —that all group members had to be Roman Catholic. Once Father Burba had begun the first Lithuanian parish at Plymouth, he and his followers found they could be perfectly compatible with their former ethnic adversary. One cannot be certain when Burba first considered that Polish priests might be his allies, but by 1894 he was working with a Polish priest in planning how to deal with the anti-Catholic charges of his erstwhile comrade, Šliupas.[9]

A variety of evidence suggests that the Lithuanian clerics

[7] The breakup was indeed upsetting as the votes were nearly equal. L. Andriekus, *Metraštis, 1950* (Kennebunkport, Maine, 1950), 138; Mykolas Biržiška, *Amerikos Lietuviai* (Kaunas, 1932), 36. The recent standard account is Antanas Kučas, *Lietuviu Romos Kataliku Susivienjimas Amerikoje* (Wilkes-Barre, Pennsylvania, 1956), 94–116, especially 102–103.

[8] Kučas, *Lietuviu,* 95–96, 113; Vaclovas Biržiškas, "The American Lithuanian Publications, 1875–1910," in *Journal of Central European Affairs,* 18: 398–402 (January, 1959); V. Bartuśka, *Les Lituaniens d' Amèrique* (Lausanne, Switzerland, 1918), 16, 21; Kruszka, *Historya,* 12: 69–70.

[9] *Varpas* (September, 1894), 95.

were siding closely with their Polish colleagues. In the early 1890's a group of Lithuanian priests were working to persuade their many countrymen who had joined the Polish National Alliance to leave the society not so much on the basis of nationality—that a Lithuanian was not a Pole—but more because the fraternal was anticlerical.[10] In this case, both Lithuanian nationalists and religionists drew support for their position from Polish allies. Other evidence of a strong, interethnic clerical bond was the continuing existence of a Lithuanian subgroup within established Polish institutions. In 1895 a Lithuanian priest began teaching his language and building a Lithuanian library at the major Polish Catholic seminary in Detroit.[11]

Like the Poles, the Lithuanians' largest colony was in Chicago, and the dramatic ordeal that took place there was nearly a replay of the Polish experience. Religionists maintained that the Catholic pastor was supreme in parish affairs and had a paramount loyalty to American and Polish Catholicism; lay nationalists regarded themselves as spokesmen for their own Lithuanian congregation and felt that the cleric was too much the servant of non-Lithuanian Catholic superiors. It was out of this contest that a realization of Lithuanianness would take root and spread among the masses.

At the parish level, the Lithuanian disorders were similar to the Barzynski-Alliance feud of the 1880's. One cleric, the Reverend Matas Kraučiūnas, arose as the Lithuanians' most powerful ethnic priest. He presided at the group's Chicago mother church, St. George. His protagonists were a few parish lay leaders and nationalists led by Antoni Olszewski, publisher of *Lietuva*. There was a continual battle for church control which actually dated from the very beginning of local religious institutions in the late 1880's, even before Kraučiūnas came. It lasted for over a quarter-century and affected not only the

---

[10] Gineitis, *Amerika,* 271, says they had been lured into joining. See also Audyaitis, "Catholic Action," 33.

[11] *Ibid.,* 14. Compare Arunas J. Alisauskas, "Catholicism, Nationalism, and Reform among Lithuanian Immigrants . . . ," a paper presented to the Hopkins-Harwichport Seminar in American Religious History, August 23, 25, 1973, pp. 6, 8.

group's first parish but also almost every Lithuanian settlement in the city. Although the earliest Lithuanians in Chicago were members of St. Stanislaus, there was no discernible friction with the Polish settlement. In fact Father Barzynski, the Polish pastor on the north side, and the archdiocese treated the embryonic colony generously. When the recently formed Lithuanian St. Casimir's Society requested in 1887 that Barzynski obtain a priest who could hear confessions in Lithuanian, the Polish cleric arranged for the Reverend Walenty Čižauskas to come periodically from South Bend.[12]

The visiting priest system continued for several years, until another Lithuanian nucleus developed rather rapidly on the west side, in Bridgeport. Then representatives sought Čizauskas and another Lithuanian priest's assistance in beginning a separate parish. Again Barzynski and the archbishop blessed Čizauskas's efforts to gather funds, and in 1892 Church authorities appointed the Reverend George Kolesinskis pastor of the new St. George Church.

The arrival of Kolesinskis at Chicago's first Lithuanian parish inaugurated a twenty-five-year struggle between him (and later his successor) and members of the congregation for church control. Unquestionably Kolesinskis was both a cleric and a patriot. He had just arrived from Russia, where he had been persecuted for his enthusiasm and his ethnic loyalty.[13] He was also a religionist, who conceived of his role as that of group leader instructing his parishioners that to be a Lithuanian meant to be a Roman Catholic. As his later action showed, he could serve his bishop loyally; follow his regulations, including adherence to the property stipulations of the Baltimore Council; maintain close ties with his fellow Polish Catholics; and still consider himself a Lithuanian. Some, but not all, of the parish fathers who had requested his presence took a differing view of

---

[12] I cannot determine from sources if Čižauskas, also called Czyzewski, was Polish or Lithuanian by birth, but he did speak the latter language. *1877–1927 Album Złotego Jubileuszu Parafji Św. Jadwigi w South Bend* (South Bend, Indiana, 1927), 54.

[13] A detailed biography can be found in *1892–1942, Golden Jubilee, St. George's Church* (Chicago, 1942).

his position. They regarded themselves as the people's representatives, who were to run the parish administration; the priest was responsible to them. Ethnicity, not religion, was the basis of their parish. The differing interpretations collided from the very beginning, and friction developed when Kolesinskis purchased lots for the church and registered the real estate, according to Church rule, in his name and the name of his bishop, instead of that of the parish committee.[14] The pastor's action divided the congregation. "Some wanted to throw the Priest out. Others wanted to throw the committee out of the parish. And thus . . . there was the greatest disorder."[15] Father Kolesinskis enlivened the controversy by frequently showing his contempt for the hostile parish committeemen. He condemned his critics regularly at mass and further infuriated them by his close relations with the Poles, especially by insisting upon living in a neighborhood Polish rectory. Eventually, in November, 1893, the parish committee convinced the archbishop, who himself was suspicious of Kolesinskis' financial dealings, to force him to resign. The diocesan head replaced Kolesinskis with the Reverend Matas Kraučiūnas, a cleric whom lay leaders hoped would be a more pliant, amenable religious leader.[16]

The trustees' hopes were soon dashed. Father Kraučiūnas was even more iron-willed and religionist than his predecessor. Like his Polish colleague on the north side, Barzynski, Kraučiūnas too had been a Russian emigré, and thus a nationalist; but basically he was a religionist who insisted that Lithuanians, like Poles, were Roman Catholic and must submit to Church authority. He demonstrated his close admiration for his Polish colleagues from the beginning, acting as vicar at a Polish parish shortly after coming to America.[17] After he assumed the pastorate at St. George, he continued the anti-trustee campaign of

---

[14] *Istoria Chicagos Lietuvių Ju Parapijų ir Kn. Kraučiūnas Prova Su Laikraisciu "L"* (Chicago, 1900), 46–49.
[15] *Ibid.*, 49, 53.
[16] His first entry in the parish records was on December 24, 1893; see St. George's records, Chicago.
[17] *Tevyne* (Rugsejis, 1899), 4: 320. See also *St. George's Church* and *Dziennik Chicagoski*, obituary, June 13, 1914.

his predecessor with a more sweeping strategy. He sought to bend the parish committee to his own will and purge the congregation of all its anticlerical elements. For the next decade and a half, until Kraučiūnas' death in 1918, the first Lithuanian parish in Chicago (and the largest in the nation) was the center of a clericalist-nationalist struggle that was going on throughout Lithuanian America.

The parish committee acted first to secure the upper hand in the church, even before Kraučiūnas officially took his position, by drawing up a parish constitution that sharply limited the pastor's authority in financial matters. But not only did Kraučiūnas refuse to sign these by-laws; he had learned of the committee's action and forestalled it by naming his own parish committee in May, 1894.[18] For the next four years, despite frequent objections to his policies, he ran parish affairs in a decidedly authoritarian manner. In particular he administered the church treasury himself to assure the construction of his church rectory and school. He also conducted an energetic religionist campaign among the various parish societies, ordering them to expel non-Catholic members. He refused to allow non-Catholic Lithuanian groups to use parish facilities, a traditional practice, and later even set up competing, clerically based fraternal societies.

At the time he was purging the parish of what he considered anti-religious and non-Lithuanian organizations, Father Kraučiūnas maintained warm relations with Polish and American Church officials. Like Bačkauskas in the 1870's and 1880's and Burba in the 1890's, Kraučiūnas behaved like a Polonophile. Not only did he spend the several months before coming to his parish at a Polish south side church, he also contributed to the Lwów Exposition of Polish America in 1894; participated in the first Polish Catholic congress in Buffalo in 1896; and invited Polish nuns, and later Lithuanian members of the same order, to teach in his parish school in 1897. Even after 1897 his non-Lithuanian Catholic ties continued strong. He sponsored an address by Archbishop Symon when he visited the Polish-

18 The details are in *Istoria*, 68ff.

American colonies in 1905. For his loyal and devoted Church activities, the archbishop of Chicago in 1909 bestowed upon him the same special title that Father Pitass of Buffalo was given, "Dziekan." It was no wonder, then, that on the silver anniversary of his ordination in 1914, the leading Polish religious organ, *Dziennik Chicagoski,* praised the leading Lithuanian pastor as "a popular priest in Polish circles."[19]

Kraučiūnas' conception of his ethnic community stimulated opposition from two factions—outspoken nationalists, who viewed their movement to establish an independent homeland as more than a clerical activity, and lay parishioners, who chafed at Kraučiūnas' authoritarian conduct. As the 1890's progressed these two camps coalesced (many Lithuanians may have been originally in both). The most articulate spokesman for both these groups was the major Lithuanian institution in the city, the weekly *Lietuva,* and Antoni Olszewski, its editor. Olszewski emerged as the most influential Lithuanian layman in Chicago by the mid-1890's. He ran the group's major newspaper, conducted a nationality bank, and was the leading advisor to scores of immigrants.[20] By the end of the decade the struggle between the clericalists and nationalists was symbolized by the bitter personal conflict between Olszewski and Father Kraučiūnas, the two leading Lithuanians in Chicago.

From the very beginning *Lietuva,* which was located in the St. George neighborhood, in Bridgeport, criticized Kolesinskis and Kraučiūnas for their overly Catholic definition of Lithuanian character. Olszewski, like his friend Šliupas in Pennsylvania, charged that the Roman Catholic priests were in fact hampering true nationality enlightenment by catering so obsequiously to non-Lithuanian superiors.[21] In 1893 the paper advised that by deeding the church to the archbishop, the pastor was exploiting Lithuanians. *Lietuva* stated flatly that one need

---

[19] *Dziennik Chicagoski,* June 13, 1914.
[20] His progressive, nationalistic philosophy, a part of his biography, is in Petras Jurgela, ed., *Antanas Olšauskas ir "Lietuva"* (Sodus, Michigan, 1934). See also Document 22, Chicago Communities Documents, Chicago Historical Society; *"Aušros" 40M. Sukakturese* (Philadelphia, 1923), 227–231.
[21] N. B. Jurgela, *Olšauskas,* 28.

not be Catholic to be Lithuanian, for in fact the Church was the enemy of ethnic nationalism. The religious institutions already had damaged if not destroyed both Polish and Italian nationalism. If Lithuanian pastors really cared for their own people, they would guard their parishioners' hard-earned money, not use it for selfish or nongroup purposes.[22] The implication was that clerics vitiated ethnic consciousness by considering parish property as Catholic rather than Lithuanian. (Several years later Olszewski leveled the same charges at Kraučiūnas personally.) In the mid-1890's *Lietuva* was reporting nationalist ceremonies sympathetically, especially in 1895 when it became the official organ for a nationalist society which Kraučiūnas was attacking.[23] It became even more contentious by 1897, agitating disgruntled St. George parishioners and giving voice to the congregationalist and patriot position.

The paper's more overt intervention in parish affairs in 1897 on a democratic-nationalist basis brought the issue down to the level of the ordinary parishioners, who were not yet entirely ethnic-conscious but who were already suspicious of their pastor's money handling. With the encouragement of some Lithuanian journals outside Chicago, *Lietuva* attacked Kraučiūnas' financial administration as extravagant, unrepresentative, and, by implication, hierarchical (Roman Catholic), not congregational (Lithuanian).[24] The paper supported a petition by six parish societies asking the bishop to remove Kraučiūnas. This so infuriated the pastor and his party that in February, 1898, he sued Olszewski for slander. Olszewski countered with five suits of his own. Kraučiūnas also established a clericalist newspaper, *Katalikas,* to answer *Lietuva* directly.

In 1898 the major issue debated was Kraučiūnas' arbitrary use of church funds. *Lietuva* criticized the pastor for being responsible only to himself. He furnished no clear accounting to the laity of how he spent the tens of thousands of dollars he

22 *Lietuva,* February 4, 25, October 21, 1893, *FLPS.*
23 *Ibid.,* October 12, 1895.
24 *Istoria,* 87–88.

collected, and he would not permit an impartial examination of the records.[25] A short time later Olszewski introduced the nationality issue by charging that Kraučiūnas spent Lithuanian money on non-Lithuanian items, destroyed national traditions by supporting diocesan ownership of the property, and brought in Polish nuns to teach Lithuanian children. In an open letter to his readers, Olszewski asserted in December, 1898: "Such [title] assignment [to the bishop] is not right," and since the Polish teachers "do not know the Lithuanian language, they cannot teach the Lithuanian children." Then, addressing his antagonist, "You [venerable Father] and your nuns are destroying Lithuanianism. . . . We are against the Polonization of our children."[26]

Katalikas made the standard religionist response: since the Catholic priest was the spiritual leader of a nationality that was itself Catholic, Olszewski's remarks were objectively anti-Lithuanian, anti-Catholic, and immoral. It pointedly stated that Olszewski was as "godless" as his friend Šliupas.[27] The heated exchange between the two leaders and their newspapers continued through the early years of the century, sometimes confusing but nonetheless educating the Lithuanian laity to a new level of ethnic consciousness.[28]

After considerable delay Kraučiūnas completed his magnificent new church, but, especially after 1898, he alienated a large number of his parishioners. He continued to harass nationalist societies, even to the point of refusing to hear Easter confession from *Lietuva* sympathizers. Some religious organizations of the church formally complained to the bishop in March, 1899, about their pastor's action. By this time a large number of petitions both for and against Kraučiūnas were circulating at St. George. *Lietuva* sneered that the only supporting signatures

---

[25] The editorial had the candid title, "Our Priest's Pockets are Deep," *Lietuva*, August 16, September 26, 1898, *FLPS*.

[26] *Ibid.*, December 23, 1898.

[27] *Katalikas*, January 5, February 10, June 1, September 14, 1899, *FLPS*.

[28] Note the pathetic lament of one parishioner, wrongly accused of being an Olszewski supporter, in *Lietuva*, August 26, 1898, *FLPS*.

Kraučiūnas could get would be Polish.[29] During a lull in these seemingly interminable parish disputes, *Katalikas* lamented that[30]

> the lack of . . . harmony and solidarity is one of the saddest manifestations among the Lithuanian American intelligentsia at the present time. . . . We do not want to see our [community] go to pieces. . . . We must create harmony. . . . We hope that peace will reign and all controversies will end forever among our Lithuanian brothers.

Unfortunately this earnest wish for peace foundered upon even greater divisions.

As the conflict in Chicago worsened with law suits, petitions, and appeals to the bishop, some progressive, nationalist parishioners decided upon other courses of action. A few joined the Polish independent movement, which, ironically, guaranteed full ethnic autonomy for Lithuanians. At first affiliation with that apostate group made them outcasts. A meeting of all Chicago Lithuanians at St. George in early March, 1897, condemned "those [independent] heretics as the product of the Satanic and Russian Hell [who are] Russian spies and . . . the sellers of God and the Fatherland."[31] Two years later, however, in the midst of the deepening clericalist-nationalist split, *Lietuva* sympathized with the "heretical" Lithuanians, who, it said, were driven to take such radical steps by Kraučiūnas' refusal to account for parish property.[32] It concluded that the Lithuanian pastor himself was the one who spread atheism by "forcing every Lithuanian from the church."[33]

For most dissident parishioners, leaving Roman Catholicism to escape a dictatorial pastor was too drastic a course. A less extreme alternative, one taken at the Polish St. Stanislaus Church almost thirty years before, was to start an entirely sep-

---

[29] *Katalikas,* May 18, 1899; *Lietuva,* May 12, 19, June 9, 30, 1899, *FLPS.*
[30] *Katalikas,* June 15, 1899, *FLPS.*
[31] *Lietuva,* March 13, 1897, *FLPS.*
[32] *Ibid.,* February 20, 1899.
[33] *Istoria,* 126.

arate Roman Catholic parish with a more flexible, democratic, and nationalistic pastor. Outwardly this step was justifiable on other grounds. St. George was overcrowded, and some parishioners had to travel from the growing Lithuanian colony on the distant near west side, around Halsted and 18th streets, to that one Lithuanian parish. To alleviate the inconvenience of traveling so far, a St. George society called Providence of God, which was also working to replace Krauciunas as its religious leader, wanted its own house of worship. The Lithuanian pastor constantly blocked the project, however.[34]

The archbishop finally approved the society's application for a new church with its name, Providence of God, in March, 1900, but, to the dismay of those who sought complete independence, he selected Krauciunas' own candidate, his assistant the Reverend Edward Steponavicius, as pastor. To combat their new cleric, the Providence of God leaders, who now constituted the parish committee, devised a sharply restrictive constitution which made the new pastor hardly more than a parish employee. The archbishop took no interest in the new church by-laws, since the committee had met his demand to deed the church property to him.[35] When Steponavicius signed the constitution and a large number of disgruntled St. George parishioners joined the new church, the parish committee felt satisfied that they had secured an ethnic place of worship beyond Krauciunas' control.

The trustees underestimated the wily old priest. With the help of some parishioners, who formed essentially a clericalist party at the new parish, Krauciunas persuaded diocesan authorities to discharge Steponavicius, ostensibly for not knowing Lithuanian well enough, and to replace him with the Reverend Petras Peza, who was more loyal to Krauciunas. This coup instigated another pastor-parishioner conflict in the Lithuanians' second Chicago parish. At his very first service, Peza argued with a committeeman over who had the right to collect

---

[34] *Lietuva,* July 7, 1899, *FLPS.*
[35] *Lietuva,* which had supported the new parish, had advised against title transfer to the archbishop. The succession of the events is in *Istoria, 555–563.*

money from the congregation. The contest ended quickly, for seeing he had little popular support, Peża took the prudent step of quietly returning to the sanctuary of St. George. After a hiatus of several months, in November, 1900, Steponavičius returned to his original position.[36]

Again the parishioners may have felt they at last had a cleric "of the people," but Steponavičius was soon embroiled in a decade-long struggle with his parishioners over financing the construction of a new sanctuary. The troubles became manifest in March, 1905, when the pastor informed the parish committee about a heavy mortgage of $42,000 that he had assumed without their knowledge. In fact, with the aid of the archbishop, Steponavičius had seized the parish account books and set up a new, more tractable board of trustees. The matter assumed more serious form in February, 1906, when the archbishop reaffirmed his support of the pastor, but the old parish committee refused to surrender the weekly collections. On February 9, Father Steponavičius, under police escort, forced the custodian of the church to give him the funds.

At mass the following Sunday, when the pastor tried to make a collection from the congregation, someone in the rear shouted, "Don't give a cent to the shoemaker!" Apparently this was a signal, for one woman hit the pastor with the collection plate and another clouted him with a bottle. In the mass confusion which followed, Father Steponavičius locked himself in the rectory. The police guard which came to his defense was "seriously hampered by . . . an attacking party . . . of [several hundred] women and girls," wielding hatpins, bottles, rocks, and boards. Seriously scratched, stabbed, or otherwise injured, the police officers called for reinforcements. Seventeen patrol wagons with over a hundred more men came, but the crowd was not intimidated until the police fired into the air. When the smoke of battle cleared, the rectory had been severely damaged, Father Steponavičius was in his quarters suffering from

[36] *Dievo Apviezdos Par. Sidabro Jubiliejaus Atminjmas 1900–1925* (Chicago, 1925), 13ff. *Lietuva*, August 3, 10, 17, September 14, 1900, *FLPS*, stated that Kraučiūnas pushed Peża into the sister parish to do "his dirty work" of controlling the new nationalist colony.

nervous prostration, and four rioters lay badly injured, one Lithuanian having been shot by the police. The parish priest later swore out arrest warrants against forty of his parishioners, particularly the custodian and a local saloonkeeper, who had led the old parish committee and whom he suspected had incited the riot. The following Sunday some parishioners outside the church broke windows during Steponavičius' sermon.[37]

All this congregational protest against ecclesiastical authority gave *Lietuva* much satisfaction, because it regarded the basic issue as clerical suppression of ethnicity. Not only did the parish disorder reaffirm the Church's anti-Lithuanian, anti-nationalist policy; the incidents also verified advice the paper had given in 1900 when it suggested that the trustees not deed the property to the bishop but keep it for themselves. Later, when a minority of parishioners threatened to leave Roman Catholicism permanently, the paper encouraged the dissension, charging that "the Catholic bishop . . . cares about the Lithuanians as little as we care about the Chinese." Finally, *Lietuva* advised Lithuanian Catholics who sought a worthy project to give their money to build a hall for the nationalist Lithuanian Alliance. (SLA).[38] The pastor's opponents continued the conflict until Steponavičius left a decade later, and at one point they brought the issue into litigation to keep the funds out of the pastor's hands.[39]

The contests in Chicago's second Lithuanian colony and at St. George affected other neighborhoods in Chicago and other cities as well. As with the Poles, parish unrest among the Lithuanians was part of a nationwide social upheaval. Unfortunately, unlike the Polish case, there was no satisfactory resolution of the controversy by Church authorities. No Roman Catholic bishop brought a Lithuanian into the American hierarchy.

Almost immediately after the Providence of God disturbances in 1900, disorders occurred elsewhere in Chicago. Rev-

[37] The account is from a compilation of *Chicago Inter-Ocean*, February 12, 1906; *Dziennik Chicagoski*, February 12, 15, 1906, and "Bullets and Blood in Big Church Riot," in *Chicago Record Herald*, February 12, 1906.

[38] *Lietuva*, February 23, March 9, 1905, *FLPS*.

[39] *Ibid.*, November 23, 1906; March 29, 1907; August 22, 1909; *Dievo Apviezdos . . . 1900–1925*, 12.

erend Pėža went to a new church in South Chicago where he again faced lay opposition to his authoritarian policies. Hostilities between Lithuanian pastors and parshioners occurred also in Westville, Illinois, at Waterbury, Connecticut, and in Philadelphia before 1901; in Scranton that year; in Waukegan, Illinois, in 1904; at All Saints (Chicago) and St. George (Shenandoah, Pennsylvania) in 1908; at Our Lady of Vilna (Chicago) in 1909; and in the Roseland area of Chicago and at Lawrence, Massachusetts, between then and 1914.[40] The enmity between factions became particularly pointed in mid-1906 when Father Kraučiūnas led five fellow-priests in issuing a formal warning to parishioners not to attend the imminent Lithuanian Alliance (SLA) convention in Chicago under penalty of excommunication.[41]

Oddly enough, the constant friction between religionists and nationalist laity produced only a minor independent movement among the Lithuanians. One reason for this may have been the absence of charismatic clerics such as Kozłowski, Kamiński, and Hodur. A few Lithuanians did support independentism. Individually these group members joined Polish independents in the late 1890's. Later, a small National Catholic branch of Lithuanians emerged prior to American entrance into World War I. Some of their attempted parishes failed in 1906 and 1914 in Chicago; others succeeded in Scranton in 1906 and in Chicago and Lawrence, Massachusetts, in 1916.[42]

For the ordinary Lithuanian immigrant, the experience of living in an American community between 1880 and 1918 must

[40] *Katalikas*, March 27, 1900; *Lietuva*, May 18, 1900, June 22, July 8, November 2, 1904; March 13, 1906; October 2, 1908; November 5, 1909; February 28, 1913, *FLPS. Shenandoah Lietuvių . . .* , 208ff. Note especially the detailed narrative in Reverend John Gallagher, *A Century of History: The Diocese of Scranton, 1868–1968* (Scranton, Pennsylvania, 1968), 252ff. I view all these disturbances, of course, not as isolated events, but as expressions of popular sentiment.

[41] It was an empty threat. *Lietuva*, March 9, 16, 30, June 1, 1906, *FLPS*.

[42] Joseph Krisciunas, "Lithuanians in Chicago" (master's thesis, De Paul University, 1935), 52, 70; *Naujienos* (Chicago), June 10, 1914, *FLPS*; End notes of Lithuanian section, *FLPS*. According to Mykolas Biržiška, *Amerikos Lietuviai* (Kaunas, 1932), 45, by 1924 the Lithuanians had their own National Catholic bishop under Hodur; by 1932 they had six parishes.

have been a trying one. He had arrived with no clear ideas about his ethnic identity, and with little desire to discover it; yet within a short time he was witness to, and perhaps a participant in, a bitter parish-level struggle between Lithuanian nationalists who urged congregational autonomy and Roman Catholic clericalists who demanded religious loyalty. Apathy, even neutrality was difficult to maintain in the face of strident appeals from both camps that theirs was the "true Lithuanian heritage." Whichever faction the immigrant supported—whether the nationalists under Olszewski and Šliupas, or the clericalists led by Burba and Kraučiūnas—the immigrant received excellent instruction in what it meant to be a Lithuanian. But he paid a price for his ethnic education. The widespread unrest, the never-ending cleavage between fellow countrymen, the occasional outbreaks of violence all cast a shadow over the Lithuanian community in America. Prior to World War I the effects of nationalist agitation were upsetting and largely divisive. Occasionally religionists did participate in a patriotic celebration; once a group of clerics even hesitantly petitioned the Catholic hierarchy for a Lithuanian bishop, but they quickly withdrew their request.[43] By and large, it was not until 1918 that Lithuanian Catholic leaders, impelled by the nationalizing pressures of the war in Europe, united with Lithuanian patriots to work for an independent homeland.[44]

[43] Audyiatis, "Catholic Action," 107.
[44] Roman Catholics, however, had accepted the principle as a goal as early as 1914. Bartuśka, *Les Lituaniens*, 104; Senn, *Emergence of Modern Lithuania*, 22–23.

NINE

1908 and After: Resolution and Assessment

THE ORDINATION of the Reverend Paul Rhode as a Roman Catholic bishop on July 28, 1908, was a landmark in the history of Polish America—similar to, but more fulfilling than, the celebration of Polish Day at the Columbian Exposition or the unveiling of the Kościuszko statue in Humboldt Park. To the Poles of Chicago who witnessed it, and to the Poles of every other American community who read about the event, Bishop Rhode's elevation to the Church hierarchy symbolized permanent Roman Catholic recognition for their emerging nation. To be sure, it did not satisfy every Pole to the same degree; a few clerics and laymen, and a small but growing number of Polish socialists, continued to argue that the appointment of one bishop could not meet the needs of the entire nationality. But Rhode's ordination calmed the anxieties of what had become a restless and fragmented community: clericalists who feared further schisms and therefore sought *równouprawnienie;* nationalists who demanded a Polish bishop in order to attain ethnic respectability; and disturbed members of the Polish rank and file, who were still bewildered by all the preceding internal struggles. Like a shaft of sunlight following a storm, the event warmed and illuminated all Polonia.[1]

---

[1] My interpretation of the Church's response to ethnicity qualifies that of Rudolph Vecoli, "Prelates and Priests: Italian Immigrants and the Catholic

162

The preparations for Rhode's ordination day welded old factions into a new harmony. The participants included all organized elements except socialists and independents. Representatives of Chicago's many Polish parishes gathered on June 29 at St. Adalbert hall to plan for the occasion. The members of St. Stanislaus and Holy Trinity were conspicuously present. The major spokesman was the well-known John Smulski, a banker, city treasurer, leading nationalist, and member of Holy Trinity, who urged every Polish neighborhood to decorate its homes and send an escort to the diocesan Cathedral to accompany Rhode. On July 21 *Dziennik Chicagoski* reported that a variety of societies—the more nationalist, such as the Women's Alliance, and the Falcons, along with the Polish Roman Catholic Union—were making elaborate plans to take part in the ceremonies. Four triumphal arches were to be constructed along the parade route to St. Stanislaus Hall.

Participants who arrived in the days just prior to the consecration further demonstrated the wide geographic interest in the event, as well as its broad, ideological acceptance. Polish parish representatives came from as far away as Hartford, Connecticut, and Scranton, Pennsylvania. Polish-American journalists called a national convention of their own in conjunction with the affair. Finally, the Church gave the Poles new status by sending many representatives—so many, in fact, that the consecration became a showcase of American Catholicism: Archbishops Sebastian Messmer of Milwaukee and John Ireland of St. Paul; twelve bishops from as far east as Pittsburgh and as far west as Kansas (including the highest Slavic-American cleric, the Right Reverend Joseph M. Koudelka, auxiliary bishop of Cleveland); and 400 other clerics. Lay people from all over the United States and Canada, representing many other Catholic nationalities—Lithuanians, Italians, Slovaks and some Frenchmen—also made the pilgrimage to Chicago.

July 28 dawned hot and clear. The Polish north side was

Church," in *Journal of Social History*, 2: 262n, 268 (Spring, 1969). Vecoli views the institution as hostile to Italians and possibly to Poles. I suggest that his conclusion is more valid for Italians than for the Slavs; he does not refer to Rhode.

decorated to welcome a hero; red-and-white bunting hung from homes and lampposts. Despite the heat, a crowd was waiting at 7 A.M. around St. Michael Church on the south side, where the bishop-to-be was staying. Another large group gathered before Holy Name Cathedral, where Rhode was to be consecrated. The young priest arrived there at 10 A.M. Archbishop Quigley officially ordained him before hundreds of Church and lay officials, including two major (and heretofore hostile) Polish fraternal societies—the entire PRCU administration and most of the PNA officers.

Even more gratifying to the Polish community were two events at the noonday banquet, which was attended by a host of Catholic clerics. One was the performance of the Polish-Lithuanian chorus, which deliberately sang Polish compositions which were familiar to group members but unknown to the non-Slavs at the banquet.[2] The other was the congratulatory address of Archbishop John Ireland, who several years earlier had been a leader of the Church's assimilationist campaign. Now, before prominent Poles and other Catholic officials, he reversed his stand and sympathized with the ethnic yearnings of Polish-Americans. To the obvious delight of the PNA, he particularly commended their efforts to establish a national homeland.[3]

The remainder of the day the Poles had Bishop Rhode to themselves. He visited several neighborhoods which had been eagerly awaiting his arrival, including his own parish, St. Michael, where the steelworkers, let off for the afternoon, gave him a tumultuous welcome. An observer wrote, "The bands blared out a quickstep, the people cheered, the church bells pealed, and even the mighty whistles of the nearby steel mills shrieked out a welcome and congratulations."[4]

In the evening a procession on the north side under banners and arches leading to St. Stanislaus ended the historic day. Nearly 300 automobiles and carriages and over 20,000 people

[2] *Dziennik Chicagoski*, July 25, 1908; and, especially, *The New World*, August 1, 1908.
[3] *Dziennik Związkowy*, July 30, 31, 1908.
[4] *Ibid.*, July 20, 1908.

took part. Many held up placards in the two-hour-long procession reading *Niech Zyje* (Long Live the Bishop) and *Niech Zyje Polska.*[5] As the first section of marchers arrived at the city's oldest Polish parish, the church bells began to peal. Bishop Rhode addressed the multitude in a manner that recalled their ethnic heritage: he spoke in the language of their early ancestors, Old Polish.[6] At the evening banquet in St. Stanislaus, the celebrated John Smulski observed that it had been a glorious day for the entire Polish community.

In addition to the general enthusiasm and popular support at the receptions and parades, religiously oriented well-wishers expressed their enthusiasm for the new bishop with gifts, flowers, and wreaths. Among them were a set of Polish figurines from St. Adalbert parish, a portrait album of all the diocesan priests from the Pittsburgh clergy, an expensive canister from the East Coast Polish clerics, vestments from four other Chicago parishes, and the symbols of his office—the ring, mitre, and cross—from Archbishop Quigley himself.[7] A Chicago parish, St. Casimir, presented him with a very formal commendation in the appropriate context, which read in part:[8]

> On such a glorious day, so greatly desired and awaited . . . a day announced not only for Your Excellency but for the entire Polish nation, let us citizens signed below and in the name of the entire St. Casimir parish in Chicago, Illinois . . . assert willingly our utmost happiness and sincere wish for many years of blessed work for the Church and Polonia in America.
> [Signed by the parish committee and the pastor]

Any joyous and popular event normally stimulates some kind of literary manifestation, and the consecration of a Polish bishop soon acquired the character of a folk legend. One sonnet, widely broadcast by the Polish press, actually originated among Irish Catholics and merits quotation in full because of the great

---

[5] *Dziennik Chicagoski,* July 30, 1908.

[6] *Ibid.,* July 30, 1908.

[7] *Dziennik Związkowy,* July 31, 1908; *Dziennik Chicagoski,* July 21, 1908.

[8] *Ibid.,* August 3, 1908. See also the specific reaction of the South Bend Poles in *1877–1927, Album Złotego Jubileuszu Parafju Św. Jadwigi w South Bend* (South Bend, 1927), 188.

satisfaction and status that it provided the Poles. Though weak
in literary merit, it reminded all readers of the historic common
bond that tied Celts to Slavs—that of defending Christendom:[9]

> Hail, youthful prelate, son of the fair land
> That to the world a Sobieski gave,
> From Islam's power Christendom to save
> Where Kościuszko and his gallant band
> For Freedom's cause made memorable stand
> And prince and priest and peasant, true and brave,
> Unflinching faced the dungeon or the grave
> Rather than tamely fear the helot's brand
> 'Tis meet a prelate boasting Irish blood
> Shall give to thee the consecrating rite
> For, like fair Poland, Ireland aye has stood
> So ever linked may Celt and Pole be true
> To God and home as symbolized in you.

Despite the more religious than secular character of the
ceremonies, Polish nationalists extended their good wishes to
the new bishop. The nationalist organ saw the deeper significance of the day for all Poles; it noted what it believed was the
"arrival" of the Polish nationality in the American Church.
Specifically, what was taking place was the end of an era of
intragroup struggle and the beginning of an era of full Catholic
recognition. While admitting that the day was largely one for
Polish Catholics, as distinct from Polish nationalists, the Polish
National Alliance also termed it "one of the most agreeable . . .
in the history of the Polish emigration," for it was "not divested
of prominent nationalistic significance. . . . A new era of hierarchical co-operation with Poles [has arrived which] follows a
resolute change in the treatment of the [ir] clergy by Roman
authorities [who are] influencing favorably the position of the
Poles in America."[10]

The nationalists' interpretation of the event was an expression not only of their and the clericalists' reaction but also that
of the Polish populace as a whole. Admittedly, certain elements

[9] From *The New World* in *Dziennik Chicagoski*, July 27, 1908. See also
ibid., August 3, 1908, on microfilm in *Dziennik Chicagoski* files at the Polish
Museum.

[10] *Dziennik Związkowy*, July 29, 1908.

refused to view Bishop Rhode's appointment as satisfactory recognition of the nationality. Independents and National Catholics had established their own ethnic church outside of Roman Catholicism, so his elevation did not interest them. The bitterly anticlerical Polish socialists admitted grudgingly that the Catholic hierarchy had taken a step in the proper direction: "Our man will take better care of 'our mangers.' " But they added that the appointment of a group prelate, as with all Church positions was essentially undemocratic and a burden to the poor. The new bishop would only add to the exploitation of the worker. "Thousands of dollars are being poured out by the hard working people [to honor the man]. . . . Even today they talk about buying an automobile and building a palace for [him], our countryman."[11] The ordination was a disappointment to even a few of the most spirited Polish patriots. They grumbled that for a number of reasons the appointment really did not signify full group recognition: the new cleric was the only group bishop for the millions of Polish-American Catholics; he was not a full bishop, only an auxiliary; and he had a German-sounding name, not a Slavic one.[12]

At the time of the consecration no one knew whether, as bishop, Rhode would further stimulate ethnic consciousness among Polish Americans. Indeed, he was a Pole with a Teutonic name so he might not be an enthusiastic group nationalist. Actually in 1908 no one really knew Rhode's inner thoughts about his future duties. The man himself had been a relatively inconspicuous cleric to his people. Only a few Poles, mostly in Chicago, had been acquainted intimately with him prior to his nomination for candidacy. In fact, that he had not been prominent or controversial and had no strong enemies may have been his best recommendation for the position. He had shown little nationalist sentiment; specifically, earlier at a rare moment of voicing his opinion, his attitude toward *równouprawnienie* had been somewhat hostile. (Ironically, he had denigrated Kruszka's

11 *Dziennik Ludowy,* July 3, 1908, *FLPS.*
12 Note the comment in *Nowiny Polskie* (Milwaukee) from *Dziennik Chicagoski,* June 23, 1908.

visit to Rome, the very action that eventually resulted in his own election.) On the whole, in the period up to 1908, Rhode's innermost feelings on the nationalist-religionist controversy were unclear. Those closest to him described his manner as simply *chico* (quiet) and *skromny* (modest).[13]

Undoubtedly his most attractive attribute to his peers and the Church hierarchy and the one which was to catapult him into prominence was a genius for parish administration—especially his ability to handle funds expertly, without antagonizing his people. In 1895 he had rescued his first Chicago church from near bankruptcy, and later he brought St. Michael out of debt to be one of the most prosperous parishes in the city.[14] In that era of widespread parish disorders over funding and finances, successful property management by the pastor was certain to bring rewards.

Despite all this previous modesty and quiet competence, once Rhode was elevated to bishop, he altered his conduct by becoming a determined ethnic enthusiast. To the delight of Polish immigrant nationalists, he immediately conceived of his office as *the* Polish representative within the American Church. He became a generator of Polishness, and, like Kruszka before him, a vigorous proponent of a highly pluralistic Catholicism. Expediency rather than sincere conviction may have dictated his projecting the ethnic dimension of his faith; that is, he may have been trying to prevent further defections to National Catholicism. But whatever his motivation, down to World War I Bishop Rhode campaigned hard for the idea that a Polish Roman Catholic could support and work as a nationalist for an independent Polish state. By so doing, he helped to reduce further and substantially the old nationalist-religionist tension. In the process he continued to raise the ethnic consciousness of all Polish Catholics.

In his first formal address as bishop, at the evening banquet

[13] The characterizations were from his home parishioners. *Album Jubileuszowa 25-cio lecie dziejów Parafii Św. Michała Archanioli w South Chicago, 1892–1917* (Chicago, 1917).

[14] *Przegląd Katolicki*, 6: 372–373 (June, 1919); *Dziennik Chicagoski,* June 20, 1908; *The New World,* July 25, 1908.

held in his honor at St. Stanislaus Hall in 1908, Rhode inaugurated his new policy. He first expressed the hope of synthesizing the religious and ethnic qualities of his people. He then reminded his listeners of their greatest American cleric Barzynski who, he said, would be his model, not as the authoritarian Catholic patriarch loyal to his superiors (omitted from his text) but as a true ethnic patriot, the personification of *Polskość*.[15] In effect, this speech was the first indication that he felt he must become the group's major patriot-priest.

In the following year, at the Cleveland convention of the Polish Roman Catholic Union, he officially launched his nationalistic campaign, announcing his "unity alliance." This alliance was to weld all Polish clerics, conservative loyalists as well as congregational patriots, into an active bloc in the Church. After some effort he was able to organize the Polish Priests' Union in 1912 and to initiate an all-inclusive Polish federation with representation as broad as possible, within and even without the Church. The latter was institutionalized in 1913 as the Polish National Department, consisting of the major nationalist and clericalist societies, mutually dedicated to realizing an independent homeland.[16] It was no surprise that when the new Polish state did arise a few years later, it honored this American prelate with its Star of Polonia Restituta.

As Rhode himself viewed his position, he was not simply an auxiliary bishop in the Chicago archdiocese; he considered himself the designated leader of all Polish Catholics in America. He sought to stimulate conscious nationalist sentiment throughout the nation, and to unify the diverse elements among his Polish-American constituency. His constant efforts on behalf of the Old Country, especially his extensive traveling through Polish America, moved Kruszka, the older patriot-priest, to refer to him sympathetically as "in constant motion." The most knowledgeable historian of Polish America concluded that Rhode's ecclesiastical diocese was not just Chicago but all

15 *Dziennik Chicagoski,* July 30, 1908.
16 See the still warm nationalist-clericalist debate in *Dziennik Związwoky,* November 2, 8, 17, 21, 27, December 12, 1911, *FLPS,* which indicates the remaining suspicions.

Polonia.[17] Thus the American Church's Polish hero, the one who was the most Catholic of all Poles in the years up to World War I, had brought God and Country together. Bishop Rhode essentially resolved that aggravating internal tension over Polishness that had begun within Polish America in the middle of the previous century. In the process of this achievement he contributed to a more advanced level of ethnic consciousness for the Polish-American rank and file.

*   *   *   *

Any study dealing with a new and broader group consciousness among ordinary people must concern itself with social psychology—the personal behavior of an individual as a part of a larger collectivity. The focus of this work has been on that subject, that is how and to what degree the individual Polish and Lithuanian immigrants leaving local villages and regions became more cognizant of their membership in the larger, distinctive ethnic group. Polishness and Lithuanianness meant more to the rank and file in 1910 than these sentiments did in 1870 or 1890. Thus this work has hypothesized about a social-psychological process among immigrants.

If this were a work about present-day ethnic feeling, it could employ rather sophisticated social science methods, such as surveys and other statistical devices to measure changing behavior. However, the ethnic historian who treats the Polish and Lithuanian immigrant past finds quantitative analysis deficient, at least this time, to record ethnic identification. Immigration records such as the federal census did not begin to isolate Poles from Lithuanians or either from other East Europeans with any accuracy until near the turn of the century, the end of this period of study. So this work rests on the traditional methodology of extrapolating from events, basing its contention of rising ethnic consciousness upon the manifest persistence of a pervasive intragroup tension.

Previous students of nationalism among American immi-

[17] Miecislaus Haiman, "Rev. Bishop Paul P. Rhode, His Life and Deeds [in Polish]," in *Przegląd Katolicki*, 9: 19–20, 23, 26, 37 (March–April, 1934).

grants already have detected this process of group enlightenment, and they have attempted to trace it over time. But none have provided much empirical historical evidence for their judgment as to how the individual foreigners experienced that sociopsychological feeling of ethnic identification. The best-known observers of the ethnic experience in the New World simply extended the general idea that nationalism and its earlier stage, ethnic awareness, resulted from the contact between immigrants and outsiders.

One of the earliest students of immigrant psychology was the American sociologist Robert E. Park. Writing in about 1920, during the era of overt hostility toward "hyphenated Americans," he used, coincidentally, a Polish example to show that it was the cultural differences between the immigrant and the native that stirred his ethnic consciousness:[18]

> Every Polish peasant, from whatever Polish province he comes . . . when transferred to a foreign soil among foreigners develops a Polish sentiment and a consciousness of his nationality character. This phenomenon is incomprehensible for those who saw the peasant at home without a consciousness of his nationality duties. And yet it is quite natural. *National consciousness originates in him spontaneously in a foreign country in consequence of the striking difference between his speech, his customs, his conceptions, from those of the people who surround him.*

He added a refinement to that notion, saying that some additional factor must be present to produce within each individual an understanding, more than just an awareness, of that difference.

Writing at about the same time, Horace Kallen, another student of American pluralism, agreed with Park. For Kallen, too, a person's ethnic awareness stemmed from his group's relations with another group, though he differed slightly with his colleague, asserting that ethnic intergroup contacts characteristically took place in an unpleasant, hostile atmosphere. It was not merely observable differences that produced ethnic consci-

---

[18] Emphasis added. Robert E. Park and Herbert Miller, *Old World Traits Transplanted* (New York, 1921), 135.

ousness, but, especially for non-Protestant groups, Anglo-American discrimination. Further, such an experience was a regrettable violation of democratic values: "[The individual] encounters the native American to whom he is merely a Dutchman, a Mick, a frog, a wop, a dago, a honky, a sheeny and no more; and he encounters these others who are unlike him, dealing with him as a lower and outlandish creature. Thus, [if] he be even the rudest and most primeval peasant, heretofore totally unconscious of his nationality . . . he must inevitably become conscious of it." He concluded pointedly: "It is the shock of confrontation and the natural feeling of aliency reinforced by social discrimination and economic exploitation that generate in them an intense consciousness."[19]

A more recent student of American ethnicity believes that the individual responds to competitiveness between ethnic groups. He suggests that all members of the recently arrived nationalities earnestly sought respectability and individuality in American society, and that it was this urge which caused them to realize and assert their own national identities. He does not clearly separate national consciousness from nationalism, but implies that both emerged because individuals made constant group comparisons.[20]

An underlying assumption of all these observers is the unquestioned notion that the new arrival had to face a hostile environment. Certainly Anglo-America was hostile and intol-

---

[19] Horace M. Kallen, *Culture and Democracy in the United States* (New York, 1924), 94–95, 102. Compare the amazingly similar Robert F. Hill and Howard F. Stein, "Ethnic Stratification and Social Unrest in Contemporary Eastern Europe and America," *Nationalities Papers*, 1: 1–28, especially 17 (Fall, 1972). Recent white minority resentment against Anglo-Protestant domination appears to verify the Kallen view. Nevertheless, present-day spokesman for these nationalities have yet to show whether the immigrant generation really felt the way that Kallen describes. For the most popular articulation of ethnic feeling, see Novak, *Rise of the Unmeltable Ethnics.*

[20] He admitted that his observation needed hard evidence. See Glazer, "From National Culture to Ideology," in Berger, *Freedom and Control,* 171. The most recent study of immigrant nationalism returns briefly to the Park-Kallen idea of consciousness formation in the case of the Irish. Thomas N. Brown, *Irish-American Nationalism* (Philadelphia, 1966), 19ff, and especially 23–24.

erant toward East Europeans, but the bulk of ordinary Polish and Lithuanian immigrants were not directly affected by this discrimination. It was not the Anglo-American community which first acclimated these East European strangers; after a very short transitional period the immigrants lived and worked in their own ethnic communities, neighborhoods, parishes, and fraternals. This was so even if they moved from New York to Chicago, Buffalo, Pittsburgh, or elsewhere. It is that ethnic subculture, the submerged but vital Polish and Lithuanian America, that observers must scrutinize in assessing the rise of group consciousness.

Karl Deutsch, a recent political scientist interested in nationalistic sentiment, has constructed a useful theoretical framework in which to consider ordinary Polish and Lithuanian immigrants and to examine their growing awareness of their Old World ethnic heritage. His study, *Nationalism and Social Communication*, explains the rise of nationalism in an individual, that is, the enthusiastic commitment to one's avowed national state. Only marginally does it deal with the antecedent of nationalism, ethnic or nationality consciousness. Deutsch is relevant, however, when he asserts that ethnic self-consciousness grows out of the information that is transmitted on each person's internal communications network. In other words, feelings of national consciousness begin when a person begins to attach secondary symbols of nationality to the primary information he receives. His national awareness is heightened when he begins to distinguish, for example, between "religion" and "Polish religion," and to recognize that he is part of the latter.[21] For most Polish-Americans the crucial period for achieving this awareness, and acting upon it, came between 1860 and 1914; for Lithuanians the period was between 1880 and the same terminal date. In both instances, the important fact was that the perception and acceptance of certain ethnic-national symbols emanated from within the immigrant communities rather than from without.

This psychological process of enlightenment—of perceiving

[21] Karl Deutsch, *Nationalism and Social Communication* (2nd ed., Cambridge, Massachusetts, 1966), 172.

that they belonged to an ethnic people, a nation—affected not only the intellectual and patriotic elite but the immigrant community as a whole. The shopkeeper, the miner, the steelworker, the seamstress, the housewife, right down to the lowliest day laborer all felt the pressure and the mounting tension of ethnic and nationalist ideas which spread to every corner of Polish or Lithuanian society. The average immigrant had brought from Europe an abiding reverence for land and a felt need for religious expression. Upon arriving in America, he experienced increasing difficulty in satisfying the two, because both were contended over by opposing factions in his community. Two factions argued over whether local church property ought to be basically the possession of Roman Catholic authorities, or instead be community-owned property. The dispute was entirely new to the immigrant, for in the Old Country his Catholic institutions had also been ethnic. In America the two interests clashed.

Before 1880 the disagreement was not particularly disturbing; only Chicago's north siders suffered the disruptive social results of the struggle. The rest of the Polish and Lithuanian newcomers merely watched and read about the disagreement from afar. But in the 1890's this quarrel over the control of their parishes, and thus over nationality identity (ought the people to think of their church basically as Catholic or ethnic?), assumed more immediate and real form for the ordinary immigrant in group colonies all over America. At that point disturbances erupted in almost every Polish neighborhood. By 1911 most Lithuanian parishes were similarly embroiled. The controversy seriously interfered with the functioning of the local church, so that merely by attending his neighborhood house of worship the parishioner became involved in the conflict. Some of his countrymen supported congregational, that is lay or ethnic, ownership of the parish and demanded an accounting of funds by the pastor. The resulting furor raised the ethnic consciousness of all parishioners, for rather than submitting to their nongroup authority some people resisted by extremely disruptive measures. Using the nationalist rationale, and with the help of a few sympathetic clerics, they erected an independent and later a National Catholic religious movement.

At this point in the crisis of the immigrant community the most naïve parishioners began to understand what was at issue. The struggle over who really controlled the parish forced all to view their community in the new context of nationality. When nationalists, independents, and other disgruntled church members demanded that the group faith be congregational rather than episcopal in structure, and thereby disrupted normal religious activities, every churchgoer began to see himself, his congregation, and his neighborhood as a part of an ethnic nation. He was now able to distill secondary symbols of nationality from his primary sources of information. For those Poles who arrived after 1900, the nationalist work of Kruszka, an occasional parish disorder, and Bishop Rhode's appointment and leadership continued to agitate the sensitive issue of religion and ethnicity, stimulating and nurturing ethnic consciousness. Fortunately, the ethno-religious conflict did not continue interminably. Rhode's elevation did much to resolve the tension between religionists and nationalists, and the two camps—indeed virtually all Polish-Americans—took satisfaction from the Church action. The Lithuanians, too, suffered from community divisions and tensions, though their resolution came later in World War I when clerics generally embraced group nationalism.

While inner struggles stimulated ethnic awareness, there were, to be sure, other external factors which sensitized the individual immigrant to cultural differences between his group and American society at large. Anglo-Americans considered East Europeans and other white minorities inferiors; even the Irish and German Catholic leaders exploited and abused the "Hunky" at times. Such intergroup friction was not, however, the major source for the rise of ethnic and national group consciousness among Poles and Lithuanians, whose contact with outsiders was, on the whole, infrequent and more harmonious than hostile. The constant and upsetting factor in the immigrant's personal communications network was a sustained internal tension. It was that struggle, and its impact among his own people, and especially between his pastor and his fellow parishioners over the question of neighborhood control, that raised Polish and Lithuanian ethnic awareness.

*   *   *   *

This exploration of immigrant history has concerned itself to this point almost solely with Polish-Americans and Lithuanian-Americans, making only fleeting references to other groups with whom they came into contact. It is, however, additionally instructive to view at least briefly these East European communities in America from a comparative perspective as well, to place their experience in the larger social settings of which they were a part—American Catholicism and American society in general. Comparativity has the virtue of distinguishing to what extent the Polish and Lithuanian consciousness formation was on the one hand unique and on the other a part of a general pattern among related groups. The comparative treatment will offer a fuller impression of ethnic group factionalisms and tensions.

The history of American Catholicism is replete with what appear to be the same local parish troubles that plagued Polish-Americans and Lithuanian-Americans. These were so-called "trusteeship" conflicts between clerics and laymen evident at least among Germans, French-Canadians, Slovaks, and Greek Catholic Ukrainians.[22] Lay trustees frequently quarreled with their bishops over control of church property. Further, these local parish disorders began early in the history of the Church in America, in the late 1700's, so the latercoming Poles and Lithuanians did not introduce the local disturbances. The congregational bias of Protestant America which was built into

---

[22] The general treatment is in the surveys, Rev. John Tracy Ellis, *American Catholicism* (Chicago, 1956), 44–46, and the more orthodox Theodore Maynard, *The Story of American Catholicism* (2 vols., paperback edition, New York, 1960), 1: 177ff. See also James J. Zatko, "The Social History of the Slovak Immigrants in America, 1823–1914" (M.A. thesis, University of Notre Dame, n.d.), for the Slovaks, and Alexander Simirenko, *Pilgrims, Colonists, and Frontiersmen* (New York, 1964), 39–47, on the Ukrainians (Russians).

state law made such difficulties for the American Church almost inevitable.[23]

While any conclusive judgment about the nature of the many trusteeship troubles must await further research on the construction of Catholic parishes, sufficient evidence is available on two other ethnic groups among whom it has been said the issue was widespread to distinguish their troubles from those of East Europeans. The conflicts were quite evident, too, among German and French-Canadian parishes in particular. From the review of their experiences which will follow, it is clear that the struggle was between the group and the hierarchy and thus unlike the situation in the Polish and Lithuanian settlements. The disorder in the East European parishes was far more bitter and disruptive because the conflict was internal, actually civil war which pit Pole against Pole, Lithuanian against Lithuanian.

For example, the earliest German ethnic dissatisfaction with higher Church authority, that is before 1802, occurred in only two parishes, one in Philadelphia and the other in Baltimore. Thus the scope of the German issue was very limited. Further, the matter in Philadelphia was not ethnic at all, but rather concerned differing interpretations of Church law, *jus patronatus,* whether the bishop or the trustees had the right to choose the group pastor. The controversy was short-lived. For three-quarters of the nineteenth century no widespread German Catholic sentiment developed or was maintained against American Church leaders. The particularly disturbing issue among East European parishes of ethnic ownership of property was rarely at issue.[24]

This lack of any German Catholic crisis before 1880 may be attributable to the ability of the ethnically sensitive German quietly to exchange Lutheranism for Catholicism while still

---

[23] Patrick J. A. Dignan, *History of the Legal Incorporation of Catholic Church Property in the United States, 1784–1932* (New York, 1932) is an old but still illuminating discussion of the problem.

[24] The details of the early German Catholic unrest are in Dignan, *History,* 96, 129, 171, and *passim;* and V. J. Fecher, S.V.D., *A Study for the Movement for German National Parishes in Philadelphia and Baltimore, 1787–1802* (Rome, 1955), 1–10, 15–64, 83–86, 193–195, and *passim.*

retaining his Germanism.[25] Such an alternative was not possible
for the fervent Polish or Lithuanian Catholic. Unlike the German he could not leave his traditional church, for ethnicity and
religion were too intimately entwined. He had to resolve the
dilemma within his faith, producing considerable tension. Of
course after 1880 the outspoken German Catholic criticism of
the Church's assimilationist policy did erupt, but the discontent
was not the feeling of a "suppressed" group as was the case
among East Europeans. German Catholics by that time already
had captured a number of dioceses for themselves.

A related factor in the less disruptive German and French-
Canadian trusteeship cases was the absence, or at any rate the
silence, of group defenders of the nongroup bishop. Germans
and French-Canadians were not factionalized, they had no
loyalist camp as did the Poles and Lithuanians. This is not to
say that non-East European dissatisfaction with the Church
hierarchy did not reach high levels of intensity. It did in the
case of the French-Canadians. Some lay leaders were so critical
of their bishop's antigroup policy that they were excommunicated in 1911. Although this dispute probably did raise the
ethnic consciousness of many French communicants, no deep
split appeared within the ethnic group over whether to side with
church critics or the hierarchy.[26]

This comparison then of the parish disorders of the other
Catholic ethnic groups suggests that ethnic consciousness spread
faster and more widely when ethnic group leaders disagreed
over proper policy (the Polish and Lithuanian cases) than when
they presented their grievances as a bloc (the French-Canadian

[25] Colman J. Barry, *The Catholic Church and German Americans* (Milwaukee, 1953), 10, 20. Philip Gleason, *The Conservative Reformers: German
American Catholics and the Social Order* (Notre Dame, Indiana, 1968), views
the pre-1802 disturbances as more ethnic than Fecher; however, he readily
admits that his reference is only suggestive.

[26] Mason Wade, "The French Parish and Survivance in Nineteenth Century
New England," in the *Catholic Historical Review*, 36: 163–189 (1950–1951),
offered a thorough account of the early French Catholic troubles. He referred
to the Franco-Americans, like the German-Americans, as having an ethnic
bishop of their own early, in 1852, with no intragroup divisions in that century.

case). It is ironic that a more potent heightening of ethnic consciousness was achieved by a divided rather than by a united group elite.

* * * *

The unique ordeal of the Polish and Lithuanian immigrants does lead the student of ethnic consciousness to refer to a related and more important aspect of the identity question: how the East Europeans may have understood themselves as Americans. By 1910 the Polish-American and Lithuanian-American did realize that he was a member of an ethnic group, but the experience helped him little to comprehend that greater awareness. Actually prior to 1900 few East European immigrants had to confront a group-wide issue about their Americanism. It was not until World War I that such a crisis developed in which they had to adjust their traditional and adopted identities. While this account does not deal directly with the larger consciousness of membership in the American nation, it does suggest that the Polish and Lithuanian immigrants could have a dual identity, as ethnic and American. Since their deepened realization of their ethnic community came from within and not as a reaction to outside hostility, it would be a simple matter for the immigrants to consider themselves as Americans of Polish or Lithuanian descent.[27]

[27] I develop this idea of a dual identity further in my "Slavic American Nationalism, 1870–1919," in Anna Cienciała, ed., *American Contributions to the Seventh International Congress of Slavists,* Volume III: *History* (The Hague, 1973), 197–215. It was suggested by Oscar Handlin in his *Race and Nationality in American Life* (New York, 1957), 193–200.

BIBLIOGRAPHICAL ESSAY

This book deals with two American ethnic groups which have received inadequate scholarly attention. Academicians have neglected Polish- and Lithuanian-American life even more than they have that of other white minorities. To help remedy this oversight and to encourage historians to fill this lacuna, the following bibliographical review will not only evaluate specific sources consulted by the author but also assess the several developing archives and research centers dedicated to the preservation of Polish- and Lithuanian-American materials, collections which have changed rapidly in the last few years.

This review will also critically evaluate the significant studies of the Poles and Lithuanians in America; it will not cover the studies of immigrant nationalism which are discussed at some length in the text. The essay will also eschew mention of the more familiar studies that interested readers can easily locate in general immigration surveys or in profiles of some of the other new immigrant groups. A comprehensive textual and bibliographical overview of the subject can be found in either Maldwyn A. Jones, *American Immigration* (Chicago, 1960) or Philip A. M. Taylor, *The Distant Magnet* (New York, 1971), both of which give a good introductory outline as well as an encompassing bibliography in English-language references. Current immigration history research is covered in the *Immigration History Newsletter* (vols. 1——, 1968——), published by the Immigration History Society with the support of the

Minnesota State Historical Society. A more recent, brief listing is Perry Weed, comp., *Ethnicity and American Group Life: A Bibliography* (rev. ed., New York, 1973), which is available from the American Jewish Committee.

ARCHIVES AND LIBRARIES

United States

Although the social historian Marcus Hansen and a few of his colleagues pioneered in developing immigration and ethnic history as early as the 1920's, during most of the twentieth century only a handful of professional academicians, and therefore only a few academic institutions, have been committed to preserving ethnic group materials. In recent years, however, the demands of nonwhite and white minorities have influenced libraries to begin to gather systematically records concerning cultural pluralism. The result has been the establishment of new ethnic collections in universities and historical societies and the reinvigoration and reorganization of established group repositories.

The most important Polish-American library is at the Polish Museum in Chicago. Organized in 1935 by journalist Mieczysław Haiman, with the support of the Polish Roman Catholic Union, it soon became a magnificent treasure trove of Polonica. After Haiman's death the library lay nearly dormant through the 1950's until in recent years it was reactivated by the Polish Roman Catholic Union and a new staff. It has an incomparable file of parish jubilee albums, extensive holdings of group periodicals, the correspondence of many Polish clergy in the 1920's and 1930's, and two large collections—the records of the Polish National Department in World War I and the American Relief to Poland Organization in World War II.

The Immigration History Research Center of the University of Minnesota, under the direction of Professor Rudolph Vecoli, is now probably the largest repository of Eastern and Southern European immigrant materials in general. It was established in the early 1960's, just prior to the current "new" ethnic movement and has extensive published and manuscript holdings on the Balkan, Slovak, and Ukrainian groups in particular (see University of Minnesota Libraries, Immigrant Archives, *Guide to Manuscript Holdings,* August, 1974). Its major Polish-American materials include the files of two leading group journals, *Dziennik Chicagoski,* the Resurrectionist daily, and *Ameryka-Echo,* the popular organ of A. A. Paryski of Toledo. It also has the papers of a leading Polish-American protestant social worker, the Reverend Paul Fox.

Another academic institution which has developed a large Slavic-American collection is the Lovejoy Library of Southern Illinois University at Edwardsville. Built and developed through the efforts of Professor Stanley Kimball, the materials (mostly published calendars, almanacs, and the like) are of East European colonies chiefly in the Midwest, especially in the St. Louis area. The bulk of the collection is Czech-American (see Stanley B. Kimball, ed., *Slavic American Imprints: A Classified Catalog of the Collection at Lovejoy Library* [Edwardsville, 1972]).

There are smaller Polish-American libraries which possess valuable specialized materials. In addition to its own organizational files, the Polish National Alliance in Chicago has a large number of sources and publications on group nationalism, including the complete file of *Orzeł Polski,* the first Polish-American newspaper. The library of the Polish Catholic Sts. Cyril and Methodius Seminary, at Orchard Lake, Michigan, has a sizable collection of printed materials on Polish Catholicism. The Alliance College of Cambridge Springs, Pennsylvania, which is supported heavily by the PNA; the Polish Institute of Arts and Sciences; and the Kościuszko Foundation of New York have more modest libraries of Polonica and Polonia Amerykańska.

A new academic center for the study of immigration and ethnicity is the well-endowed Balch Institute of Philadelphia. Dedicated in 1974, it will be one of the most important recipients of new-immigrant materials on the East Coast. The Institute already has included in its activities the sponsoring of reference publications, such as a list of doctoral dissertations in ethnic history and a series of ethnic group bibliographies.

Some state and local historical societies, especially those in highly pluralistic urban and regional centers, have responded to their ethnic communities by including white minorities in new acquisition programs. Probably the most successful effort in the Polish-American field is that of the Buffalo Historical Society under the direction of its ethnic specialist, Dr. Stephen Gredel. The society has received the valuable diary of the major Polish patriarch in the early immigrant years, the Reverend John Pitass, and extensive papers of the group's leading layman, Dr. Francis Fronczak. Dr. Gredel has also assembled a huge card index of ethnic individuals in the metropolitan area. In addition, the Minnesota Historical Society, the Western Reserve Historical Society, the Pennsylvania Museum and Historical Commission, and the Institute of Texan Cultures are energetically pursuing Polish and white ethnic materials.

Most of the archival and source materials on Lithuanian Americans remain at group institutions, either in libraries or the offices of Lithuanian organizations. The World Lithuanian Archives, housed in the Lithuanian Jesuit Fathers Provincial House in Chicago, has many published works, especially church albums, on Lithuanian Roman Catholicism. The Balzekas Museum of Lithuanian Culture, also in Chicago, received the bulk of its holdings, especially its periodical literature, from recent Lithuanian immigrants. A large repository of more purely Lithuanian-American materials is the ALKA Archives on the grounds of the Lithuanian Marian Fathers near Putnam and Thompson, Connecticut. It contains much of the private library of Monsignor Francis Juras of Lawrence, Massachusetts. Other useful, smaller collections of books and periodicals are at the St. Casimir Sisters' Motherhouse in Chicago and in the newspaper offices of *Darbininkas* (Brooklyn), *Draugas* (Chicago), *Garsas* (Wilkes-Barre), and *Naujienos* (Chicago). The State Historical Society of Wisconsin, Madison, now has the valuable early years of *Lietuva* (Chicago) for 1892–1910.

Poland

Millions of ordinary Poles have long admired the United States, referring to it as the "Land of Washington," and even today they continue to hold Americans in high esteem, but the Polish government has only recently permitted formal, academic recognition of American or Polish-American studies because of longtime unfavorable and financial considerations. Lately a clear change in policy has become evident; a Fulbright exchange agreement in American history and a center of American Studies have been established at the University of Warsaw. Further a few other academic institutions, such as the institute in Poznán under Professor Lech Trzeciakowski and the center at the Jagellonian University in Kraków, have just begun to realize an interest in emigration and Poles overseas.

Two exceptional institutions, the Towarzystwo Łącznosci z Polonia Zagraniczna (the "Polonia" Society) and the Instytut Gospodarstwo Społecznego (IGS) in Warsaw, have had a long-standing interest in studying Polish emigration. The Society, in co-operation with a committee of the Polish Academy of Sciences (PAN), sponsored a scholarly journal, *Problemy Polonii Zagranicznej* (1960–1973, vols. I–VIII), which contained the results of important research on migration. Although the Academy has recently reorganized the publication, the yearbook has always promoted and maintained a small international community of scholars who have been committed to Polish migration studies.

Since its beginnings in the 1920's, the IGS has aided Polish sociologists and economists interested in the assimilation and material welfare of their overseas countrymen. In the mid-1930's the Institute encouraged Poles to send in written memoirs about their movement to and settlement in foreign lands. The result was the gathering of a large file of hundreds of such reminiscences, and the Institute is editing and publishing the more significant autobiographies for each section of the world. The volumes on the French and Latin American contingents appeared before World War II, and the Canadian number came out in 1971. The file of eighty-eight memoirs (called *pamiętniki*) from the United States is being edited and should be published soon.

The large, well-established research libraries in Poland such as the Biblioteka Narodowy and the University of Warsaw in the nation's capital, the Jagellonian University in Krakow, and the Kórnik Library outside Poznán all have some important individual publications on emigration. But none have made a significant effort to amass an archival center on the subject. Recently there has been some talk about constructing an American library on the estate of Count Casimir Pulaski in Warta, south of Warsaw. The current celebration of the American

Revolutionary Bicentennial might seem an appropriate opportunity, but the project is yet to be realized.

SOURCE MATERIALS

Bibliographies and Other Reference Aids
   Since immigration study itself is a neglected field in American history, published reference works are few and generally dated. The familiar immigration history surveys usually cite the available English-language sources, which constitute only a fraction of the extant group literature. Virtually every American immigrant group and especially those from Eastern and Southern Europe badly need some comprehensive and widely available reference publication. In addition to the inaccessibility of many ethnic sources on both sides of the Atlantic, a major drawback to such a work is the plethora of ephemeral materials, pamphlets, brochures, calendars, and the like which are difficult to gather and catalog, as well as read. It is hoped that the forthcoming lists of the Balch Institute and the current federal funding for ethnic studies curriculum aids will fill this great need.

   The available East European-American bibliographies are inadequate, though the Lithuanians are better served than the Poles, possibly because their literature is smaller and thus more manageable. A model but selective work is Jonas Balys, comp., *Lithuania and Lithuanians: A Selected Bibliography* (New York, 1961). Balys, an employee of the Library of Congress, annotates and gives the location of many of the sources. In addition, a remarkably complete bibliographical periodical which appeared quarterly for a short time was *Knygu Lentyna* (1948–1966, vols. I–XIX) compiled by Aleksandras Ružaniec-Rusancovas. Two other helpful works are Elena Stanka, "Lithuania: A Selected Bibliography, with a Brief Historical Survey" (Master's thesis, Catholic University of America, n.d.) and Casimir V. Baltramaitis, *Lithuanian Affairs: An Index of the New York Times . . .* (New York, 1945).

   No author has assumed the task of enumerating the multitude or even a comprehensive selection of Polish-American publications. A few published library catalogs come close, but they are now incomplete and inaccurate. Because of the catalogs' age and the recent extensive reorganization of ethnic archives, these publications now have value only as bibliographies. Dr. Alphonse Wolanin, Haiman's assistant, compiled two volumes, *Polonica in English* (Chicago, 1945) and *Polonica Americana* (Chicago, 1950), on part of the Polish Museum collection. Unfortunately, in the Museum's dormant period a number of the enumerated works were either misplaced or lost. Wolanin also compiled a similar bibliography in several issues of *Polish American Studies,* beginning in 1945. In addition, the Polish National Alliance put out a catalog of its rich collection, *Katalog Biblioteki, Związku Narodowego Polskiego, Rok 1923* (Chicago, 1923). I. T. Firkins, *Slavs in the United States* (Boston, 1915) is useful but dated; Joseph Roucek, *American Slavs: A Bibliography* (New York, 1945) refers solely to English language publications.

Two recent listings are of high quality and indicate the great promise of Slavic- and Polish-American studies. Jan Wepsięc, *Polish American Serial Publications, 1842–1966: An Annotated Bibliography* (Chicago, 1968), is an exceptionally thorough union list of Polish-American periodicals, which, unfortunately, appeared privately. The author is a professional librarian, and his work will remain a standard for some time to come. The other valuable publication is the work edited by Kimball, *Slavic American Imprints,* mentioned above.

The biographical dictionary is another helpful reference tool. Indispensable but not entirely reliable is the ambitious work of the Reverend Francis Bolek, ed., *Who's Who in Polish America* (3rd ed., New York, 1943). Andrzej Kapostas and Andrzej Karwowski, eds., *Polski Slownik Biograficzny* (Kraków, 1966) has only a few Polish-Americans but is more authorative. A detailed directory of America's first major Polish Catholic Order was prepared by the Reverend Edward Janas, C.R., *Dictionary of American Resurrectionists, 1865–1965* (Rome, 1967). Through the nineteenth century very few English language *Who's Who*s or city "histories" included East European Americans because the authors did not consider them noteworthy citizens. The increasing respectability of these nationality personalities in the early twentieth century is reflected in the coverage given several leaders in Weston A. Goodspeed and Daniel Healy, *History of Cook County, Illinois* . . . (2 vols., Chicago, 1909).

A few encyclopedias give some attention to Polish and Lithuanian Americans. Reverends Francis Bolek and Ladislas Siekaniec, eds., *Polish American Encyclopedia, A-B* (Buffalo, 1954) is a courageous but rather uneven attempt at a comprehensive group compendium. Although the articles in this work vary widely in quality, the succeeding volumes which are in manuscript ought to be published. Joseph Roucek, ed., *The Slavonic Encyclopedia* (New York, 1949) contains a surprisingly large number of brief but informative essays on various Slavic groups, especially the Poles, in the United States. Two other helpful survey articles are Felix Seroczynski, "The Poles in the United States," in *Catholic Encyclopedia* (15 vols., New York, 1911), 12: 204–212, and M. Biržiška, "Chicagos Lietuviai," in *Lietuviškoji Enciklopedija* (9 vols., Kaunas, 1933–1937), 5: 270–275. There are also pertinent articles in *Lietuviu Enciklopedija* (36 vols., South Boston, 1953–1969), which is to be translated into English.

Contemporary Newspapers and Periodicals

The ethnic press is an essential source. Fortunately any Chicago ethnic study has the advantage of extensive press review through the *Foreign Language Press Survey,* a Federal Works Project Administration effort of the late 1930's, which consists of translated excerpts of the city's diverse ethnic press dating back a century. While it is difficult to use because of an involved topical outline, the excerpts taken in sum are a sensitive record of the little-known ethnic societies. The editors of the project gave extended coverage to the God and Country issue that affected Poles and Lithuanians. This is an invaluable source for any investigator interested in East European Americans or any other of the more conspicuous Chicago nationalities.

Fortunately the files of a number of leading Polish newspapers are or will be widely available. An extensive run of *Dziennik Chicagoski,* the major Catholic organ, is now at the University of Minnesota Immigrant Archives, and the Polish Museum has *Niedziela* (Detroit), and *Naród Polski* (Chicago), the PRCU paper. *Zgoda* (1881——) the nationalist organ at the PNA Library and the *Kuryer Polski* of Milwaukee, an outspoken and more independent patriotic voice, at the Milwaukee Public Library, are both highly informative. The Immigration

History Research Center at the University of Minnesota and the Center for Research Libraries, which also has large files of immigrant newspapers, are sponsoring a massive microfilming project with the Polish-American press as its first priority. The English language press of Chicago, especially the *Chronicle, Inter-Ocean, Daily News, Record,* and *Record-Herald,* all of which can be found in the Chicago Historical Society, paid unusually close and frequently dispassionate attention to the presence and troubles of the Polish and Lithuanian quarters. The official archdiocesan paper, *The New World,* has disappointingly limited coverage of social events. All the extant Lithuanian papers are either at the archives already mentioned or in the offices of their publishers.

Immigrant Letters and Memoirs

Another important genre of immigration documents are the intimate, private immigrant letters which relatives and friends sent to each other. English language scholars already have translated, published, and edited the letters of English, Welsh, and Norwegian migrants to America, but to date no similarly comprehensive work has been prepared for the Lithuanian or Polish migrants. Some correspondence, *Listy* in Polish, has appeared in translation. Family letters constituted an important source for the classic William I. Thomas and Florian Znaniecki, *The Polish Peasant in Europe and America* (5 vols., Chicago and Boston, 1918–1920). However, Herbert Blumer, "An Appraisal of Thomas and Znaniecki's *The Polish Peasant in Europe and America,"* in *Social Sciences Research Bulletin,* No. 33 (New York, 1939), criticizes the collection for its bias. Another, more important collection of letters, Witold Kula et al., eds., *Listy Emigrantów z Brazylii i Stanów Zjednoczonych, 1890–1891* (Warszawa, 1972), although limited in time and including non-Polish migrants, is of particular value because it includes letters from migrants not only abroad but also in transit.

A related type of evidence, the memoirs of immigrants written long after their transfer, apparently constitute a highly respected source among Polish scholars. Note in particular the journal of the Towarzystwo Przyjaciół Pamiętnikarstwa, *Pamiętnikarstwo Polskie,* begun in 1971, edited by Dr. Franciszek Jakubczak. Also the Instytut Gospodarstwa Społecznego published several volumes entitled *Pamiętniki Emigrantów* in 1939, 1958, 1965, and 1971. In spite of their intrinsic value the scholar should consult these *Listy* and *Pamiętniki* with caution because they tend to represent the more articulate, successful, and enlightened segment of these Polish and Lithuanian groups.

SECONDARY WORKS

European Background

No satisfactory account of Polish and Lithuanian motivation for emigration exists in any language, although there are some recent localized studies. One obstacle is the difficulty in separating these ethnic groups from their neighboring nationalities—the Germans, Russians, Austrians, and Ukrainians. A further drawback is that most Slavic historians in both Europe and America concentrate upon political questions of nationalism rather than the social and economic conditions of the masses. The best work on the political emigrés in the U.S. and Europe is Jerzy W. Borejsza, *Emigracya Polska na Powstania Styczniowym* (Warszawa, 1966), which is superior to Florian Stasik, *Polska Emigracja Polityczna w Stanach Zjednoczonych, 1831–1864* (Warszawa, 1973).

To find some mention of emigration conditions in English one must return to dated works, such as Thomas and Znaniecki, who regrettably tend to oversimplify the subject. Sula Benet, *Song, Dance and Customs of Peasant Poland* (New York, 1952) is helpful because the author deals with the larger matter of Polish national character as well as peasant folklore. Jan Slomka, *From Serfdom to Self-Government,* trans. William J. Rose (London, 1941) and especially Emily Greene Balch, *Our Slavic Fellow-Citizens* (New York, 1910) give added insights into peasant psychology and migration, although Balch deals with only the Austro-Polish sector and Slomka's views are of a small Russian-Polish village.

After a long hiatus Polish scholars have turned their attention to the migration question, in part as a result of the heightened interest in statistical and demographic analysis. An early, conscientious effort which deals with the effect of mailed money orders is Zygmunt Gargas, *W Sprawie Ruchu Pieniężnego Między Ameryka a Galicya* (Kraków, 1907). A valuable sociological study of motivation and assimilation are the interviews of American returnees in K. Duda-Dziewierz, *Wieś Małopolski a Emigracya Amerykańska* (Poznań, 1938). Renewed general interest in migration became apparent in the mid-1950's but Boguslaw Drewniak, *Robotnicy Sezonowi Na Pomorzu Zachodnim, 1890–1918* (Poznań, 1959); Krysztof Groniowski, *Kwestia Agarna w Krolestwia Polskim, 1871–1914* (Warszawa, 1960); and Kazimierz Wajda, *Migracje Ludnóści Wiejskiego Pomorza Wschodniego w Latach, 1850–1914* (Warszawa, 1969) all have difficulty in isolating first Polish emigrants *per se* and then those destined for the United States. A reliable demographic breakdown is J. Zubrzycki, "Emigration From Poland in the Nineteenth and Twentieth Centuries," in *Population Studies* (March, 1953), 6: 248–272.

The origins of the earliest Polish contingents from Silesia to America are described by Andrzej Brożek, especially in his *Ślązacy w Teksasie* (Warszawa, 1972), which reveals the continual close tie between Silesians and their countrymen in Texas. Joanna Sadomirska, "Z Dziejów Śląskiej Emigracji do Ameryki Połnocy," in *Studia Śląskie*, 10: 271–275, gives additional information, and Bogdan Gzelonski, "Początki Polskiej Emigracji Zarobkowej do Stanów Zjednoczonych," in *Kwartalnik Historyczny* (1973), Nr. 3, 378–382, improves on both. Little exists for Lithuanian conditions. Anicetas Simutis, *The Economic Reconstruction of Lithuania After 1918* (New York, 1942) is excellent on its subject but marginal on the prewar period.

Early Polish-American History

Despite the group's large size and significance as an American ethnic group—over three million immigrants and eight million descendants—there is no adequate Polish-American history in English. The two books by Dr. Joseph Wytrwal, *America's Polish Heritage* (Detroit, 1961) and *Poles in American History and Tradition* (Detroit, 1969), are occasionally illuminating but generally filiopietistic and slight. The most gratifying general impression of Polonia Amerykańska past and present remains the monumental X. Wacław Kruszka, *Historya Polska w Ameryce* (13 vols., Milwaukee, 1905–1908). Although highly opinionated and critical of the Church hierarchy at times, Kruszka maintained exceptional standards of historical scholarship in his thorough "settlement" perspective. For understanding

Polonia after Kruszka's time, Dr. Mieczysław Szawleski, *Wychodźtwo Polskie w Stanach Zjednoczonych* (Lwów, 1924), is unsurpassed. Other stimulating contemporary impressions are Emil Duniwokski, *Wśród Polonii w Ameryce* (Lwów, 1898), who visited the major Polish colonies in the 1890's; Ludwik, Krzywicki, *Za Atlantikiem* (Warszawa, 1895); Stefan Barszczewski, *Polacy w Ameryce* (Warszawa, 1902?), who deals with the question of assimilation; and nationalist Zygmunt Miłkowski, *Opowiadanie z Wędrówki po Koloniach Polskich w Ameryce Połnocznej* (Paris, 1901). Karol Wachtl, *Polonia w Ameryce* (Philadelphia, 1944) is another group profile of Poles in America with a decided pro-Roman Catholic and institutional bias; Stefan Wloszczewski, *History of Polish American Culture* (Trenton, New Jersey, 1946), although outwardly similar, is really a localized but revealing glimpse of Polish-American agriculturalists in New England and Long Island. Paul Fox, *The Poles in America* (New York, 1922) is a satisfactory guide, but the later sections betray his assimilationist bias.

A number of other specialized views of the group are sound and informative. Some of the best are J. Mierzynski et al., *Polacy w New York* (New York, 1908); Rev. Joseph Swastek, "The Formative Years of the Polish Seminary in the United States," in Rev. F. Domanski, ed., *The Contribution of Poles to the Growth of Catholicism in the United States,* Tom VI, *Sacrum Poloniae Millenium* (Rome, 1959), which offers more than the title implies; Jozef Chałasinski, "Parafja i Szkoła Parafjalne Wśród Emigracji Polskiej Ameryce," in *Przegląd Sociologiczny* (1935), 3: 633–636; and Jan Perkowski, "The Kashubes . . . " in *Polish American Studies* (January–June, 1966), 23: 1–7.

There are many graduate student theses on Polish-American life, and some merit further development and publication. Only the more suggestive can be mentioned here. Very sound community profiles can be found in Sister Mary Inviolata Ficht, "Noble Street in Chicago" (master's thesis, De Paul University, 1952); Frank Renkiewicz, "The Settlement of St. Joseph County, Indiana, 1855–1935" (doctoral dissertation, University of Notre Dame, 1967); Joseph Parot, "The American Faith and the Persistence of Chicago Polonia, 1870–1910" (doctoral dissertation, Northern Illinois University, 1971); and Carol Golab, "The Polish Communities of Philadelphia . . ." (doctoral dissertation, University of Pennsylvania, 1971). Ms. Golab uses comparative and statistical data to show the smaller Polish migration to her city. Daniel Marsh, "The Problem of Polish Immigration . . ." (master's thesis, Northwestern University, 1907) is interesting only because it is a lively, prejudicial condemnation by a social worker. The sociological study by Helena Znaniecka Lopata, "The Function of Voluntary Associations in an Ethnic Community 'Polonia' " (doctoral dissertation, University of Chicago, 1954) is an attempt to show that there was institutional assimilation, a position with which I do not agree.

Early Lithuanian-American History

Little of the Lithuanian-American experience is recorded in English. Once again the major work in English, Alfred E. Senn, *The Emergence of Modern Lithuania* (New York, 1959), investigates Lithuanian nationalism. An early but broad group profile similar to Kruszka's for the Poles is Fr. Jonas Žilius, *Lietuviai Amerikoj* (Plymouth, Pennsylvania, 1898). It is more descriptive than interpretive. The Reverend Antanas Miliukas of Philadelphia, a more impassioned and prolific religious nationalist wrote several historical works, including *Amerikos Lietuviai XIX Šimtmetyje* (Philadelphia, 1938), volume 1. Dr. Vincas Bartuśka, *Les Lituaniens d'Amerique* (Lausanne, 1918); Kazys Gineitis, *Amerika Ir Amerikos Lietuviai* (Kaunas, 1925); and V. K. Rackauskas, *Amerika . . .* (New York, 1915) are largely American handbooks for Lithuanians in the home country. S. Michelsonas, *Lietuvių Išeivija Amerikoje, 1868–1961* (South Boston, Massachusetts, 1961) is a socialist interpretation.

Selected specialized publications are Vaclovas Birziska, "The American Lithuanian Publications, 1875 to 1910," in the *Journal of Central European Affairs* (January, 1959), 18: 396–408, which is far more than a simple listing; Professor F. Kamesis, "Ideologines Kovas Lietuviškoje Šiaures Amerikos Išeivijoje," in *Krikščionybe Lietuvoje* (Kaunas, 1938), 112–130, which exposes the bitterness of the nationalist-clericalist struggle; and Fr. Jonas Žilius, *Kun. Aleksandras Burba* (Plymouth, Pennsylvania, 1898), a laudatory biography at the time of Burba's death.

Jubilee Albums

The serious historian tends to view suspiciously official institutional histories and commemorative publications because they are usually uncritical, exaggerated, and even self-serving. Ultimately, however, they force themselves upon the attention of academicians by their huge numbers, their easy availability, and their occasional sophistication. Almost all offer some factual information about a neighborhood settlement, dates and names of local pioneers, and a chronological outline that would be difficult to obtain elsewhere. Since works of this sort really vary widely in form, content, and quality, the user must judge each individually.

The official PNA and PRCU histories are typical of the normal commemorative publication. Stanislaw Osada, *Historya Związku Narodowego Polskiego* . . . (Chicago, 1905), the only chronicle of early PNA activities, was published on the association's silver anniversary. Mieczysław Haiman, *Zjednoczenie Polsko-Rzymsko Katalickiego w Ameryce, 1873–1948* (Chicago, 1948) is an unusually dispassionate review of the PRCU with full scholarly apparatus. Dr. Antanas Kučas, *Lietuvių Romos Kataliku Susivienijimas Amerikoje* (Wilkes-Barre, Pennsylvania, 1956) provides a chronological examination of the Lithuanian brotherhood. Two other essential jubilee albums in Polish-American historiography are Romuald Piatkowski et al., eds., *Pamiętnik Wznieszenia i Odsłonecia Pomników Tadeusza Kościuszki i Kazimierza Pulaskiego . . . w Washington, D.C.* (Washington, D.C., 1911), which memorializes the first Polish-American nationalist congress, and *Księga Pamiątkowe "33" . . . Powstania Polsko Narodowego Katolickiego Kosciola . . .* (Scranton, 1930), a historical directory of the Polish National Catholic Church.

There were 1,000 or so Polish and Lithuanian parishes in America at the height of their ethnic community, and almost all published at least one local history on their silver, golden, or diamond anniversary. Even the most informative are too numerous to be listed. A sampling of the broader, regional accounts includes Anthony Tomczak, ed., *Poles in America: Their Contribution of* [Chicago] *Progress* (Chicago, 1933); *Pittstone Lietuvių Istoria, 1885–1935* (Pittston, Pennsylvania, 1935); Thaddeus Borun, ed., *We, The Milwaukee Poles* (Milwaukee, 1946), and Rev. Milton J. Kobielski, *Millenium of Christianity of the Polish People, 966–1966, Buffalo Diocesan Observance* (Buffalo, 1966). The individual parish albums themselves are the best neighborhood profiles, not so much for what they tell directly as for what they imply about the character of the locality. They give, in detail, descriptions of the pioneers in their local setting, and brief sketches of businessmen, religious leaders, and societies. The best examples for Chicago are Karol Wachtl, ed., *1867–1917 Złoty Jubileusz Najstarzej Polskiej Parafii Świetego Stanisława Kostki* . . . (Chicago, 1917) and Rev. Alfred Abramowicz, *Diamond Jubilee Immaculate Conception B. and M. Parish, 1882–1957* (Chicago, 1957) for the Poles; and *1892–40–1932, Šv. Jurgio Parapijos 40-ties Metų Jubiliejus* . . . (Chicago, 1932), *1892–1942, Golden Jubilee, St. George Church* (Chicago, 1942), and *Anno Domini, 1900–1950, Banketas* . . . *Dievo Apviezdos Parapijos* . . . (Chicago, 1950) for the Lithuanians. Curiously these publications were of far more value than the parish birth, marriage, and death records, which were consulted with little success.

The biographies of group leaders generally come under the commemorative designation, for many were written either to honor the subjects' achievements or as eulogies. Nevertheless, this literature is valuable, too, because it is rich in evidence unavailable elsewhere. Two examples are Rev. Stanisław Siatka, C.R., *Krótki Wspomnienie o Zycie Działalności Ks. M. Wincentego Barzynskiego* (Chicago, 1901), a worshipful review written just after the Rev. Vincent Barzynski's death, and Petras Jurgela, ed., *Antanas Olšauskas ir "Lietuva"* (Sodus, Michigan, 1934), written on the occasion of Olszewski's seventieth year.

Catholic Histories

Until the last few years historical reviews of American Catholicism have ignored the faith's East European constituency and have skipped lightly over the vexing nationality issue that later immigrants presented. It was not until the 1950's that a few authors began at least to allude to the problem of pluralism within the Church, notably Msgr. John Tracy Ellis, *Life of James Cardinal Gibbons* (2 vols., Milwaukee, 1952) and *American Catholicism* (Chicago, 1956); and Colman J. Barry, *The Catholic Church and German Americans* (Milwaukee, 1953). The most recent official diocesan histories show a particular sensitivity toward the lesser-known ethnic communicants, but at the same time maintain a pro-hierarchical interpretation. Two examples are Henry Caspar, *History of the Catholic Church in*

Nebraska: Chapters in Nebraska Immigration (Milwaukee, 1966), and the fuller account of Rev. John Gallagher, *A Century of History: The Diocese of Scranton, 1868–1968* (Scranton, 1968). Historians eagerly await the official history of the Chicago Archdiocese, the largest in the nation. *The Archdiocese of Chicago: Antecedents and Development* (Des Plaines, Illinois, 1920) and *History of the Catholic Church in Chicago and Directory* (Chicago, 1898–1899?) are little more than reference guides.

Polish and Polish-American religious orders have their own rich historical literature which describes the intra- and intergroup contact in the New World. The two major male and female communities in America are the Resurrectionist Fathers and the Felician Sisters. Both have a wealth of historical publications. For the Resurrectionists the earliest recollections are by Rev. A. Bakanowski, *Moje Wspomnienie* (Lwów, 1913) and X. Hieronim Kajsiewicz, *Rozprawy, Listy z Podoży* (3 vols., Kraków, 1872). Recent anniversary volumes are Ks. Wladyslaw Kiatkowski, C.R., *Historia Zgromadzenia Zmartwychwstania Panskiego . . . 1842–1942* (Albano, Italy, 1942) and Rev. John Iwicki, *The First One Hundred Years: A Study of the Congregation of the Resurrectionists in the United States, 1866–1966* (Rome, 1966). The latter is based on extensive archival materials, but is decidedly uncritical. Adequate accounts of the Felician Sisters can be found in *Historja Zgromadzenia SS. Felicjanek na Podstawie Rekopisów* (3 vols., Milwaukee, 1924, 1929, 1932); Alexander Syski, *Ks. Jozef Dąbrowski; Monografia Historyczna* (Orchard Lake, Michigan, 1942), a biography of their host in America; and the initial volume of the centennial series, Sister Mary Theophane Kalinowski, C.S.S.F., *Felician Sisters in the West* (Milwaukee, 1967).

Chicago History

Chicago possesses perhaps the richest sociological and historical literature of any urban center in America. Various observers, social workers, sociologists, and social historians concerned with the impact of industrial development on humans have viewed Chicago as an ideal laboratory. For example, early social workers investigated and exposed the deleterious effects of urban life on the poor, largely the recent immigrants; thus a large number of early publications reveal the living and working conditions of Poles and Lithuanians. Grace Abbot, "The Chicago Employment Agency and the Immigrant Worker," in *The American Journal of Sociology* (November, 1908), 14: 289–305; Antanas Kaztauskis, "From Lithuania to the Chicago Stockyards—An Autobiography," in *The Independent* (August 4, 1904), 57: 241–248; and Leila Houghteling, *The Income and Standard of Living of Unskilled Laborers in Chicago* (Chicago, 1927) offer evidence that supports their demand for minimal middle-class standards of living.

Additional material on the newcomer's daily life is in more formal official reports, such as the testimony found in U.S., Industrial Commission, *Reports of the Industrial Commission on Immigration* (57 Congress, 1 session, serial 4345) and U.S., Immigration Commission, *Abstracts of Reports of the Immigration Commission* (61 Congress, 3 session, serials 5865-5866). Raw statistical data, on individually held property especially, are in the ninth and tenth federal manuscript censuses, 1870 and 1880, at the Chicago Historical Society. The Chicago Communities Documents 2, 4, 10–16, 19, and 22 at the society have good oral accounts of social life, too. The ordinary laboring situation in the city is graphically told in Illinois, Bureau of Labor Statistics, *Seventh Biennial Report*, 1892 (Springfield, 1892). Immigrants' home purchases is a topic that awaits extended investigation. The official account, H. Morton Bodfish, ed., *History of Building and Loan in the United States* (Chicago, 1931); the home-building industry journal, *Financial Review and American Building Association News;* and the Illinois, Auditor of Public Accounts, *Reports of the Building and Loan Association of the State of Illinois* (1892——) hint that this vital American institution was particularly important in Chicago. Two helpful efforts to show the significance of the home-buying urge among Chicago newcomers are Mary F. Bruton, "A Study of Tenement Ownership by Immigrant Workmen in Chicago" (master's thesis, University of Chicago, 1924) and Julius F. Ozog, "A Study of Polish Home Ownership in Chicago" (master's thesis, University of Chicago, 1942).

INDEX